VOYAGEUR S

BOOKS THAT EXPLORE CANADA

Michael Gnarowski — Series Editor

The Dundurn Group presents the Voyageur Classics series, building on the tradition of exploration and rediscovery and bringing forward time-tested writing about the Canadian experience in all its varieties.

This series of original or translated works in the fields of literature, history, politics, and biography has been gathered to enrich and illuminate our understanding of a multi-faceted Canada. Through straightforward, knowledgeable, and reader-friendly introductions the Voyageur Classics series provides context and accessibility while breathing new life into these timeless Canadian masterpieces.

The Voyageur Classics series was designed with the widest possible readership in mind and sees a place for itself with the interested reader as well as in the classroom. Physically attractive and reset in a contemporary format, these books aim at an enlivened and updated sense of Canada's written heritage.

OTHER VOYAGEUR CLASSICS TITLES

FORTHCOMING

VOYAGEUR CLASSICS

BOOKS THAT EXPLORE CANADA

THE MEN OF THE LAST FRONTIER

GREY OWL

INTRODUCTION BY JAMES POLK

DUNDURN PRESS
TORONTO

Project Editor: Michael Carroll
Copy Editor: Matt Baker
Design: Jesse Hooper
Printer: Marquis

Library and Archives Canada Cataloguing in Publication

Grey Owl, 1888-1938
    The men of the last frontier / by Grey Owl ; introduction by James Polk.

Also available in electronic format.
ISBN 978-1-55488-804-7

    1. Canada, Northern--Description and travel. 2. Canada, Western--Description and travel. 3. Natural history--Canada. 4. Frontier and pioneer life--Canada. 5. Indians of North America-- Canada. I. Title.

QL791.G7 2010   917.19   C2010-902301-3

1 2 3 4 5   15 14 13 12 11

 Conseil des Arts du Canada Canada Council for the Arts   Canada    ONTARIO ARTS COUNCIL CONSEIL DES ARTS DE L'ONTARIO

We acknowledge the support of the **Canada Council for the Arts** and the **Ontario Arts Council** for our publishing program. We also acknowledge the financial support of the **Government of Canada** through the **Canada Book Fund** and **Livres Canada Books**, and the **Government of Ontario** through the **Ontario Book Publishers Tax Credit** program, and the **Ontario Media Development Corporation**.

Care has been taken to trace the ownership of copyright material used in this book. The author and the publisher welcome any information enabling them to rectify any references or credits in subsequent editions.

J. Kirk Howard, President

www.dundurn.com

Dundurn Press	Gazelle Book Services Limited	Dundurn Press
3 Church Street, Suite 500	White Cross Mills	2250 Military Road
Toronto, Ontario, Canada	High Town, Lancaster, England	Tonawanda, NY
M5E 1M2	LA1 4XS	U.S.A. 14150

CONTENTS

In the amphitheatre of the dusky hills, where is silence, unbroken and absolute, a hush that has held sway since time began ...

INTRODUCTION

BY JAMES POLK

Published in 1931, *The Men of the Last Frontier* was Grey Owl's first book, the kickoff to an unparalleled international career as a Native celebrity, a bestselling writer, and a popular lecturer on preserving the wilderness. On December 10, 1937, a mere six years after his first book, he reached the top, invited to speak to King George VI, Queen Elizabeth, and the two princesses in a private audience at Buckingham Palace. This command performance lasted three hours and concluded with the world's most celebrated First Nations figure shaking hands with the king, calling him "Brother," and wishing him luck.

The Men of the Last Frontier was welcomed by almost everyone in a Depression-weary Britain. As London's *Times* rhapsodized: "It is difficult to recall any record of the great North so brilliantly and lovingly handled." The surprised and surprising publisher was the upmarket and tweedy British magazine *Country Life*, which, in a ham-fisted introduction to the first edition, seems to be nervous about inflicting a wild Canadian onto civilized readers. If Grey Owl's language seems "unnatural," the editors warn, "the manuscript has not been easy to follow," and one must remember that it was produced in bad-weather conditions and "typewritten by a French-Canadian who knew little English."

It should be explained that the author is a half-breed Indian, whose name has recently become known throughout the English-speaking world. His father was a Scot, his mother an Apache Indian of New Mexico, and he was born somewhere near the Rio Grande forty odd years ago. Grey Owl is the translation of his Red Indian name, given to him when he became a blood brother of the Ojibway, and his proper legal style.

A drawing by Grey Owl from the original Country Life *edition of* The Men of the Last Frontier.

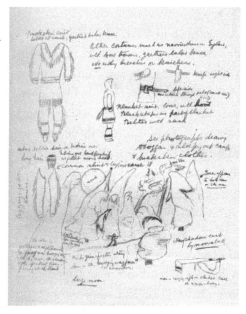

Almost none of the above information is true, although supplied by the author himself. Grey Owl's father was indeed of Scottish descent, but his mother, Katherine (Kittie), was never an "Apache Indian." Instead, she was a shy, fifteen-year old English barmaid. The author was not born "somewhere near the Rio Grande" but several thousand miles away in the prim seaside resort town of Hastings, Sussex, on the English Channel.

Grey Owl's real name was Archibald Stansfeld Belaney, he had enjoyed a privileged British upbringing, and possessed not one drop of aboriginal blood.

George Belaney had been the dissolute black sheep of a respectable line of Scottish farmers and businessmen, a feckless drunk who, very soon after his son's birth, skipped out on the young mother and fled to the colonies, much to the family's relief. Tall, handsome, clever, and alcoholic, George had already abandoned one family before Archie and Kittie, after passing his younger days squandering the family fortune. He apparently was to die later in a bar brawl in the United States, and was never a U.S. Army scout in the West — another of his son's fantasies. Kittie Belaney, the teenage mother, unskilled and impoverished, gratefully gave up Archie to the care of his aunts, Carrie and Ada, who had been horrified at the wastrel example of their brother. There had been men of distinction in the family, notably a cleric who had written on animals and against vivisection. (There had also been a doctor charged with poisoning his wife.) The aunts clothed Archie in gloves and an Eton suit; they looked after his education in a good school; they indulged his interest in bringing home animals — snakes, birds, hares — in the hope that he might grow up to be a scientist and not take after Dad. It did not quite work out that way.

In old photographs, Archie looks the very picture of a starched Victorian schoolboy, but he was not much interested in his good school, or church attendance, or even friends and games. Instead, he preferred to live on fantasies of adventure, of Buffalo Bill's Wild West Shows and other current mythologies of the Far West: *Hiawatha*, James Fenimore Cooper. Throughout adolescence it seems that young Belaney, abandoned by his father and mother, grew into a loner who preferred the woods and his animal pets to sporting with chums — unless it was playing at Red Indians, which in some sense he did for the rest of his life. He left school before graduation, and after a failure clerking at a local lumberyard, began pestering his aunts to let him go to Canada. Always persuasive with women, Archie was allowed to go, and at seventeen, arrived in Canada in 1906, eager for northern derring-do and finding instead Toronto, then a no-nonsense, mercantile city of five hundred thousand hard-working souls.

For a time, Archie sold men's haberdashery at Eaton's Department Stores, marking time until he could head to the wilderness, to Cobalt, Ontario, where a silver mine was opening up dreams of wealth and employment to many Canadians. Jobs and money were not at all the stuff of Belaney's dreams: instead, he found what he wanted: the forest primeval, where Native people flourished in the pine-scented fresh air among savage rocks and pure lakes. He picked up some work around the camps to get along and learned the fur trapper's trade, but preferred to spend time with his newfound Ojibway friends, drinking too much and getting into fights. He even began learning some of the Ojibway language, if, it appears, quite imperfectly. The Indians seem to have put up with him. He married a lovely young Ojibway girl, Angèle, and there was a child, and then two children. Then Archie abandoned his whole young family, moving on — his father's son, after all.

With the Great War, a restless Belaney enlisted; first, apparently, in Montreal (he immediately deserted, he later said) and then more definitively in Halifax, where he joined the 13th Battalion of the Royal Highlanders of Canada — later to be the Canadian Black Watch. He served briefly in France but got shot in the foot, a war wound that sent him back to an English hospital and recovery from an amputated toe. At home in Hastings the aunts were attentive, but it seemed as if life had come full circle, back to dreary civilization, with its small lives and little glory. He married an English rose named Ivy without bothering to mention his Native wife or the children, then took off alone for Canada, promising to send for his bride when things got settled. Ivy waited in Sussex for four years, by which time her wandering husband had written, confessing bigamy, whereupon she, sensible English girl, sued for divorce. Archie did not contest.

Rootless in Canada, mostly jobless, Archie spent much time around Biscotasing and other rough Northern Ontario towns, trapping, drinking, and brawling; but also entertaining the gang with his tall tales and his alleged "ancient Indian songs," made up on the spot. He was beginning to dress like an Indian, and with his long Scots Belaney face, his shiny black hair braided in pigtails, his patrician hawk nose, his complexion duly tanned, the buckskin fringe and the moccasins and feathers, he could and did pass. He created an Indian name, Wa-sha-quon-asin, which he said meant "Grey Owl" in Ojibway. (Linguists suggest instead that it's "White Shining Beak.") "He Who Walks by Night" was another preferred nickname: we are not far here from Fenimore Cooper and the *Boys' Own Annual*. Playing the Red Indian,

Grey Owl in full First Nations regalia in Niagara Falls, Ontario, in July 1937.

Belaney could be insulting and snappish with uppity whites. He was fast becoming a local character, a faux-Indian wreck.

Nobody around Bisco would have believed that in twelve years "Archie Grey Owl" would be revered everywhere as a famous author, friend to the beaver and the Indian, preaching the gospel of the great wilderness to the king and queen of Britain. How did it happen?

Grey Owl's salvation, as he later acknowledged, was a young, frisky, and beautiful waitress named Gertrude Bernard, by far the most appealing figure in Belaney's wayward biography. She was nineteen years old and at least partially Indian: Iroquois, with a Mohawk grandmother, despite her stout Anglo name, but Grey Owl soon changed "Gertie" to Anahareo, another quasi-Native manufacture. She stuck with her own nickname, Pony, and with common sense and strength of character somehow managed to transform Archie, slowly, at age thirty-six, from a colourful northern screw-up into a wilderness hero, writer, and performer. At first Anahareo went fur trapping with Archie, but the iron jaws of the traps, the agonies of the ensnared prey, disturbed her deeply. She played upon Archie's feelings for animals and his concern for the beaver, which was then being overhunted. In *The Men of the Last Frontier*, Grey Owl defends the cruelty of trapping: since animals are naturally cruel to one another, they deserve the cruelty of the trap, he says. One can imagine Anahareo's response to this. Such weak solipsism vanishes by the later chapters when the couple finds and adopts the beaver kits who are too cute not to live and who will become prototypes for the classic characters in Belaney's later *The Adventures of Sajo and Her Beaver People*.

Trapping had become abhorrent to both of them, and in fact it was now illegal for Archie, given a new Ontario rule that only genuine status Indians could set traps. Drifting around the north, the couple with their beaver pets moved into Quebec, all the way eastward to the New Brunswick border, living in tents and off the land, and somehow making do. With the wolf at the door and Pony's promptings, Archie began writing stories and articles about the wilderness, and later, at Métis Beach, on Quebec's St. Lawrence River, a resort town for English Montrealers, he drummed up the courage to lecture in Indian gear on his experiences, albeit desperate and petrified. (Public speaking made him feel, he said, like "a snake who had swallowed an icicle.") The tourists loved him. The beaver kits were adorable, and their handler was a gifted storyteller who looked like everyone's fantasy Indian: tall and hatchet-faced, in moccasins, braids, and occasionally even a feathered (Plains Indian) war bonnet. If we can now detect the Scottish genes writ large in his long, dour face and blue eyes, he convinced many, who saw what they wanted to see: a Noble Savage turning gracefully in his beads and fringe, J-stroking a canoe packed with a fat beaver.

Left to right: Unidentified person, Grey Owl, Anahareo, and Sir Charles G.D. Roberts at Riding Mountain National Park in Manitoba in the fall of 1931.

The Métis Beach lectures and the magazine articles became the genesis of *The Men of the Last Frontier*, and the entire Quebec episode marks the turn in Belaney's fortunes. He attracted a sponsor, Harry Spence from Montreal, who promised financial support for further sustained writing. His local fame inspired a Canada's Parks Branch commissioner to think about showcasing this eloquent Indian for publicity purposes, as a conservationist and tourist attraction in the newly created Riding Mountain National Park in Manitoba. Thus Belaney was suddenly offered a Parks job, salaried and stable, manna from heaven in Depression Canada, 1931. As the *Montreal Star* noted, Grey Owl "clearly knows the ways of both the white and red man," which was true enough, and moreover "has a vocabulary that would put many of his paleface brethren to shame."

The fledgling writer sent much of his early work to *Country Life*, a magazine he no doubt remembered from his Hastings childhood, and a curious choice for nature writing. However, the magazine's posh readers devoured the articles about pines and breezes and pure lakes in a threatened northern paradise, and wanted more. With promises of book publication, cheques in the mail, the beneficence of National Parks, and contented beavers slapping their tails on the lake, Grey Owl buckled down to assemble a long piece. Anahareo restlessly came and went, shut out, as she loudly and often complained, by his absorption in paper and pen. Finally, at age forty-three, wild, hard-drinking man of the woods Archie Belaney put together *The Men of the Last Frontier*, his long, beautifully written meditation on Canadian nature, with its prophetic warning about the dangers of civilization: the trappers, developers, miners, railways, and woodcutters that threatened our last Eden.

Ever consistent in its meddling, *Country Life* decided to change Archie's original title, *The Vanishing Frontier*, without bothering to inform the author. The author was not best pleased, as he wrote the publisher:

> That you changed the title shows that you, at
> least, missed the entire point of the book. You

still believe that man as such is pre-eminent, governs the powers of Nature. So he does, to a large extent, in civilization, but not on the Frontier, until that Frontier has been removed. He then moves forward, if you get me. I speak of Nature, not men; they are incidental, used to illustrate a point only.

Also *Country Life* had rewritten Belaney's prose to be "less colourful," as they said in their introduction, to Archie's fury. For his next bestselling books, Archie left *Country Life* and went to another publisher, Lovat Dickson, a Canadian from Alberta who founded his own publishing house in London in 1932, and who became Belaney's loyal friend, defender, and biographer, as well as his long-time publisher, first at Lovat Dickson & Thompson and then as the director of Macmillan and Company. Still, the original *Country Life* edition of *The Men of the Last Frontier* is a striking production, with endpapers reproducing Belaney's sketches of Indian clothing and artifacts, and many photographs of the Canadian wilderness of the time, with descriptive captions by the author, the black-and-white snapshots of mountains and streams adding to the impression that the wilderness is indeed majestic, pristine, and doomed.

The Men of the Last Frontier is not really about men, beyond a few brief character sketches, and is not typical of the later Belaney. Nowhere in the book does the narrator pretend to be an Indian. He is rather our experienced and conscientious guide into the wild, pointing out to us, the tourist, what it is about the northern forest world that makes it worth saving. There is no "plot" per se. Each chapter gives us a locale to explore, or typical wilderness situations: getting lost in the woods, braving the winter, shooting treacherous rapids. Our guide can be amusing about his own personal failures roughing it in the bush, but there is also a grim, Scots, overarching gloom about the struggle to keep the natural world intact: "Side by side with the modern Canada there lies the last battle-ground in the long-drawn-out, bitter struggle between the primeval and civilization," he warns. Civilization is "the fringe of burnt and lumbered wastes adjacent to the railroads," and civilization is winning.

Retreating to the woods, the American Henry David Thoreau, almost a century earlier, meditated on the fate of nature, but his *Walden* is infused with the optimistic breath of American transcendentalism and ends with spring regenerating the land. Belaney is more the skeptical Canadian, although precise and poetic as Thoreau in his observations of nature: The North in winter is a moonscape where "the cold grips the land with the bite of chilled steel" and "trees crack in the frost like scattering rifle-fire." He describes the northern lights, "swaying in a lambent, flickering horde to the tune of the unheard rhythm that rocks the universe." Some of the literary vocabulary seems dated today: the forest as cathedral, the goblin dances of sprites, the Grim Spirit of the Silent North, et al. Also the recurring elegiac tone can seem all but Victorian, although laments for a nation are a time-honoured Canadian genre.

Also Canadian is the narrator's immense sympathy with real animals. Grey Owl knows his beavers and respects their wildness. A British author might have dressed Miq and Maq up in little clothes and set them to tea; an American might symbolically hunt them down; the French would have them moralize in rhymed couplets. But Belaney reflects the reality of the natural world as experienced first-hand, in the tradition of the best Canadian nature writers, from Susanna Moodie, Anna Jameson, and Catharine Parr Traill to Roderick Haig-Brown, Ernest Thompson Seton (whom Belaney knew and admired), Sir Charles G.D. Roberts, and Farley Mowat. In the best sections of *The Men of the Last Frontier* — I'd pick anything with animals or Indians, or set in a canoe — Belaney's prose is rich, accurate, fresh, and original: much as he may have hated his studies, he owed much to the Hastings Grammar School.

The Indians flit through the book, amused, friendly, but often endowed with a mysterious otherness, as our guide notes the sobering presence of charred bear skulls and moose shoulder bones. Chapter 10, *The Trail of Two Sunsets*, is a thoughtful analysis of the condition of the modern Native, beginning with the flight into Canada from Custer's Last Stand ("the ill-advised fiasco"). Belaney speaks with concern of a people he knows, his hunting companions, his friends; he talks considerately of their integrity and courage, but also acknowledges the "attendant degeneracy" of Indians adopting the white man's ways, the struggles, the paradoxes of tribal life in an urban world. Although "left to his own devices in civilization the Indian is a child let loose in a house of terrors," he remains "the freeman of a vast Continent, the First American." Belaney praises the Native spiritual gift as an

Grey Owl with his beloved beaver Jelly Roll at Prince Albert National Park in Saskatchewan.

"almost Oriental mysticism" in a passage reminiscent of Seton's somewhat over-the-top view of the "red-man" (a term Belaney disliked) as the spiritual heir to Socrates or Jesus. Nonetheless, *The Men of the Last Frontier* is not an "Indian book." The tribes are a phenomenon of the vanishing frontier, like the lakes and woods: noble, splendid, but threatened. This first book is not part of the Wa-sha-quon-asin Native masquerade, and in fact was sweetly dedicated to his English aunt in Hastings.

As celebrity began to settle in on Belaney after this first book, he slowly became imprisoned by his Indian persona, pushing himself hard to stay in character and in costume, speaking mock-Ojibway, resorting to hair dye for the black pigtail and henna makeup for the (pale) face. Pony left him, fed up with his absences and drinking, and he impulsively married again, to a beautiful French-Canadian girl, but he never settled down. Travelling constantly, as if pursued by demons, Grey Owl experimented with film and made several excellent movies, documenting his life in the North but exhausting himself in a two-week-long film shoot of a canoe trip down the Mississagi River. He toured Canada. He toured America, theoretically the land of his birth. He toured England and got in trouble with the BBC for his blunt views on fox hunting. He met other celebrities and was welcomed by Governor General Lord Tweedsmuir, John Buchan, Canada's other popular author. He knew royalty and made money: it seemed on the surface a rich and productive career, but he was living a lie. Fuelled by alcohol, he fought with his friends and was belligerent to strangers: about U.S. Customs, where the blue-eyed Indian was questioned keenly about his past, he ranted "I was the only true American on that ship." Journalists were beginning to wonder about those pale eyes, his elegant prose style, his classical education. A man in a bar called him a fake. The Department of Indian Affairs in Canada began investigating his background.

Drained, ill, and alone, he at length retreated to the Ajawaan Lake cabin in Prince Albert National Park, Saskatchewan, where he died on April 13, 1938, at the appallingly young age of forty-nine. It was pneumonia, they said, but the man was simply used up. A few weeks later the *North Bay Nugget*, an Ontario newspaper, broke the story they had long been sitting on, exposing Belaney's Anglo Sussex past. There was plenty of evidence, including that missing toe from the war years. Now the whole world knew the truth.

Today, some eighty years afterward, the Indian play-acting seems harmless, even admirable, and even at the time, Grey Owl was not pilloried. We were fooled, read the headlines, more amused than horrified. Whether a Scot or Ojibway or half-breed, he had written good books and entertained, and he was celebrating the Indian and the wilderness in an honest and popular way. He well served the beaver, he charmed the young, and brought a man of the wilderness into a Depression that needed a hero. His deception still fascinates, as in the recent book, *Great Canadian Imposters* (part of an "Amazing Stories" series). The Caucasian secret identity is also the key to the plot of Richard Attenborough's 1999 movie *Grey Owl*, replete with stunning photography of the radiant Quebec woods and offering an idealized hero, pure of heart, word, and deed, but troubled within. A very white Pierce Brosnan, looking like Richard Nixon, enacts the hero, uncomfortable in pigtails and deerskins, pretending to be a white man pretending to be an Indian. The actress playing Anahareo is forced to deliver lines like: "Why do I have to do the loving and leaving?" Everybody seems miscast, including the beavers.

Whatever its authenticity, Grey Owl's Indian act filled a need of the day, which was also met by Pauline Johnson paddling her canoe and lecturing in beads (she had Mohawk blood but was hardly a Savage Princess), or Chief Buffalo-Child Long-Lance, of mixed blood from North Carolina, who outrageously played the Native chief in Alberta and got away with it. Ernest Thompson Seton's Indian obsession led to the Woodcraft Movement and his college of Indian wisdom in New Mexico. There had been, through the nineteenth and early twentieth centuries, a long tradition of Indian epics (*Hiawatha*), Indian operas (*Natoma* by Victor Herbert), novels (*Ramona*), classic photographs (Edward Curtis), Indian love calls (When I'm calling you — ooo — ooo), and a rich legacy of Hollywood westerns, all the way up to *Little Big Man*, *A Man Called Horse*, and *Dances with Wolves*.

It is probable that Belaney's Cree and Ojibway friends knew all along that he was faking it, but why would they sabotage their champion? A lot of people — aunts, journalists, buddies, critics — suspected. What distinguishes Belaney now, and what saves him from being a period curiosity, is the work itself. His five books are solid literary achievements, quite readable, although not yet, scandalously, canonized as CanLit. His most popular titles — *Pilgrims of the Wild*, *The Adventures of Sajo and Her Beaver People* — sold well at the time and are still in print. He was an evocative prose stylist soaked in the English classics: *The Men of the Last Frontier* is buttressed with echoes and epigraphs from Robert Louis Stevenson, John Bunyan, the Bible, the Greeks, Lord Byron, Alfred Tennyson, Henry Wadsworth Longfellow. His life is a paradox. On one level he seemed driven to relive his own father's sad biography, with the drinking, brawling, and abandoned families. By the end, Archie had acquired at least four wives, perhaps five, as well as several children. Yet somewhere along the way, wastrel Archie became a creative force in the world, a charismatic performer, and a writer with an important message.

We now, more than ever, have to heed his warning, delivered long before Greenpeace or Al Gore or PETA. Grey Owl forcefully reminds us that we are creatures of the natural world and cannot trifle with our environment. In this first book, he has no hopes that we will listen. The epilogue of *The Men of the Last Frontier* shows us a forlorn white man and an Indian, looking out over farms, foresters with axes, skylines, massed machinery, and smokestacks belching a "dark canopy" over all. Belaney tells us flatly that "all wild life is over." This in 1931! What would he have made of today's oil spills, melting glaciers, flash floods and forest fires, clear-cuttings, polluted waters, declining fish stocks, trashed oceans, climate change, poisonous greenhouse emissions, the scandal of our environmental indifference? Across the Alberta border, not far to the northwest of Grey Owl's Prince Albert lakeside cabin, now stretch the black domains of the Athabasca Tar Sands.

WITH US AGAIN WITH WONDERFUL FILMS!

After a brilliant and overwhelmingly successful tour

of

The British Isles and the United States

and

A Command Performance at Buckingham Palace

GREY OWL

WILL SHOW HIS PICTURES AND TALK ON

"BACK TO MY BEAVER PEOPLE"

— AT —

MASSEY HALL, SATURDAY, MARCH 26th

Commencing 8 p.m. sharp. Doors open 7.30.

RESERVE YOUR SEATS EARLY AND BRING YOUR FRIENDS!

Tickets: $1.00 and 50c.

Remember! If you want your seats in blocks book early!
Tickets may be secured by telephoning Mr. Eric Gaskell, RA. 2867, or Mrs. King, HU. 1441.

THE STUDENT'S IMPRESSION OF GREY OWL!

The Toronto Branch of The Canadian Authors' Association offers two prizes for the best essays by any high or secondary school student on the theme of Grey Owl's appearance and remarks while on the Massey Hall platform on the evening of March 26th.

FIRST PRIZE!

ANY TWO OF GREY OWL'S BOOKS (AUTOGRAPHED)

"Tales of an Empty Cabin"   "Sajo and Her Beaver People"   "Pilgrims of the Wild"
"Men of the Last Frontier"   "The Tree"

SECOND PRIZE!

ANY ONE OF THE FIVE

Preferred length 300 words. Limit 500 words. Entries to reach Mr. Eric Gaskell, 40 Nanton Ave., Toronto, by April 9th. Presentations will be made at the Canadian Authors' Association Annual Dinner May 14th.

UNDER THE AUSPICES OF THE TORONTO BRANCH
OF THE CANADIAN AUTHOR'S ASSOCIATION

A circular announcing Grey Owl's lecture at Toronto's Massey Hall in 1938.

"The Canadian romance of nature is over," Grey Owl tells us long ago in his poetic and timely first book. Protect it, or lose it, he warns. We have done our utmost to lose it, but perhaps the time has finally come to attend to the message of this strange, self-destructive, deplorable, but somehow magnificent fake. It was Grey Owl's gift to see both the darkness and the light in the probable fate of the natural world, and in this, his first book, *The Vanishing Frontier* (as it should have been called), he begins a lifelong argument to persuade us to look after our salvation as a species and as a planet, and to do it now.

Further Reading

The essential biography of Grey Owl is Donald B. Smith's splendid *From the Land of Shadows: The Making of Grey Owl* (Western Producer Prairie Books, 1990) to which I am much indebted. It is in paperback (GreyStone, 1999) and is a must-read. For a good shorter version of the life, Jane Billinghurst's *Grey Owl: The Many Faces of Archie Belaney* (GreyStone, 1999) is well worth a look. Lovat Dickson's early biographies, *Half-Breed* (P. Davies, 1939) and *Wilderness Man* (Macmillan of Canada, 1973), are a bit dated but still enjoyable and informative, by the man who was Belaney's publisher after *Country Life* and who knew him well. There is a wealth of other materials: a photography book of Grey Owl country, a prose poem, appreciative essays, memoirs, and several biographies.

Later books by Grey Owl after *The Men of the Last Frontier* include his entertaining bestseller *Pilgrims of the Wild* (Dundurn Voyageur Series, 2010), which dramatizes the beavers and includes a valuable biographical introduction by Michael Gnarowski. *The Adventures of Sajo and Her Beaver People*, long a children's favourite in many editions, is nonetheless a satisfying read for adults. (The title is *Sajo and the Beaver People* in the United States.)

For the role of the Indian, Daniel Francis's *The Imaginary Indian: The Image of the Indian in Canadian Culture* (Arsenal Pulp, 1992) is stimulating, as is Betty Keller's account of the Mohawk princess, Pauline Johnson, *Pauline* (Douglas & McIntyre, 1981). Cheryl MacDonald's *Great Canadian Imposters* (James Lorimer, 2009) is more scholarly than its title suggests and includes a short biography of Chief Leroy, as well.

Ernest Thompson Seton's last chapter in *The Book of Woodcraft and Indian Lore* (Doubleday, 1921) offers a sixfold "Message" from Indian experience (as the prophet of outdoor life, the beautiful, the sacred) with comparisons of Native philosophy to the thought of Socrates and Jesus, among others: the cult of the idealized Indian at its most intense.

The Richard Attenborough movie *Grey Owl* (1999) is available on DVD. The photography is exceptional. I recommend Anahareo's lively *Devil in Deerskins* (New Press, 1972), if it can be searched out. I met her at the book's launch and found her alert and delightful company. My own *Wilderness Writers* (Clarke, Irwin, 1972) talks about animal-story writers. See also Margaret Atwood's *Survival* (House of Anansi, 1972).

THE MEN OF
THE LAST FRONTIER

ORIGINAL PUBLISHER'S NOTE

The publisher feels that a short foreword is necessary in offering this book to the public.

It should be explained that the author is a half-breed Indian, whose name has recently become known throughout the English-speaking world. His father was a Scot, his mother an Apache Indian of New Mexico, and he was born somewhere near the Rio Grande forty odd years ago. Grey Owl is the translation of his Red Indian name, given to him when he became a blood brother of the Ojibways, and his proper legal style. He trekked, in his early twenties, into Canada and followed the life of a bush Indian, trapping, fire-ranging, and guiding. During the Great War, he enlisted in the 13th Montreal Battalion, became a sniper, and saw service in France. On his return he took up his old life as a trapper, but presently found his chief interest in the preservation of the beaver, which was on the verge of extinction, and his efforts in that direction have been recognized by the Canadian Government. He tried his hand at writing an article on Canadian Wildlife, and his letters to his publisher, from time to time, were so original, so full of the local colour of his surroundings, that, in 1929, the suggestion was made that he should write this book. Difficulties have been many, both for author and publisher. The book was written in many camps, often the author was a hundred miles from the nearest post office, and frequently weather conditions made any journey impossible. His MS., by no means always easy to follow, was further complicated by the fact that it had been typewritten by a French-Canadian who knew little English.

Among the pile of letters and MS. which, in the course of time, accumulated at the publishers, were several rough but extraordinarily vivid sketches drawn by the author in pencil on pages torn from an exercise book; one of these is reproduced here and others appear as the end papers of this book.

At Grey Owl's own request, and because the publisher felt very strongly that much of the value of his work lies in its individuality, the editing of his MS. has been reduced to a minimum and alterations have only been made to clear possible ambiguities or where a phrase would have read too strangely. This will explain to any reader who may find the author's language anywhere unnatural that the fault does not lie with Grey Owl.

Dedicated as a tribute to my aunt, whom I must thank for such education that enables me to interpret into words the spirit of the forest, beautiful for all its underlying wildness

PROLOGUE

A deep slow-flowing river; silent, smooth as molten glass; on either bank a forest, dark, shadowy, and mysterious.

The face of Nature as it was since the Beginning; all creation down the eons of unmeasured time, brooding in ineffable calm, infinite majesty, and a breathless and unutterable silence.

So it has lain for countless ages, dreaming, dwelling on the memories of untold tales no longer remembered, wise with the wisdom of uncounted years of waiting.

Overhead an eagle manoeuvres in the eye of the sun, and in the shadows on the shore an otter lies asleep.

Far-off in midstream appears a tiny dot, growing larger and larger as it approaches, and presently a bark canoe, yellow as an autumn leaf; and floating as lightly, speeds by. The sun glints sharply at regular intervals on paddles swung with swift and tireless strokes, by six brown, high-featured savages. Eagle feathers bob in unison, copper-hued backs bend and sway, driving forward the fragile craft, high of prow and stern, with a leaping undulation that is the poetry of motion.

In the centre stands a white man, bedizened with the remnants of the lace and ruffles of the courts of Europe. His cheeks are hollow and his frame gaunt. His skin is streaked with blood from the bites of myriad flies, but he recks not of it; his burning gaze is fixed ahead: Westward, Westward, from whence the river flows.

A few minutes and the bump and swish of paddles become inaudible. The canoe diminishes again to a speck and disappears into the unknown. And the tiny waves of its passing find their way to shore, and so die. The two wild creatures stare in idle curiosity, and return each to his occupation: the eagle to his undisturbed soaring, the otter to his interrupted sleeping: and little know that, for a moment, they have gazed on History.

And so, unostentatiously, without pomp or ceremony, all unknown to the teeming millions of the Eastern Hemisphere, the long closed portals of the Western World swing open.

I

THE VANGUARD

I live not in myself, but I become
Portion of that around me; and to me
High mountains are a feeling, but the hum
Of human cities torture; I can see
Nothing to loathe in Nature, save to be
A link reluctant in a fleshly chain,
Class'd among creatures, when the soul can flee,
And with the sky, the peak, the heaving plain
Of ocean, or the stars, mingle, and not in vain.

— LORD BYRON

A chief of the Sarcee dressed in all the regalia to which his rank entitles him.

During the last twenty years or so, with emigration pouring its thousands of newcomers into Canada to seek fresh homes, the world has been wont to consider the Dominion as a settled country, largely shorn of its forests, and given over almost entirely to farming, mining, manufacturing, and like industries.

Certainly the Canada of today can boast of unlimited opportunities for those who are willing to work, and there can be found in her cities and small towns a civilization as prosaic and matter-of-fact as exists in many older and longer-settled countries. There is big business; there are mining developments and engineering projects second to none in the world. Several finely equipped railroads span her from coast to coast. The mountains have been conquered, mighty rivers dammed, and vast reaches of prairie and woodland denuded of their game and brought under the plough. There are few improvements or inventions of modern times that are not in common use, even in sparsely settled districts.

All this is known to the world at large, and the word "Canada" is synonymous with "Prosperity" and "Advancement." These things coupled with the almost unequalled natural resources yet remaining at her command, have placed Canada in the forefront of the colonies that help to make the British Empire.

Those of us who enjoy the high privilege of participation in the benefits accruing from the development of a land of such riches, and unequalled opportunity, are apt to think but little, or fail, perhaps, even to be cognizant of the ceaseless warfare that for three centuries has been carried on in the van of the Great Advance. Without it the triumphant march of today might have been long deferred, or at least limited to a far smaller area. This bitter contest is still being waged without intermission, by a thin handful of devoted souls, on the far-flung borderland beyond the fringe of Civilization, where they are still adding additional, and alas, final, verses to the soul-inspiring saga of the Great North-West.

The mechanical mind of the efficient engineer who designs marvelous bridges, constructs huge dams, lays out our railroads, or makes extensive surveys — however well suited to his particular calling — very seldom possesses that sixth sense which seems to be the peculiar attribute of the pathfinder. Many of the mountain passes, and skillfully selected routes bearing the names of prominent men supposed to have discovered them, were the century-old trails of trappers and other frontiersmen whose names we never hear.

Not for the borderman are the rich rewards of honour, material profit, and national prominence, which fall rather to those who follow with the more conspicuous achievements of construction, and, too often, destruction. Not for gain does he pursue his thankless task, for he is satisfied if he makes the wherewithal to live; neither for renown, for he lives obscurely, and often dies a strange death, alone. And no press notices sing his praises, and no monument is raised over his often unburied body.

He who leads the precarious life of skirmisher or scout on the No-Man's-Land beyond the Frontier, becomes so imbued with the spirit of his environment, that when the advance guard of the new era sweeps down on him with its flow of humanity and modern contrivance, he finds he cannot adapt himself to the new conditions. Accustomed to loneliness and seclusion, when his wanderings are curtailed, he forthwith gathers his few belongings and, like the Arab, folds his tent and steals silently away. Thus he moves on, stage by stage, with his furred and feathered associates, to fresh untrammelled horizons; where he explores, lays his trails, and unearths secret places to his heart's content, blazing the way for civilization, and again retiring before it when it comes.

This is the spirit of the true Pioneer. This is the urge that drove Champlain, Raleigh, Livingstone, and Cook into the four corners of the earth; the unquenchable ambition to conquer new territory, to pass where never yet trod foot of man.

Of all the various kinds of bordermen that pass their days Back of Beyond, undoubtedly the most accomplished and useful as a pathfinder is the trapper. He antedates all others. Men of the type of Boone, Crockett, Bridger, and Cody still exist today, undergoing the same hardships, eating the same foods, travelling by the same means, as did their forerunners, and talking languages and using methods handed down from the dim obscurity of the past, by the past-masters in the first and most romantic trade that North America ever knew, that of the hunter. The trapper of today has no longer the menace of the hostile savage to contend with, but he is in many ways under infinitely greater difficulties than was the woodsman of an earlier day.

From the time of the conquest of Canada until about fifty years ago, the land now under cultivation was covered with hardwood and pine forests with little or no undergrowth or other obstructions to retard progress. The woods-runner of that period had the best of timber for manufacturing his equipment. As a contrast, I once saw in the far North a party of Indians equipped with tamarac axe-handles and poplar toboggans; a condition of affairs about on a par with using wooden wheels on a locomotive, or cardboard soles on boots. The woods in those days were full of deer, a more prolific animal than the moose, far more easy to handle when killed, and with a much more useful hide. The old-time trapper had not far to go for his hunt, once settled in his district, and he had no competition whatsoever.

The modern hunter has to cover more ground, largely by means of trails laboriously cut through tangled undergrowth, sometimes not setting over three or four effective traps in a ten-mile line. The country so far North is more broken, the rivers rougher, the climate more severe; the forest, amounting in some places to little more than a ragged jungle, offers resistances unknown to the traveller of earlier days. Steel traps have supplanted to a large extent the wooden deadfall, and the snare, and better firearms have simplified still-hunting;* but game is scarcer, and harder to approach, except in very remote sections.

Conditions have changed, and the terrain has shifted, but the kind of a man who follows the chase for a living remains the same; the desire to penetrate far-away hidden spots, the urge to wander, is there as it was in his prototype of two hundred years ago. The real trapper (by which I mean the man who spends his days up beyond the Strong Woods, not the part-time hunter, or "railroad" trapper out for a quick fortune) is as much an integral part of the woods as are the animals themselves. In tune with his surroundings, wise in the lore of the Indian, he reads and correctly interprets the cryptograms in the book that lies open before him, scanning the face of Nature and forestalling her moods to his advantage. Dependent entirely on himself, he must be resourceful, ready to change plan at a moment's notice, turning adverse circumstances and reverses to what slight advantage he may. The hardships and privations of the trapper's life have developed in him a determination, a dogged perseverance, and a bulldog tenacity of purpose not often necessary in other walks of life. At the outset, before the

---

* Stalking.

commencement of the hunt, the trapper may have to spend one or two months in getting supplies to his ground, after spending most of the summer searching for a likely spot. His exploration work is of great value to those who follow him, but it is all lost time to him. He expects, and receives, nothing for his labours, but counts it all in the day's work, and hopes his ground will produce the goods. On such trips these men are sometimes called on to perform seemingly impossible feats, and probably no trip coming inside my recollection would illustrate this better than the journey undertaken by a white man and an Indian, three winters ago in Northern Quebec.

These men came from further south and, having made no allowance for the difference in climate, on their arrival found the freeze-up already in progress. Travelling during this period is considered by even the most enduring as being almost, if not quite, impossible.

Nothing daunted, these two hardy souls commenced their pilgrimage, for it was nothing less. Each had a canoe-load of about 600 lbs. On the first lake they found ice, which, whilst not capable of bearing a man, effectually prevented the passage of a canoe. This had to be broken, the two men armed with poles first breaking a channel in an empty canoe, from one expanse of open water to another. This entailed the unloading of 600 lbs. of baggage on any kind of shore, into the snow, and the reloading of it on the return of the empty canoe; work enough, if frequently performed. They proceeded thus at the rate of about three miles a day, carrying the loads and canoes over seven portages. It snowed steadily day and night, increasing the difficulties on portages, making camping out a misery, and preventing at the same time the ice from becoming thick enough to walk on.

For five days they continued this struggle, making camp every night after dark, soaking wet and exhausted. It now turned colder, and this did not improve the ice under its clogging mass of snow water, while in the channel so laboriously broken, the cakes of ice and slush often cemented together, during the return trip, into a stronger barrier than the original ice had been. Held up at length on the shores of an eight-mile lake by these conditions, they passed around the entire shoreline of one side of the lake on snowshoes, the ice being too weak to carry them otherwise, and even then, within a few feet of the shore, driving their axes through the ice at one blow every few feet. A full day was consumed on the outward journey, and they returned by the light of a clouded moon, splashed to the head, their garments freezing as they walked. But they were well repaid, as the water flooded the ice around the holes they had cut, and slushed up the snow on it. The whole mass froze through, forming a kind of bridge, over which they passed in safety, drawing the canoes and loads in relays on improvised sleighs.

This style of progress, alternating with the usual portages, continued for several more days, one man going through the ice in deep water, and being with difficulty rescued. The men were in no danger from starvation, but wrestling with hundred-pound bags of provisions under such trying conditions, and carrying ice-laden canoes over portages on snowshoes, was too severe a labour to be long continued. Worn-out and discouraged by their seemingly hopeless task, too far in to turn back, not far enough advanced to remain, faced by the prospect of passing the best part of the winter on a main route denuded of game, these companions in tribulation plodded with bitter determination, slowly, painfully, but persistently ahead.

Mile by mile, yard by yard, foot by foot, it seemed, those mountainous loads proceeded on their way, as two steely-eyed, grimfaced men opposed their puny efforts to the vindictive Power that vainly inhibited their further progress.

Their objective was a fast-running river, some forty miles in from the steel,* knowledge of which had caused them to retain

* Railroad.

their canoes, in the hopes of finding it unfrozen. This proved to be the case, and on its current they travelled in ease and comfort, as far, in two days, as they had previously done in the two weeks that they had been on the trail. When the water no longer suited their direction, they camped several days to rest up; and winter coming on in real earnest, they cached their now useless canoes, and making sleighs moved on into their ground by easy stages.

My own first introduction to a district celebrated for its topographical irregularities was a muskeg two miles long, of the same width and of indeterminate depth. These muskegs are frequently little more than moss-covered bogs that offer not one solid piece of footing in miles. Between two of us we juggled close on nine hundred pounds of equipment and provisions across this morass, besides a large freighting canoe, taking three days to complete the task. It rained the whole time, so we were wet on both sides, at both ends, and in the middle. Two nights camp had to be made on a quaking bog, where a small cluster of stunted spruce offered shelter and a little dry wood, whilst mosquitoes in countless myriads swarmed on us from the pools of slime on every side.

At no place in this swamp could we carry over a hundred pounds, owing to the treacherous nature of the footing, this increasing the number of trips.

On one occasion, bogged to the knees, I was unable to extricate myself; and, unwilling to drop my load in the mud, had to wait in this position till my partner passed on his return trip. The whole thing was a hideous nightmare. Four trips apiece we made by quarter-mile stretches, and the labour involved was nothing short of terrific. Yet the feat, if so it could be called, excited no comment; such things are commonly done.

★ ★ ★

Men following the trap line become so inured to the severe conditions prevailing, and the unremitting exertion connected with the continuous travelling, that they can undergo, without serious inconvenience, discomforts and hardships that would kill an ordinary man. The exigencies of a life devoted to wrestling a living from an unyielding and ungenerous wilderness, make frequent feats of endurance a matter of course; yet the severity of the life itself; unartificial, healthy, aboriginal almost, engenders the nervous force necessary to the performance of them. Laziness under these conditions is an impossibility, as even to exist requires, at times, a daily expenditure of energy not always given by the wage-earner to a day's work.

In the summer long trips have to be made by canoe and portage into the interior in search of hunting grounds, whilst swarms of mosquitoes and black flies make life almost unendurable. In late summer, or early Fall, canoes are loaded down with little less than half a ton of supplies, and have to be run down rapids, or poled up them according to direction, and paddled over big lakes in all kinds of weather, into the selected territory. At every portage the whole outfit must be unloaded, packed across the carry by means of a leather headpiece attached to two ten-foot thongs and known as a "tump line," in loads of from one to three hundred pounds each trip, according to the kind of trail. The canoe is then reloaded and the paddling renewed. No rests are taken on these portages; recuperation is supposed, on the sound theory that a change is as good as a rest, to take place on the return trip for another load.

In these late days game is far to seek, and it is sometimes necessary to go in two or three hundred miles over thirty, forty, or fifty portages, only perhaps to find, with the coming of snow, that what had appeared to be a rich territory when visited on an exploration trip, is now barren, the game having migrated in the interim. The hunter who finds himself caught in such a predicament may be hard put to it to make his expenses, and his whole year is a loss.

The hunting ground reached, a log cabin is built, trails laid out, caches of provisions distributed to outlying points, where tents or other shelters for one-night stands are to be located. Traps are set, meat killed and brought in. Once the snow commences to fall, trails have to be kept open, and traps examined and broken out after every storm, to the number of perhaps two hundred or so, extending over an aggregate of thirty or forty miles of lines. And this is over and above the constant cutting of wood, cooking, tanning of hides, and other routine work.

Expeditions have to be made into far districts with a toboggan loaded with a tent, stove, blankets, and a few provisions, drawn by dogs. This outfit will be set up every night on top of the snow, the only preparation being to tramp the surface solid with snowshoes, and to lay on it a thick layer of balsam brush. Every morning this will be all pulled down again, and loaded, and trail broken ahead of the dogs for another day; and so on for a week at a time.

A man if alone, and going far, needs all the available space in his canoe for provisions, and must often do without dogs, having no room for them. On these side trips he must therefore draw his own toboggan. As he has also to break his own trail, he travels light, taking only a sheet of canvas for a windbreak, and one blanket, sleeping out all night in temperatures often as low as 60 degrees below zero.

Making camp thus is a matter of two or three hours' hard work, and this after a day's hard travelling. The snow has to be dug out over an area of about ten feet each way, as the fire would speedily sink below the level of the camp to the ground otherwise; and not the least labour is the cutting of the large quantity of wood required. Nor dare the trapper lose time to cook, eat, or rest until the last job is done, lest he be caught in the dark with insufficient wood, or otherwise unprepared for the blistering deadly cold.

For there is One who is watching him, has watched him since he entered the woods, waiting for just some such contingency:

the grim Spirit of the Silent North, who stalks each lonely traveller's footsteps relentless and implacable, whose will is law in the White Silence. They who enter his Kingdom do well to tread with circumspection.

Once fixed for the night, his hunger satisfied and his pipe going, the refreshed man takes his ease. He is no longer alone, for his dancing fire serves as both friend and comforter; and as he sits and watches the billowing smoke clouds make pictures in the air, he thinks not the labours of the day just done, but plans the morrow's trip with enthusiasm. Thus he is content, and his scheme of existence, shorn of all the multitudinous complexities of modern life, suffices him; he retains his peace of mind and thinks the cost in hardship well repaid.

During the dead days of mid-winter, when game does not run, the time hangs heavy, and loneliness is often such that only high-pressure activity keeps the mind from wandering into the black abyss of introspection. So that, as a man is more alone with himself in the confinement of the camp, he stays out during all the hours of daylight, and often many of those of darkness, in all weathers, traversing the empty streets of the forest, where the tracks of beasts are as messages from friends, and the very trees seem living entities.

A man so much alone looks kindly on the numerous small birds and animals that congregate around his cabins and camping places. Squirrels that eye him knowingly from the eaves of his roof, chattering and quivering with some violent emotion the while, are tolerated until they become a pest. Ermine are suffered to enter the camp at will through some hidden crack, to flicker noiselessly around in flashes of white, bobbing up almost simultaneously in widely separated spots, thus giving the impression that there are two of them, where there is only one, or that they are able to appear in two places at the one time. Chickades in little flocks chirrup their "Don't-give-a-darn — Don't-give-a-darn" at him at every stop, and — trail companion that sticketh closer than a brother — the whiskey-jack, commits, unpunished, his numerous depredations. This whiskey-jack is a small bird, about the size of a blackbird, but he has more mischief in his small body than there is in a whole bag of cats. He is a scamp, but a likeable rascal, at that. He mocks the calls of other birds and steals bait, or any small articles left around the camp. He loves human company, and, at the first smoke of a campfire, he appears mysteriously from nowhere, like a small grey shadow, and perches on a limb, generally right over the trapper's lunch place, knocking snow down his neck or into the cooking as he lights. He has a foolish little song he whistles which is supposed, no doubt, to charm the hunter into giving him a part of his meal. This he generally gets, but does not eat, carrying it away and caching it; so he is never full, and stays until the last morsel has disappeared.

A lonely man cannot resist the little bird's begging, and he, as he gets fed, becomes bolder and, should the man move away to fix the fire, will even steal out of the lunch bag. If shoo'ed away, Mr. Whiskey Jack will fly up squawking into a branch and maybe knock some more snow down the trapper's neck, or on to his mitts which he is carefully drying.

A pleasant hour having been spent in this way, the trapper moves on, thinking himself well rid of this impish familiar, and continues baiting his sets. Friend whiskey-jack follows silently and invisibly behind, flying from tree to tree. When the trapper stops and baits his trap, the nuisance watches until he is gone, and just as carefully unbaits it, removing the meat piece by piece, and caching it — and so all along the line for miles. And when the trapper returns to his fire place, there is his chum, sitting innocently up on a limb, singing his crazy song, waiting for some more to eat. At one camp I had, there were five or six of these birds, and they used to follow me out on the trail in this way; and in selecting their portion from any moose-meat there was, believe me, they knew the steak from the neck. A man alone for months is glad of their company, in spite of the trouble they make; and for me their friendliness and cheerful whistling have brightened many a lonesome camp fire.

By some dispensation of Providence the unpleasant happenings, the freezings, the burnings, the starvation trips, and the terrific labour are soon forgotten, only the successes and triumphs are remembered. Were it otherwise, not one man in ten would return to the bush after the first trip. A man may be soaking wet, half-frozen, hungry and tired, landed on some inhospitable neck of the woods, vowing that a man is a fool to so abuse himself. Yet, let him but make a fire, get a sheet of canvas between himself and the elements, and a dish of hot tea under his belt, and his previous state of misery will fade from his mind; and he will remark to his partner, his dogs, or his tea-pail, that "Home was never like this," or that "This is the life."

He overcomes his difficulties by skill and cunning, rather than by force, taking a leaf from the Indian's book, thus husbanding his energies against the time when he is tried by the supreme tests of endurance, which occur frequently enough. A saving sense of humour eradicates all feeling of self-pity in times of stress, the only feeling being that elation which one lone man may experience at prevailing against overwhelming odds, and the only comments passed arc a few quaint remarks on the queer tricks of Fate. The more lurid flows of profanity are reserved for trivial occurrences, where the energy thus expended will not be missed.

This optimistic state of mind must be carried to the point where — if he lose a canoe-load of goods through miscalculation, or incorrect handling in a rapids, or should a toboggan piled with necessaries, and what few luxuries he permits himself, go through the ice after being hauled eighty miles or so — he must be glad it was not worse, see only the silver lining, and remember he did not drown. Also that he is lucky to, perhaps, have saved a few matches in a waterproof case, or that he kept his hat dry maybe.

He who lives by the hunt must be patient, and of a monumental calm. The constant petty annoyances incident to everyday travel, trivial in themselves, become by constant repetition exasperating to a degree, and would soon drive an irritable man to the verge of insanity. Being much alone, this modern Spartan subjects himself to a discipline as severe as that demanded of any soldier, for he cannot allow his emotions ever to gain the upper hand, lest they get complete control, and that way madness lies. His unceasing vigilance and watchfulness, by constant practise, become almost automatic. Even in sleep this awareness of what is transpiring around him is subconsciously continued, so that a slight noise, as of the passage of some animal, or the abrupt cessation of a familiar sound, bring instant wakefulness.

They who would catch a woodsman of the old school asleep do well to come carelessly and with much noise. A stealthy approach seems to establish some telepathic communication with the subconscious mind of one who lives with Nature. This faculty is borrowed from the animals, and is common amongst Indians. To creep up on a sleeping animal, except in a canoe, is an impossibility. Domesticated wild animals, lying asleep, perhaps in the midst of all kinds of noise, will, if gazed at intently, become uneasy and awaken.

A man's progress through the woods is heralded before him as the advance of a plague would be down a crowded thoroughfare, and he who would cope with senses so much more delicately balanced than his own must needs develop, to some extent, the alertness of the beasts he chases.

Also, he must develop to a remarkable degree the tenacity of life that they possess. Deer shot through the heart have been known to rush blindly on for a hundred yards, dead to all intents and purposes. I have followed moose, shot through the lungs and otherwise wounded, that travelled doggedly on for miles before falling. So with man, it has sometimes occurred that, having lost everything by some accident, frequent enough in the unwritten history of the woods, lone bushmen have been known to stagger out of the wilderness in a dying condition, having striven painfully for days to get to some human habitation, the will to live alone having sustained them until they might safely collapse.

The case is well known of the Scotch half-breed, who was caught by the leg in a bear trap weighing perhaps twenty-five pounds, and fastened to a large tally-pole. He cut through the heavy birch clog with his hunting-knife, no mean feat even for a well man; he then made a sling to hold the leg and trap clear of the ground, and, with the teeth lacerating him at every move, made his way to civilization on improvised crutches — only to die during the night within reach of help, just outside the town limits.

In a territory beyond the jurisdiction of the police, life is simplified down to a few basic principles. Laws become more or less unnecessary, except the few unwritten ones which are tacitly observed; and ostracism, or worse, is the penalty for infringement. In such an elementary state of society complete strangers, meeting, have no means of judging one another save by a few simple direct actions, and it is well to avoid even the appearance of wrongdoing. Witness the case in earlier days of the prospector, who, on meeting a party on the trail, reached quickly towards his hip, and was immediately shot. It transpired that he had merely been in the act of drawing his flask to offer a round of drinks, but the suspicious action, as related by the witness, entirely exonerated his assailant.

Generally speaking your woodsman does not steal.

In the first place, a man usually has all the necessaries or he could not be in the woods at all, also, he has faith in his fellow man, and in the unwritten law that he himself obeys. To take a certain amount of food, to carry a man on to the nearest base of supplies, is not considered other than excusable. In fact, deserted shacks are often found to contain a small supply of essentials, left there by the departing owners with that very end in view. Caches containing goods worth hundreds of dollars are often exposed to view, although sheltered from the weather; and passersby will make repairs to the keep-over if necessary, in the same spirit in which they expect to get it done for them by others.

Once stealing is commenced by a few amateurs and thoughtless or ignorant vandals, the tradition of centuries crumbles, the barriers are down, and stealing becomes the king of outdoor sports. A rifled cache in the woods calls for reprisals of a severe nature and, unless justice can weed out the offenders, sometimes leads to grim tragedy enacted beneath the larch and spruce trees, who keep their secret well; mute witnesses, condoning by their silence a justice as certain and inexorable as the retributions of Nature itself.

Two years ago a white trapper, situated two hundred and forty miles north of the railroad in the Abitibi district, returned one night to his camp to find it destroyed in such away as to be no longer habitable. Worse, every last ounce of his provision was gone, together with a spare canoe, a tent, and small stove, with which he could have made out to live, on a strictly meat diet, all winter. His remaining stove was smashed beyond possibility of repair.

The man was in a serious position. He had with him a little food left from his trip, enough only for a couple of days at the most. It was the time of year when, owing to ice conditions, travel by canoe was almost impossible. Soon the intense cold of winter, in that parallel, would be upon him and without shelter he must succumb, starvation or no. The time of the raid had obviously been selected with regard to this. Somehow he got out to the "Front," how is not known, except that he arrived in rags, and in a starving condition. I have talked with the man in question, but beyond stating that it "was no picnic" he will not speak of the trip.

The *casus belli* was known to be the disputed ownership of a rich hunting ground, and the intention of the raiders evidently was that he should never leave the spot alive. The following winter, in the same district, the two parties met, six men all told; threats were exchanged over the muzzles of loaded rifles, and a pitched battle seemed imminent. But the affair had attracted the attention of the Mounted Police and itching trigger-fingers had to be controlled in this instance. Arrests were made and a trial staged. Justice, unable to differentiate between the claims of either side, dropped the case; but such things are never forgotten nor forgiven.

This affair was a modification of the old "Longue Traverse," a scheme adopted by the despotic representatives of a big fur company in earlier days, whereby undesirables, such as free traders, encroaching trappers and others, were captured, their outfit confiscated, and themselves turned loose with a rifle and a few rounds of ammunition, to find their way on foot, hundreds of miles, to the nearest town. And often enough a pair of Indian killers, earning thereby, perhaps, a rebate on their debt, followed stealthily behind to watch the dying struggles of a starving man with callous apathy, or grimly stalk him day by day, and later shoot him.

A man who has successfully overcome the difficulties, and endured the privations of the trap-line for a few years, can no more quit it than the confirmed gambler can leave his gaming. Trapping is, after all, a gamble on a large scale, the trapper's life and outfit against the strength of the wilderness and its presiding genii, to win a living; and in the hazard he experiences a rare pleasure.

Nor is his life without its compensations. He may climb a mountain, and look as far as the eye can reach, out over illimitable leagues of forested hill and valley stretching into the dim distance, with a feeling of ownership, and there is none to say him nay. And to all intents and purposes it is his, therein to work his will; surely a vast enough estate to satisfy the most land-hungry, and with no taxes or upkeep attached to it. His sole title to possession is the hard-won supremacy he has attained to by unremitting toil, as potent for him as any letter's patent could be. The sense of untrammelled freedom and a wild independence, inculcated by wanderings over an unlimited area, enter his soul, unfitting him for any other walk of life. His is the sport of kings, and he is free as no king ever was.

He scans the face of the wilderness, and there gets his inspiration. The pale disc of the moon shining through the interlaced limbs of a leafless tree; the silhouette of tall distant pines against the frosty sky; the long shadows cast by a winter sunset across the white expanse of a snowbound lake, all strike a chord which finds a ready response in his breast. He may not be able, or willing, to express his feelings to the world, but they indubitably impress his unspoken thoughts. The sublimity, the immensity, and the silent majesty of his surroundings influence his character, and the trapper is often a quiet thoughtful man, set in his ways, and not overly given to conversation.

Many are the tales told of his taciturnity; exaggerated accounts, no doubt, many of them, but typical. There is the story of the old-timer, who, in years of solitary wandering, had happened on a particularly pleasant camping ground and was preparing to pass the night there. Presently he saw coming a canoe, and soon a stranger, attracted no doubt by his smoke and the knowledge of the presence of another of his kind in the interminable waste, edged his canoe ashore and landed.

"Fine evening," said the stranger, probably his first speech for months.

"Yeah," replied the old-timer.

"Gosh darned fine camping ground you got here," added the new arrival.

"Uh huh." The habit of a lifetime was not to be so easily broken.

The other man commenced to unload his canoe, and whilst he so busied himself, endeavoured to warm the chill atmosphere by cheerful conversation.

"They's a war in China; d'jy'a hear about it?" he queried.

Receiving no answer he looked up to see his newly found companion, deliberately folding his blankets, and pulling down his tent, evidently so lately erected.

"What in hell's wrong," he demanded in pained surprise. "Not goin' away, a'ir you?"

"Yes, I'm going away," was the answer. "They's too darn much discussion around here to suit my fancy."

It is related of a man of my acquaintance that on an occasion being informed politely that it was "a great day" he gave no answer; and on the remark being repeated, replied — "I'm not denying it, am I? I don't aim to have no argyment with you!"

Men who follow this life will follow no other, and the interests of the outside world, current events, the doings of the great and the near-great, affect them not at all. I remember being of a party where one of the guides was asked how he could go such long periods without news from the "front," as the railroad is called, the death of a noted film star being cited as an example of such news.

"I don't give a continental hoot," said he, "if Douglas Fairbanks eats his beans with a knife or a shovel. As for that fillum guy you say died, too much of a good thing killed him I guess. Me I'm okay here, and I won't die till I'm dam good and ready."

Those used to the polite evasions and diplomatic social intrigue of a higher state of society find the average frontiersman disconcertingly direct in speech on occasion, yet his tact and acumen have been such that in days gone by he was able to deal successfully with savage leaders, past-masters in all the arts of subtlety, where the trained diplomats of Europe failed.

Proud generals have sought his advice on the eve of decisive battles, and without his leadership the successful crossing of the western plains by the great wagon trains of fifty years ago would have been well-nigh impossible. There are no longer any savages or generals contesting for the possession of this country but he still, today, shoulders responsibilities as great and as important.

He is entrusted with the care of brigades of canoes loaded with valuable cargoes destined for the scene of important development work, and highly trained engineers turn to him for advice when map and compass fail.

Even at this late day, the arts of woodcraft are practised as originally acquired from the Indian, whose highly specialized faculties his white contemporary has more or less successfully emulated. Having for neighbours a people who carry drums to celebrate the Wabeno and wear charms to ward off evil spirits, the white trapper has naturally imbibed some of their lesser superstitions. If he has bad luck he is none too sure that he is not conjured by some enemy. He feels that there is no actual harm done by cutting out the kneecaps from the hind legs of his beaver carcasses and burning them, or by placing a small portion of tobacco in the brain box of a bear he kills and hanging the skull on a tree.

Sometimes old hands, soured by the disappointments of several bad seasons in succession, will proclaim that they have quit the game, are off the trail for life. But come Fall, the smell of a smoky wood-fire, or the sight of some portion of well-used equipment, companion of many a long and arduous journey, brings up a chain of recollection, and the hunt is on again.

One of the most successful trappers I ever knew was visited with about all the bad luck that could be crowded into one season. The beaver in his district developed a degree of sagacity unusual even in those animals. They evaded his sets persistently, springing traps, and stealing bait with monotonous regularity. A swarm of rabbits descended on the land, and on nearly every occasion on which a valuable animal entered a trap house, the rabbits were there first, getting themselves caught, and providing an excellent chain of free lunches to the fur bearers, who disdainfully refused his other lures. Omitting to remove a greased plug from the muzzle one day, he blew the end off the best rifle in the world, as he was wont to call it. Early in the Fall a cloudburst had transformed a dry creek into a raging torrent, carrying away a tent and complete outfit erected as a branch camp in an outlying district. A man of Indian training, he was superstitiously inclined, as is common; so, when, after slicing one of his feet with an axe, he found one of his dogs eating the bones of one of the few beaver he had caught,★ he commenced to figure that there was a nigger in the woodpile somewhere, and left the woods, selling most of his gear.

The next year, resolving to try his luck once more, he reassembled an outfit, and hit the trail for over the hills and far away; only to find one morning, his canoe, left overnight at the far end of a portage, completely stripped of its canvas by a bear. Apprehensive of what further disaster might lie in store, he patched up the canoe, returned to town, and sold out completely. He had been a saving man, so he built him a nifty bakeshop, and did well selling bread to the people of the village.

Coming on Fall, I tried to persuade him to come in with me, saying I would lend him the equipment, but he stood firm to his decision. As I was leaving town for the last time I paused at his little shop in passing. It was a cool day in Indian Summer, the tang of Autumn was in the air, and a bluish haze softened the outlines of the wooded hills across the lake, which, calm as a sheet of glass, reflected the forest that crowded down to its very edge in reds, yellows, and russet browns. The sun was shining brightly, but without heat, through the smoke of wood-fires from the houses of our little town, as it hung in wisps and whorls in the still air.

The old fellow was standing outside his door, looking beyond the smoke, into the distant hills, gay in their autumn colouring. I held out my hand to bid him farewell, and just then came a chill puff of wind, from nowhere at all, blowing some yellow leaves from a bush to our feet where they eddied momentarily and

---

★ Among the more primitive Indians and trappers it is considered derogatory to the beaver, on account of his high intelligence, that a dog should eat any part of the carcass, especially the bones. The carcass must all be returned to the water, or, if eaten by man, the bones restored to their element.

went fluttering and rustling down the empty street. He followed them with his eyes. Turning suddenly, he struck my hand aside.

"Hell," said he. "Goodbye nothin'! Gimme some traps an' a gun, I'm comin' with you!"

There are exceptions, but the professional hunter and woods-runner seen at the trading posts is rarely the shaggy, bearded, roaring individual depicted in the movies and some books; but a quiet, purposeful-eyed man, out in town, after the hunt, to have a good time in his own way.

Rarely does he leave the bush in the winter months, unless perhaps at New Year, and I have seen some lively times at trappers' conventions at that season. Habits of silence and watchfulness make him a somewhat taciturn person, but when in congenial company, and his tongue perhaps loosened by a few applications of the New Year's spirit, the effect of the gloom of shadowy forests fades temporarily away, and the repression of word and action gives way to a boisterous hilarity.

Some save their gains, others engage in a well-earned spree, as has been customary with frontiersmen from time immemorial. On these occasions they spend money like water, and indulge in generosities that would stagger a city worker, seeming to place little value on the money so hardly earned.

His short holiday over, some morning at daybreak the trapper loads his toboggan and harnesses up his team, amidst the barking and howling of huskies, near huskies, and just plain dogs, and is gone. He has no thought of the money he spent, the good times he had, or didn't have; true to type his mind is on the trail ahead. And as he passes the first fringe of the forest, which is never any great distance from these outposts of civilization, he enters the enchanted world of which he is as much a part as the ancient trees, the eternal snows, and the dancing Northern Lights. The magic of the winter wilderness descends on him like a cloak, and the waiting hush that covers the face of Nature, reaches out and engulfs him.

An anachronism, belonging to a day long past, he marches back down the avenues of time, a hundred years in as many steps. With a glance at the sun for direction, and eye to the lie of the land easiest for his dogs, feeling for signs of an unseen and drifted trail with his feet, he swings along on his big snowshoes, out across the Frontier, beyond the ken of mortal man, to be no more seen in the meagre civilization he has left behind, till the suns of springtime shall have melted the snowdrifts from the hillsides, and cleared the lakes of ice.

Whether treading bitter trails, or resting securely in warm log cabins; faltering over empty barrens with staring eyes; hollow-cheeked with hunger or with hands dyed to the wrist with the rich blood of newly killed meat; fighting for life with desperate strokes in the hungry white water, or floating peacefully along some slow, winding river; these men of the Last Frontier are toilsomely, patiently, but indubitably laying the stepping stones by which will pass the multitudes of future ages.

On the outskirts of the Empire this gallant little band of men still carries on the game that is almost played. The personnel changes as the years roll on, but the spirit remains the same. Each succeeding generation takes up the work that is laid down by those who pass along, leaving behind them traditions and a standard of achievement that must be lived up to by those who would claim a membership in the brotherhood of the Keepers of the Trails; bequeathing something of their courage, self-sacrifice, and devotion to a cause, to those who follow.

These are the soldiers of the Border Lands. Whether recruited from pioneer stock, and to the manner born, or from the ranks of the wage earners; whether scion of a noble house, or the scapegrace who, on account of some thoughtless act has left the haunts of men, or, perchance, a rolling stone to whom adventure is as the breath of life; each and every one is playing his allotted part in that heroic struggle which is making possible the fulfillment of the greater and more lasting purpose of the future.

We, today, of this generation, are seeing the last of the free trappers; a race of men, who, in passing, will turn the last page in the story of true adventure on this continent, closing forever the book of romance in Canadian History.

The forest cannot much longer stand before the conquering march of modernity, and soon we shall witness the vanishing of a mighty wilderness.

And the last Frontiersman, its offspring, driven back further and further towards the North into the far-flung reaches where are only desolation and barrenness, must, like the forest that evolved him, bow his head to the inevitable and perish with it. And he will leave behind him only his deserted, empty trails, and the ashes of his dead camp fires, as landmarks for the oncoming millions. And with him will go his friend the Indian to be a memory of days and a life that are past beyond recall.

II

THE LAND OF SHADOWS

Full in the passage of the vale above
A sable silent solemn forest stood
Where nought but shadowy forms were seen to move.

Side by side with the modern Canada there lies the last battle-ground in the long-drawn-out, bitter struggle between the primeval and civilization. I speak not of those picturesque territories, within easy reach of transport facilities, where a sportsman may penetrate with a moccasined taciturn Indian, or a weather-beaten and equally reticent white man, and get his deer, or his fishing; places where, in inaccessible spots, lone white pines, one-time kings of all the forest, gaze in brooding melancholy out over the land that once was theirs. In such districts, traversed by accurately mapped water routes and well-cut portages, all the necessities and most of the luxuries of civilization may be transported with little difficulty.

But to those on whom the magic lure of far horizons has cast its spell, such places lack the thrill of the uncharted regions. Far beyond the fringe of burnt and lumbered wastes adjacent to the railroads, there lies another Canada little known, unvisited except by the few who are willing to submit to the hardships, loneliness, and toil of long journeys in a land where civilization has left no mark and opened no trails, and where there are no means of subsistence other than those provided by Nature.

Large areas of this section are barren of game, no small consideration to the adventurer caught by the exigencies of travel, for an extended period, in such a district. The greater part, however, is a veritable sportsman's paradise, untouched except by the passing hunter, or explorer; those hardy spirits for whom no privation is too severe, and no labour so arduous as to prevent them from assuaging the wanderlust that grips them and drives them out into the remaining waste places, where the devastating axe has not yet commenced its deadly work, out beyond the Height of Land, over the Great Divide.

This "Backbone of Canada" so called, sometimes known as the Haute Terre, stretches across the full breadth of the continent, East and West, dividing the waters that run south from those that run north to the Arctic Sea. In like manner it forms a line of demarcation between the prosaic realities of a land of everyday affairs, and the enchantment of a realm of high adventure, unconquered, almost unknown, and unpeopled except by a few scattered bands of Indians and wandering trappers.

This hinterland yet remains a virgin wilderness lying spread out over half a continent; a dark, forbidding panorama of continuous forest, with here and there a glistening lake set like a splash of quicksilver amongst the tumbled hills. A harsher, sterner land, this, than the smiling Southland; where manhood and experience are put to the supreme test, where the age-old law of the survival of the fittest holds sway, and where strength without cunning is of no avail. A region of illimitable distance, unknown lakes, hidden rivers, and unrecorded happenings; and changed in no marked way since the white man discovered America.

Here, even in these modern days, lies a land of Romance, gripping the imagination with its immensity, its boundless possibilities and its magic of untried adventure. Thus it has lain since the world was young, enveloped in a mystery beyond understanding, and immersed in silence, absolute, unbroken, and all-embracing; a silence intensified rather than relieved by the muted whisperings of occasional light forest airs in the treetops far overhead.

Should the traveller in these solitudes happen to arrive at the edge of one of those high granite cliffs common to the country and look around him, he will see, not the familiar deciduous trees of the south, but will find that he is surrounded, hemmed in on all sides, by apparently endless black forests of spruce, stately trees, cathedral-like with their tall spires above, and their gloomy aisles below. He will see them as far as the eye can reach, covering hill, valley, and ridge, spreading in a green carpet over the face of the earth. Paraded in mass formation, standing stiffly, yet gracefully, to attention, and opposing a wellnigh impenetrable barrier to the further encroachments of civilization, until they too shall fall before the axe, a burnt offering on the altar of the God of Mammon.

In places this mighty close-packed host divides to sweep in huge undulating waves along the borders of vast inland seas, the far shores of which show only as a thin, dark line shimmering and dancing in the summer heat. These large lakes on the Northern watershed are shallow for the most part, and on that account dangerous to navigate. But in spots are deep holes, places where cliffs hundreds of feet high run sheer down to the water's edge, and on to unfathomed depths below. Riven from the lofty crags by the frosts of centuries, fallen rocks, some of them of stupendous size, lie on some submerged ledge like piles of broken masonry, faintly visible in the clear water, far below. And from out the dark fissures and shadowy caverns among them, slide long, grey, monstrous forms; for here is the home of the great lake trout of the region, taken sometimes as high as forty pounds in weight.

In places long low stretches of flat rock reach up out of the water, entering the wall of forest at a gentle incline. Their smooth surface is studded with a scattered growth of jackpines, fashioned into weird shapes by the wind, and, because standing apart, wide and spreading of limb, affording a grateful shade after long heats at the paddle on the glaring expanse of lake. These are the summer camping grounds of the floating caravans, and off these points a man may catch enough fish for a meal in the time it takes another to make the preparations to cook them.

In the spring time, in sheltered bays, lean and sinuous pike of inordinate size, hungry-looking and rapacious, lie like submarines awash, basking in the sunlight. Shooting them at this season is exciting sport, as only the large ones have this habit, and fish up to fifty inches in length are common.

Here and there, too, the sable carpet of evergreen treetops is gashed by long shining ribbons of white, as mighty rivers tumble and roar their way to Hudson's Bay, walled in on either side by their palisades of spruce trees, whose lofty arches give back the clatter of rapids or echo to the thunder of the falls.

Far beneath the steeple tops, below the fanlike layers of interlaced limbs that form a vaulted roof through which the sunlight never penetrates, lies a land of shadows. Darkened aisles and corridors lead on to nowhere. A gloomy labyrinth of smooth, grey columns stretches in every direction into the dimness until the view is shut off by the wall of trees that seems to forbid the further progress of the intruder. This barrier opens up before him, as he goes forward, but closes down behind him as though, having committed himself to advance he may not now retire; it hems him in on either side at a given distance as he proceeds, a mute, but ever-present escort. Here, in the endless mazes of these halls of silence, is neither time nor distance, nor direction.

Here exists a phantom world of unreality, where obstacles crumble beneath the touch and formless undefinable objects loom up vaguely in the middle distance, fading to nothingness on near approach. Elusive creatures whose every movement is furtive, light of foot, springy, effortless of gait, go their soundless ways; grey ghosts that materialize and vanish on the instant, melting into the shadows at the sight of man, to stand observing him from skillfully selected cover.

Above, below, and on all sides is moss; moss in a carpet, deadening the footfall of the traveller, giving beneath his step, and baffling by its very lack of opposition his efforts to progress. Moss stands in waist-high hummocks, around which detours must be made. Moss in festoons hangs from the dead lower limbs of the trees, like the hangings in some ancient and deserted temple. And a temple it is, raised to the god of silence, of a stillness that so dominates the consciousness that the wanderer who threads its deserted naves treads warily, lest he break unnecessarily a hush that has held sway since time began.

In places the dense growth of spruce gives way to sandy plains, where, more open but still a heavy enough forest, are stretches of jackpine. Here the gnarled and uncouth limbs, and the ragged grotesquely twisted tops of these deformed hybrids, throw fantastic shadows at the full of the moon on the floor of this devil's dance-hall — shadows in and out of which flit the Puck-wah-jeesh in their goblin dances, as they hold high revel to the tune of their soundless drums, and plot fresh mischief against the Indian.

There are vistas, unbelievably beautiful, to be seen beyond the boles of giant trees edging some declivity, of sun-drenched valleys, or wide expanse of plain, blue with its luscious carpet of berries. Occasional grassy glades, oases in the sameness of the sunless grottos surrounding them, refresh the mind and eye, seeming intimate and friendly after the aloofness of the stately forest.

Huge burns, of ancient time and unknown origin, lie like scars, across the landscape. Here all the foundation and structure of the earth's surface, hitherto jealously hidden, lies naked and exposed. Smooth round mountains bare of vegetation, upthrust of Keewaydin,★ the oldest known rock, rear themselves above

★ An Indian word meaning land of the N.W. Wind, or the wind itself. The name is applied generally to the North Country beyond the Height of Land, and is also the name of this rock (Keewatin) in mineralogy.

the arid waste, monuments to the mighty upheaval that belched them forth from the bowels of the earth. High broken cliffs and precipitous crags of red granite flank the boulder-strewn gulleys, and dried-out stream beds. Immense masses of rock, cracked open by the intense heat of forgotten fires, lie fallen apart, choking the valleys. No movement of a living beast, no sound of a bird, relieves the staring desolation. This is the world as it was after the age of ice, the scratches and gouges of its slow passage still visible on the now solid rocks. Here, a prospector, skilled in the science of metals, may find his Eldorado.

The culminating reward of the fruitless labour of a lifetime may stand out freely for all to see in one of those white bands of quartz that shine so glassily on the mountain side, and indication of untold riches may lie beneath the surface of a handful of gravel, to be exposed by some careless movement of a foot, or perhaps by the lighting of a fire.

There are ridges, becoming rarer as one journeys towards the Arctic Circle, of birch and poplar, cheerful with their bright trunks, and sun-spotted leafy floor, so familiar below the Height of Land. Here are singing birds and partridges, and also the main routes of moose and bears in summer; their trail, as well beaten as any portage, affording a never-failing guide to a lake or river. These are the Hills of the Whispering Leaves of the Indians, so called because of the continuous rustling flutter of the poplar leaves, shivering and trembling in the lightest current of air, in contrast to the motionless foliage of the conifers which so monopolize the landscape.

It is in such places, near a pleasant, sunny lake, or by a cheerful, shouting brook, that the red men spend the lazy days of the short north-country summer, resting from the arduous toil of the long winter. Nor are they idle, for now they are already preparing equipment for next winter's hunt; tanning hides for clothing and making their cunningly devised snowshoes and toboggans, against the time when the Hunting Winds hold sway. And during the long afterglow which precedes the coming of darkness in these high latitudes, they sit by smoky fires and listen to some white-haired teller of the tales of ancient days, when in one lift of traps a man might half-fill a canoe with beaver, or spear sufficient sturgeon for his winter needs in a single night.

In places the forest dwindles down to small trees which, giving way to moss and sage brush, thin out and eventually disappear altogether, and the country opens out into one of those immense muskegs or swamps which make overland travel in whole sections of this territory impossible in the summer time. These consist mostly of stretches composed of deep, thin mud, covered with slushy moss, and perhaps sparsely dotted with stunted, twisted trees. Bright green, inviting-looking fields show up in places, luring the inexperienced into their maw with their deceptive promise of good footing. These last are seemingly bottomless, and constitute a real danger to man or beast, excepting the lordly moose, who, by some unknown means is able to walk over, or swim through, such places unscathed. There are holes between hummocks that are filled with noisome stagnant water, which would engulf a man. The whole thing is practically a floating bog, yet the only good water to be found, perhaps for miles around, is in just such places, to be obtained in the small pitcher plants which grow thickly, with about as much as an egg-cup will hold in each.

But the main part of the country is clothed in its dark-green robe of spruce trees. They stand in serried rows around every lake, and wall in every river to the banks, darkening them with their shadows, still sentinels on guard from everlasting.

In fastnesses of this rapidly fading frontier, the last on this continent, reigns the Spirit of the North Land. Enthroned behind the distant mountains with the cohorts and legions of his last grand army massed about him, he sallies forth, brooding over the length and breadth of the land, seeking whom he may destroy, ever devising new means for the elimination of the invaders of his closen realm. His is not the spectacular kill by the shedding of blood, not the shock of honest battle in the open, but by devious ways and subtle methods he obtains his ends. Securely entrenched behind the bristling ramparts of the forest, with all the unleashed forces of the primeval at his command, he primes his deadly weapons, and spreads his entanglements, his obstacles, and his snares; nor are they always vainly set.

Through them the invader must pick his way with the delicacy and assurance of one who walks barefoot amongst naked knives. Some of his weapons are merely annoyances, irritating but bearable; others are harassing to the point of obsession, wearing out the body and mind, and lessening the resisting power of a man; others, yet, bring swift death, or the long slow agonies of those who would die but cannot.

A stiff, wiry growth of sage brush, knee-deep and tangled, cumbers the ground over large areas. Mosquitoes, black flies, moose flies, and sand flies in relentless swarms make the forest almost uninhabitable for three months of the four of which the summer consists. The immense inland seas, shallow and exposed, are frequently whipped to fury on short notice, or none at all, by terrific storms, which, gathering force over the Height of Land, lash these northern latitudes with unbelievable fury. Forest fires, irresistible, all-devouring, sweep at times through the close-set resinous timber at railroad speed, leaving in their wake a devastation of bare hills and smoking stumps; desperate indeed is the plight of the voyageur so trapped far from water. Frequently miles of rapids have to be negotiated, where only the greatest skill and courage, coupled with days at a time of heart-breaking and exhausting labour, can gain the objective. In winter snow often lies six feet deep in the woods and at the railroad, a hundred or so miles to the south, sixty-five degrees below zero (Fahr.) is no uncommon temperature. A rise in temperature often precipitates a blizzard, and these winter storms are so violent as to destroy whole areas of timber by sheer weight alone; the solitary trapper caught on the trail by one of these tempests, with little or no warning, especially if crossing any large lake, is in grave danger. His dogs, blinded and half-choked by the wind-driven masses of snow, cannot face the storm. Himself unable to break trail through the mounting drifts, or to keep his direction through the whirling white wall that surrounds him at the distance of a few feet, he may, if far from land, perish miserably.

Perhaps, wisely relying on his dogs to lead him ashore, he may, if lucky, find wood and shelter enough for his protection. A broken axe handle under these conditions would be not only an inconvenience, but a disaster with probably fatal results. Here, with his toboggan sheet for a windbreak, a bed of hastily laid brush, and a pile of wood sufficient to do all night, gathered with infinite labour, he can make some kind of a stand to live out the storm.

The howling wind fills his shelter with blinding smoke, and the fire only serves to melt the snow as it accumulates on blankets, food and clothing, wetting everything; cooking is impossible, and content with a pail of tea and perhaps some thawed-out fish intended for dog feed, he and his shivering huskies crouch by the fire all the long night. And often enough the cold light of morning breaks on a shelter half-filled with drifting snow, a fire long since extinguished, and a pack of whining wolf-dogs waiting in vain to be harnessed up, later to run wild with the wolves.

The waterways that form a network over large sections are the lines of travel of not only man, but of mink, otter, and other animals, who go their rounds as regularly as any man. Further back in the hills range fisher, marten, and wolves, in their never-ceasing hunt for meat to abate their continuous hunger. In sheltered spots among heavy timber, the giant moose yards up in small herds. Although they are six feet high at the shoulder the snow lies at times so deep in the forest that they are unable to navigate, moving only a few yards daily, eating and sleeping alternately. As they move they plough a trench through the snow about three feet wide, and maybe five feet deep, a pitfall for those who travel at night. Here they stay until spring thaws leave them free to wander back to their favourite haunts of lily ponds and marshes.

These animals grow, in the season between June and September, sets of horns of from thirty to sixty or seventy inches' spread, losing them again in January. They put up terrific battles among themselves in the fall, and dead moose are a common sight in the woods at that season, with at least one bear in attendance on the feast so provided, fattening up for the long winter sleep.

Back off main routes in lonely ponds, or on dammed-up streams in hidden gullies, communities of beaver work all summer against the coming of winter, passing the cold dead months of the year, as a reward for their prodigious labour, well fed and in comfort and warmth. The shores of lakes, swamps, and the edges of the frozen fen lands are the hunting grounds of lynxes and foxes, for in such places abound the snowshoe rabbits, their prey.

In a wilderness apparently without life there is a teeming population continuously on the move, yet a man may travel for days at a time and see nothing but the trees around him, and hear nothing save the sounds he himself makes. For here man is the only alien, the arch-enemy from whom all the dwellers in this sanctuary flee, as from pollution. Apprised of his approach by senses trained to register the least discordant note in the symmetry of their surroundings, they disappear long before he arrives in the vicinity. All along his line of travel this is going on and hardly ever is he permitted to see or hear the living creatures that surround him on every side.

Animals seem to be able to distinguish instantly the slightest noise made by man, from that of any other forest dweller. The laughing owls may hoot in uncouth cackling whoops; a beaver may waken the echoes with a resounding smack of his tail on the water; a tree may fall with a crash, or a moose walk carelessly along rattling the underbrush, or smashing dry sticks underfoot, and cause no more commotion than the shake of an ear or the flick of a tail. But let a man so much as break a twig or rustle the dry grass of a beaver meadow, and all living creatures within earshot will, each according to his kind, sink beneath the surface of the water without a ripple, fade soundlessly into the shadows, leap with astonishing bounds to cover, or freeze into immobility, if their colour scheme harmonizes sufficiently well with the immediate background.

There are two notable exceptions to this, however; the skunk and the porcupine. The latter beast is dumb cousin to the beaver, whom he resembles very closely except for the tail, the webbed hind feet, and his bristles. But it seems that when the brains were handed out between the two of them, the porcupine was absent and the beaver got them all. With no regard for personal safety, to him strange noises or the smell of cooking, are as music and ambrosia; and a camp will not be very long pitched, in a country where they abound, before a "porky" will be over to make his inspection. Save for an insatiable appetite for canoe gunwales, paddles, leather goods, provisions of all kinds, anything made of wood, canvas, paper — or perhaps it were easier to say everything not made of iron or steel — and for a bad habit he has of leaving barbed quills lying around carelessly, he is a harmless enough beast. Skunks are also friendly, and if undisturbed are as good-natured as a cat. They also have the community spirit, but this can be carried too far, as in the instance when I awoke one morning to find a number one extra large specimen curled up on my blankets. I made several attempts to rise and on each occasion he became very agitated, so I had to lie in bed until he was pleased to go.

To the majority of the dwellers in the centres of civilization the animals inhabiting the waste places are nothing more than savage creatures, wandering aimlessly about, with no thought beyond the satisfaction of one or two animal appetites. But closer observation reveals the fact that nearly all of them have more native intelligence than those animals that have spent many generations dependent on man, and amongst the higher orders among them their "personal" relations are such that the word "brute" as term of contempt is somewhat of a misnomer. Ferocious as many of them undoubtedly are when in pursuit of their prey, they all have their lighter moments, and their lives are almost as well regulated as those of human beings living under the same conditions.

They form strong attachments amongst themselves. Beaver work in shifts, keep a clean house, and hold rapid fire conversations together; coons wash their food before eating it. Most of them keep trails, especially beaver, deer, and bears, and in the case of the latter animal they blaze the boundaries of their territories in places by biting and tearing bark off trees, and it is known that they do not encroach on each other. They will climb a tree for the express purpose of sliding down again, doing this repeatedly for no other reason than the kick they get out of it. Otter also play together, and will climb a steep bank and slide down into the water uttering sharp barks of enjoyment, climb up, and slide again, much after the fashion of human beings on a toboggan slide; they, too, travel in well-defined territories, passing certain spots every eight or nine days with the regularity of clockwork. Crows, gulls, and eagles will fly into the wind during a gale, and then turning, allow themselves to be blown down wind at dizzy speed, flying back upwind and repeating the performance until satisfied. Wolves when hunting exhibit team work similar to that employed by football players, send out scouts, obey the orders of a leader, and will gambol and play on the ice precisely as do pedigreed collies on a lawn.

Man is not the only trapper in the wilderness. There are insects that dig holes into which their prey falls and is captured before he can get out. Water spiders set nets shaped like saxophones, the large end facing upstream, to catch anything floating down, and round the curve, in the small end, waits the spider. Wolves divide their forces to capture deer, and I saw one of them drive a deer across a stream, whilst another waited in the brush on the other side for him to land. I know of another occasion on which three wolves cornered a caribou on a fair-sized lake. In the timber the snow was too soft for either wolves or caribou to make much headway. It was April and the ice was clear of snow and slippery as glass. A caribou's hoof is hollowed out in such a way that it grips the ice, but the wolves had difficulty in making any speed. The caribou ran round and round the lake, a distance of several miles each trip, thinking, no doubt, to tire the wolves; but two would rest whilst one chased the caribou, taking each his turn until the deer dropped from exhaustion.

Of the creatures that inhabit the woods, by far the lesser number are of a predatory nature. The majority consists of the varieties of deer, the rodents, and the smaller birds. Nature is cruel, and the flesh-eating animals and birds kill their prey in the most bloodthirsty manner, tearing off and eating portions of meat before the unfortunate animal is dead. The thought of this considerably lessens the compunction one might feel in trapping carnivorous animals, as they are only getting a dose of their own medicine and do not undergo a tithe of the sufferings they inflict on their victims, often hastening their own end by paroxysms of fury.

Although this country offers such resistances to overland travel during the short summer of the region, with the coming of winter, with its ice and snow, which are apt to cause stagnation in settled areas, all these difficulties cease. Once the freeze-up comes, and the woods are in the grip of winter, and snowshoes can be used, usually early in November, a man may go where he will without let or hindrance. Moss, sage-brush, and muskeg no longer retard progress.

The one-time gloomy forest becomes cheerful in its bright mantle of snow, the weight of which bears down the fanlike foliage of the evergreens, letting in the sunlight, and what once were shadowed crypts become avenues of light. Swift dog-teams race down the snowy highways between the trees, where in summer men plodded wearily over the insecure footing at the rate of perhaps a mile an hour. Once snow commences to fall no creature may move without leaving the signs of his passage. All the goings, the comings, the joys, and the tragedies of the forest folk are printed there for the experienced eye to read. Nothing intrigues the imagination of a hunter so much as the sight of fresh tracks. There in the snow is a story; but, although the characters are so plainly written, he must needs be an expert who would interpret them.

Easily distinguishable to the initiated are the tracks of each variety of beast, say, the peculiar trail of an otter; three or four hops and a slide, more short hops and another slide, sometimes yards in length. The lynx leaves tracks which in point of size might well pass for those of a small lion; the leaping progression of Wapoose the white rabbit, whose exaggerated hind feet have gained for him the title of "snowshoe" rabbit, shows everywhere. These feet are partially webbed, and have a large spread, enabling him to pass without sinking over the softest snow, and where a single track shows plainly, it much resembles that of some gigantic bird of prey.

Very common are the delicate, paired footprints of the ermine; and similar, but larger, and not so numerous, are those of the fisher, and marten; common too are the neat, mincing footmarks of the fox, spaced, like those of the lynx, exactly in line, and as regularly as the "tuck" of a drum. Often can be seen where an owl has swooped down on a scurrying rabbit, his imprint plainly showing where he missed his stroke and landed in the snow, the rabbit doubling, twisting, racing, screeching with mortal fear, and the owl, in muffled deadly silence, following every twist and turn, but unable to strike. Here and there the drag of a wing, the scrape of wicked claws, show plainly the progress of the struggle. For fifty yards or so this may go on, and at the end, a torn skin, the heavier bones, and the entrails. For your owl is fastidious and skins his victims, alive, taking only the best of the meat.

From now on the trapper, with the tell-tale tracks to guide him, can place his snares to greater advantage at the various crossings and routes, now easily discovered, which animals as well as human beings devise to facilitate their ceaseless travels.

Soon comes the time of the Dead Days. The wind no longer whispers and sighs through the treetops, deadened by their load of snow, and the silence, intense enough before the coming of winter, now becomes the dominating feature of the landscape. In these padded corridors sound has no penetration, and the stillness becomes almost opaque. It is as though one walked through an endless vaulted chamber, walled, roofed and paved with silence. Unconsciously one listens, waiting, straining to hear some sound which seems imminent, but never actually occurs, and all Nature seems to stand with bated breath, waiting momentarily for the occurrence of some long-threatened incident. The swish of the snowshoes, and the light rustle of garments are thrown back thinly to the ear, and the crack of a rifle is chopped off short in a dull thud.

Storm after storm piles the snow higher and higher on the stratified limbs of the spruce, until the mounting roll of snow meets the burdened limb next above it. Other storms smooth off the irregularities with a finishing blanket of snow, and the trees become transformed into immense pointed columns of white. Those of smaller growth, completely covered, show only as squat pillars and mounds, fantastically sculptured by the keen-edged winds into the semblance of weird statuary.

Beautiful as this Arctic forest appears in the daytime, it is only by moonlight, when much travelling is done to avoid the cutting winds of the daylight hours, that the true witchery of the winter wilderness grips the imagination. Seen by the eerie light of the moon, the motionless, snow-shrouded trees that line the trail, loom on either hand like grim spectres, gruesomely arrayed, each in his winding-sheet, staring sardonically down on the hurrying wayfarer. In the diffused uncertain light the freakish artistry of the wind appears like the work of some demented sculptor, and the trail becomes a gallery of grinning masks and uncouth featureless forms, as of dwellers in a world of goblins turned suddenly to stone.

Athwart the shafts of moonlight, from out of the shadows, move soundless forms with baleful gleaming eyes, wraiths that flicker before the vision for a moment and are gone. The Canada lynx, great grey ghost of the Northland; the huge white Labrador wolf; white rabbits, white weasels, the silvery ptarmigan: pale phantoms of the white silence. A fantasy in white in a world that is dead.

And the moonlight, too, is death. The full of the moon is the period of most intense cold, and there have been men who, already exhausted by a day's travel, and carrying on by night, half-asleep as they walked, their senses lulled by the treacherous glow, decided to sleep for just a little while on a warm-looking snow bank, and so slept on forever. So Muji-Manito, the Evil Genius of the North, cold and pitiless, malignantly triumphant, adds another victim to his gruesome tally.

Then later, when the moon has set, in that stark still hour between the darkness and the dawn, the snow gives back the pale sepulchral glare of the Northern Lights; and by their unearthly illumination, those who dance the Dance of the Deadmen* perform their ghostly evolutions, before the vast and solemn audience of spruce.

And then the stillness is broken by the music of the wolves, whose unerring instinct senses tragedy. It comes, a low moaning, stealing through the thin and brittle air, swelling in crescendo to

*Indian name for the Northern Lights.

a volume of sound, then dying away in a sobbing wail across the empty solitudes; echoing from hill to hill in fading repetition, until the reiteration of sound is lost in the immensity of immeasurable distance.

And as the last dying echo fades to nothing, the silence settles down layer by layer, pouring across the vast deserted auditorium in billow after billow, until all sound is completely choked beyond apparent possibility of repetition. And the wolves move on to their ghastly feast, and the frozen wastes resume their endless waiting; the Deadmen dance their grisly dance on high, and the glittering spruce stand silently and watch.

This then is the Canada that lies back of your civilization, the wild, fierce land of desperate struggle and untold hardship, where Romance holds sway as it did when Canada was one vast hunting ground. This is the last stronghold of the Red Gods, the heritage of the born adventurer. In this austere and savage region men are sometimes broken, or aged beyond their years; yet to those who are able to tune in on their surroundings, and care to learn the lessons that it teaches, it can become a land of wild, romantic beauty and adventure.

Up beyond the wavering line of the Last Frontier lies not merely a region of trees, rocks, and water, but a rich treasure-house, open to all who dare the ordeal of entry, and transformed by the cosmic sorcery of the infinite into a land of magic glades and spirit-haunted lakes, of undiscovered fortunes, and sunset dreams come true.

This is the face of Nature, unchanged since it left the hands of its Maker, a soundless, endless river, flowing forever onward in the perpetual cycle which is the immutable law of the universe.

Not much longer can the forest hope to stem the tide of progress; change is on every hand. Every year those who follow the receding Border further and further back, see one by one the links with the old days being severed, as the demands of a teeming civilization reach tentacles into the very heart of the Wild Lands. And we who stand regretfully and watch, must either adapt ourselves to the new conditions, or, preferably, follow the ever-thinning line of last defence into the shadows, where soon will vanish every last one of the Dwellers amongst the Leaves.

III

THE TRAIL

Send not your foolish and feeble; send me your strong and your sane,
Strong for the red rage of battle; sane, for I harry them sore.

— SERVICE

The trail! You visualize a smooth, narrow path meandering in and out between stately trees; lightfooted Indians slipping noiselessly by; a highway between two points unknown; a winding road to dreams, romance, and mystery.

It can be that. It can also be the faintly discernible, at times invisible, crushing of dry moss on sun-scorched rocks, with little or no other indication of the passage there of generations of wandering tribesmen. It may be but a few broken twigs, turned leaves, or bent grasses, displaced by the single passage of some adventurer, which, slowly twisting back to their former position, are no more disturbed by the foot of man; or a well-defined, beaten main route, hard-packed by the traffic of centuries; the smooth and easy road to disaster, or the rough and arduous road to fortune.

On it may pass the wealth of a nation, from some fabulously rich Eldorado, or the staggering wreck of a beaten man, broken on the wheel of incompetence or misfortune. The Trail is the stage on which all the drama, the burlesque, the tragedy, and the comedy of the wilderness is played. On these narrow paths that thread their secret ways through hidden places, are performed epic deeds of courage and self-sacrifice, and incredible acts of treachery and cowardice.

On the Trail the soul of a man is stripped bare and naked, exposed for all to see, and here his true nature will come out, let him dissemble never so wisely. The pleasant and versatile companion of a social entertainment may exhibit unsuspected traits of pusillanimity, and weakness of character, when put to the test; and the unassuming, self-effacing "wallflower" may show an unexpected fund of resourcefulness, and by sheer strength of will perform prodigies of valour which his sturdier brethren shrink from.

Night and day the Trail makes its insistent demands on the ingenuity, the resourcefulness, and the endurance of a man. Work on the Trail is synonymous with the contact between an irresistible force and an immovable object. The issue is entirely in the air until the last incident of that particular trip is closed. The whole course of a journey may be changed, or increased hardship caused, by such apparent trivialities as a change of wind, or the passing away of clouds from the face of the sun. An hour lost may mean a day or more beyond schedule at the other end, with attendant shortage of supplies. Careless travelling is too dearly paid for to be indulged in. No rests are taken; the easier sections of the route providing sufficient respite from toil and permitting recuperation of energy to expend on the difficulties ahead. Abandoned loads, non-completion of self-appointed tasks, mistakes in direction or in selection of routes, involving delay, are all blots on the record of efficiency, for which payment is extorted to the last pound of flesh. Although the rewards of the game are rich to those who conform to the rules, the penalties of disobedience are often swift, sure, and terrible. And let not the heedless be unduly optimistic that at times the discipline appears to slacken, that the barriers seem to be down, and all is going well. This is but subterfuge, an attempt to catch him off guard, to deal a lightning body-blow, or a foul. For the Trail is like unto a fickle officer, who today apparently condones breaches of discipline, to visit sudden and disproportionate penalties for the least infringement on the morrow.

Every year takes its toll of life by bad ice, intense cold, or mis-adventure. Quarrels over hunting grounds terminating fatally are not unknown, the Spirit of the Northland meanwhile sitting by and grinning ghoulishly to see his enemies destroy one another.

Often a rifle or other imperishable article of equipment, exposed by the low water of a hot summer, or the remains of a canoe hung high and dry by spring floods, points to some error in judgment that explains an almost forgotten disappearance. Some bones and a few mildewed rags at a long-dead camp fire, discovered by a wandering Indian, will account for one canoe that failed to show up after the spring hunt.

Even the very silence, most negative of all the passively resis-tant qualities of the country, claims its victims. The unearthly lack of sound is such a strain on the nerves of those unaccustomed to it that men have been known to go insane under its influence, and have had to be brought out to the railroad.

The Trail is the one and only means of entry to the land of promise of the North, and on it all must pass a critical inspection. Newcomers must undergo the severe scrutiny of the presiding powers, and all who enter are subjected to trial by ordeal, from which only the chosen few emerge unscathed. And to those who by their own unaided efforts do so prevail the jealously guarded portals of the treasure-house are thrown open without reserve; and there is a twice-fold value on the recompense so hardly won, and, once attained to, so lavishly bestowed.

Nor are the rewards thus gained always material. Let it not be imagined that riches dog the footsteps of the successful fron-tiersman. His ambition to become supreme, get quickly rich and retire early, if he had any such idea, is soon lost sight of in the lively and unceasing contest he must enter into, if he would qualify for admission to the fraternity of the forest.

Up beyond the Height of Land, no man may expect any exemption or immunity on account of his superiority, as such; he has to prove his case. Often he exhibits less common sense than the animals, and of them all he is the most helpless in the face of the vigorous conditions that obtain. When he has conquered these he has accomplished something worth while.

The spiritual satisfaction, the intellectual pleasure, and the knowledge of power that comes with victory over a valiant but ruthless adversary, which accrue after years of submission to the acid test of wilderness life, give the veteran woodsman a capacity for a clean, wholesome enjoyment of living that riches sometimes fail to bring. And looking back on his past struggles, through which he has risen successfully to a position of equality with the dwellers of the waste lands, he would not trade his experience for wealth. He enters into his inheritance with a mind tempered to the fullest appreciation of it, and says to himself that it was worth his while.

On the Trail life is stripped of the non-essentials; existence is in the raw, where an aye is an aye, and a no, no; and no trick of speech, or mannerism or cherished self-deception, can gain one jot or tittle of preferment. Under these conditions a man subordinates that part of him that feels and suffers, to the will to conquer, retaining only that part which takes cognizance of the exigencies of travel, and the means adopted to overcome them. There is none to tell him what he shall or shall not do, yet he has the hardest master a man can well work for — himself.

Long periods of intense concentration of will on one line of endeavour, together with the entire subjection of all that is physical to the fulfillment of the big idea, produce, in time, a type of mind that can be subdued by death alone, and cases have been known of stricken men who, dead to all intents and purposes, staggered on an appreciable distance before finally collapsing.

Out from town; the warmth, the laughter, the comfort left behind. Past half-finished barns, and snowy deserts of burnt stumps; past the squalid habitations of the alien, while the inmates stare out with animal curiosity; and so beyond the works of man, to where the woods become thicker and thicker, and all is clean, and silent, and shining white — the winter Trail.

Trees filing by in endless, orderly review, opening up before, passing on either hand, and closing in irrevocably behind. That night a camp under the stars. Then, the hasty breakfast in the dark, breaking of camp in the knife-edged cold of dawn; shivering, whining huskies squirming impatiently whilst numb fingers fumble with toboggan strings, and the leather thongs of dog harness. Then away!

Strings of dogs swinging into line; a couple of swift, slashing dog fights, the shouts of the drivers, cracking of whips, and an eventual settling down to business. The swing and soft sough of snowshoes in the loose snow, the rattle of frame on frame. Then the sun rises. Glittering jewels of frost shivering on the pointed spruce-tops, like the gay ornaments on Christmas trees. The breath jets into the crackling air like little clouds of smoke, and steam rises off the dogs. Onward, onward, speed, speed, for the hands are still numb, and the cold strikes the face like volleys of broken glass; and we have far to go today.

So, for an hour; we begin to warm up. Suddenly ahead, the thud of a rifle, the answering crack leaping with appalling reverberations amongst the surrounding hills. Shouts up front; someone has shot a caribou. Good! Fresh meat for supper.

Two of the more lightly laden teams drop out, and their owners commence expertly to skin and dress the kill; as their hands become numb they will plunge them to the elbows in the warm blood for a minute, and resume their work.

More hours; steep hills where men take poles and push on the load ahead of them, to help the dogs; on the down grades, tail ropes are loosed, and men bear back with all their weight, some falling, others dragged on their snowshoes as on a surfboard, amidst the shouts and yells of the brigade and the excited yapping

of the dogs as they race madly to keep ahead of the flying toboggan. Meanwhile the Trail unwinds from some inexhaustible reel
up front, passes swiftly underfoot and on behind, while the trees
whirl swiftly by.

Then another stop; what is this? "Dinner," say the trail breakers; well, they ought to know, they are bearing the brunt of the
work. Quick, crackling fires, tea made from melted snow, whilst
the dogs take the opportunity to bite the ice balls off their feet;
most of them are wearing moccasins, evidence of thoughtful
owners; for men, red or white, have always a heart for a dog.
Pipes are lighted, and all hands relax utterly and smoke contentedly — for a few minutes.

Meanwhile, a word for the husky. Lean, rangy, slant-eyed and
tough as whalebone, hitched in teams of four; over muskegs and
across frozen lakes; tails up, tongues hanging, straining against the
harness, bracing themselves at the curves, trailwise and always
hungry, these faithful animals haul their loads all day for incredible distances. Not overly ornamental in appearance, inclined
to savagery and deadly fighting, and thieves of no mean ability,
these half-bred wolves are as necessary to transport in the North
as horses were in the West in the early days. On more than a
few occasions, they have been the means of saving life by their
uncanny knowledge of ice, and unerring sense of direction.

And now the short rest is over, and we swing into position
as the teams go by, and are away. Hours, miles, white monotony,
and a keen, steady wind; lake and portage, gully and riverbank;
sometimes the crest of a bare hill from which a fleeting glimpse
of the surrounding country is obtained. Limitless, endless, empty
distance before, behind, and on either hand.

Later a trail turns in from the left, a thin winding ribbon,
dwindling to a thread, to nothingness, across a lake, the far shores
of which show but faintly, coming from out of the Keewaydin,
the storied, mystic North. The trail is well packed by snowshoes
of all sizes, men, women, and children; Indians.

Good going now; the trail breakers, glad of the respite, drop behind. On the hard trail the snowshoes commence to sing.

Smoke ahead; teepees, windbreaks; the Indian camp. Sharp vicious barking, howling, and then an unspeakable uproar as a herd of wolf-dogs swoops down on the caravan. Shrill scolding of squaws, who belabour lustily with burning sticks, restoring comparative quiet. Black-eyed, round-faced children stand aloof, whispering in soft voices. Maidens with head shawls peep from canvas doorways; buxom old ladies declaim loudly, as they cook at open fires. A tall spare man with Egyptian features, and long black hair, intones gravely in an ancient language, and we understand that we are invited to share the campground; the place is well sheltered, and we are told, there is much wood, moose meat. But we cannot stay; the mail is with us, and travels on schedule; tonight we camp at Kettle Rapids, tomorrow at Thieving Bear.

"Will we take tea" We surely will, for who can refuse tea on the Trail ? Large steaming bowls, and strong.

Away again; more hours, more miles. The teams with the meat have caught up, and the party redoubles its speed; it is getting colder and the men commence to trot. The snowshoes sing shriller now as the *babiche*★ tightens in the frost, and speed, and more speed is the slogan. Another lake; long, narrow, and bordered by glittering spruce-trees garbed in white; the great sun, hanging low above them, dyeing their tops blood red.

And as the sun goes down, the shadows creep softly out of the woods to the feet of the runners, and beyond. The wind drops and the cold quickens. One man drops out; there is blood on his moccasins. Incorrectly dressed, his feet have chafed with the rub of the bridles and have been bleeding for an hour. Another man steps aside and joins the first; as no one of the brotherhood of trail runners can be left alone in distress; an unbreakable law. But the mail man is satisfied, so all hands stop for the night.

★ The rawhide thongs that compose the knitted filling or web of a snowshoe.

Out axes and after the drywood, boys! A mighty clamour of steel biting into wood. Large piles of spruce boughs make their appearance. Semicircular windbreaks of canvas stretched over poles cluster before a central fire, eight feet long. Smoke billows up to a certain height, to open out in a spreading, rolling canopy over the camp.

Dogs are fed with frozen fish or moose meat, this their only meal in twenty-four hours.

It has now been dark a long time, but wood is still being cut; eventually quiet settles down and the men sleep; but not the dogs. It seems they never sleep. One of them finds a morsel of something eatable; a swift rush and he is fighting at least six others. Howls, snarls, sharp, shrill yapping as of wolves; then curses, shouts, thuds, and silent scurrying retreats; for your husky does not yelp when beaten, but is a skilful dodger.

Once more, quiet. And then the moon rises, pale, and very large, and seemingly no further away than the back of the next ridge, the ragged outline of the shrouded trees standing sharply out across its face.

From around the fire, where each takes his turn at replenishing, come sounds of sleep. The bizarre shadows cast by the shifting flames dance in and out the tree trunks, and white snowshoe rabbits appear and disappear silently within the circle of light, unseen by the dogs who have crept up near the fire, dozing with the eye nearest it.

The moon rises high and resumes its normal size. The cold grips the land with the bite of chilled steel; trees crack in the frost like scattering rifle-fire. Then, later, as the moon sets, a thin wailing comes stealing across the empty wastes, wavering in strophe and anti-strophe, increasing in volume as voice after voice takes up the burden; the song of the wolves. And simultaneously, as at a given signal, in the wide dance hall of the sky above, the Dead commence to tread their stately measures. Flickeringly and hesitantly at first; but, as the moonlight disappears, the unearthly nebulous host stretches in the files of a ghostly array, which has the whole horizon for its manoeuvring, swiftly undulating, spreading and contracting, advancing and retreating in formless evolution, marching in column of route across the face of the Northern sky, swaying in a lambent, flickering horde to the tune of the unheard rhythm that rocks the universe. At times they seem to hover in the treetops, almost, it would seem within reach, and the ear seems to get the illusion of sound; so that the listener strains to hear the ghostly music, almost, but not quite audible, to which the spectral company is performing.

A little later the mail man gets up, scans the stars, and pronounces it time to rise. An hour and a half, or less, and all is ready. As the day breaks, the last team disappears around a bend in the trail. And nothing remains but a few bare poles, flattened piles of brush, and a dead fire, and, stretching either way into the chill, white silence, the Trail.

Such, in normal circumstances, is the Trail in winter. A few days soft weather, however, or a rainstorm, may bring conditions which make travelling virtually impossible. Yet a man caught out in such shape must do the impossible; he must go on. Goaded on by the knowledge of a rapidly diminishing food supply, or the certainty of more bad weather, he must keep moving; for this is the Trail, and will be served.

One season, having located a pocket of marten and lynx, which, being within a short distance of the railroad, had been overlooked, another man and myself hunted there all winter. We made frequent trips to town, a distance of twelve miles, often covering the route in four hours or less.

Hearing from a passing Indian that there was talk of a close season being suddenly declared, we decided to take out our fur, and dispose of it while it was still legal, and so avoid a heavy loss. This was late in April, and the ice was on the point of going out, but there were yet four feet of snow in the bush.

We started before daylight one morning, so as to cross most of the lakes before the sun took the stiffening out of the night's frost. There was open water of varying widths and depths around the shores of every lake, and we crawled out over this on poles, drawing the poles with us for use in making our landing. A light blow easily punctured the ice in any place, excepting on our winter trail, which, padded down solid by the numerous trips back and forth to town, formed a bridge over which we passed, most of the time erect, and with little danger. An hour after sunrise, a south wind sprang up, the sky clouded over, and it commenced to rain. The bottom went out of the ice bridges, necessitating walking the shores of each remaining lake, and on land the trail would no longer support our weight.

Where we had so blithely passed at a three-miles-an-hour gait in winter, we now crawled painfully along by inches, going through to the knee at each step, the snowshoes often having to be extricated by hand. The surface held until we put just so much weight on it, when it let us through at every step with a shock that was like to jar every rib loose from our backbones. Off the trail the snow was of the consistency of thick porridge, and progress there impossible.

We heartily cursed the originator of an untimely close season, who, no doubt, sat at home in warmth and comfort, whilst we, his victims, wet to the skin, our snowshoes heavy with slush, our feet and legs numb with ice water, crept slowly on. The water slushed in and out of our porous moccasins; but there was little we could do beyond wringing them and our socks out, and so occasionally getting relief for a few minutes, and also keeping moving. At that, we were no worse off than the man who walked all day in ice water with holes in his boots, claiming that he preferred them that way, as he did not have to take them off to empty them.

Every so often we made a lunch, and drank tea, and our progress was so slow that on one occasion, on making a halt, we could look back, and still see the smoke of our last fire, made two hours before. And this is to say nothing of the load. We took turns to draw the toboggan, which could not stay on the trail, since the sides having given out it was peaked in the centre. Thus the toboggan ran on its side most of the time, upsetting frequently, and the friction producing, contrary to common supposition, cold instead of heat, it became coated with ice, and drew with all the spring and buoyancy of a water-soaked log. Frequent adjustments had to be made to snowshoe-bridles with numb hands, the increased weight of the snowshoes breaking the tough leather repeatedly.

Resting was not desirable, except at a fire, as we became chilled to the bone in a few minutes; and, dark coming on with several miles yet to go, we pressed on as best we might. The jar of constantly going through the trail was nauseating us, and we had almost decided to camp for the night in the rain, when there loomed up in the gloom a large grey animal, standing fair in the centre of the trail ahead. We reached simultaneously for the rifle, but the animal came towards us with every appearance of confidence, and turned out to be a big Indian dog, out on a night prowl for rabbits.

Had this occurred in days gone by, no doubt we should have subscribed for a shrine at the place, in honour of some saint or other; as it was we said nothing, but seized the unfortunate beast, and quickly stripping the tump line off the toboggan, with multiple knots fashioned a dog harness, and hitched up our new-found friend. Showing no regret for his interrupted hunt, he hauled along right manfully, whilst we, unable to do enough for our deliverer, kept the toboggan on the trail, as far as was humanly possible, with poles. About that time, the wind changed to the North, the sky cleared, and it commenced to freeze, and with all these things in our favour, we made the remainder of the trip with ease, having spent seventeen and a half hours of misery to cover about ten miles up to that point.

In the woods nothing can be obtained except by effort, often very severe and prolonged, at times almost beyond human endurance. Nothing will occur of its own volition to assist, no kindly passerby will give you a lift, no timely occurrence will obviate the necessity of forging ahead, no lucky accident will remove an obstruction. Of course, a man can always give up, make fire, eat his provision, rest, and then slink back to camp, beaten and dishonoured; but that is unthinkable.

As you sit on your load to rest, searching the skyline for some encouraging indication of progress, it is borne home to you most irrefutably that all the money in the world cannot hire a single hand to help you, and that no power on earth, save your own aching feet, will cause the scenery to go sailing by, or take one solitary inch off the weary miles ahead. And as you sit in chill discomfort, your body bowed down from the weight of your load, your mind depressed by the incubus of the slavish labour yet to do, you realize that the longer the rest, so much longer you remain on the Trail. The thought goads you on to further efforts. Those packs will never move themselves, and the fact that they may contain skins worth a small fortune obtains for you no respite.

In civilization, if you showed your peltries, attention would be showered on you; willing hands would lift you to your feet. Deep in the forest your valuable pack becomes a useless burden, except for the pinch or two of tea and the few bites of greased bannock it may contain, which are worth, to you, more than all the gold in Araby.

At times you are fain to give up, and abandon your hardly won treasure, of which you would give the half for one mile of good footing, or the privilege of going to sleep for an hour. But you must struggle on; exhaustion may be such that further movement seems impossible, or you may have injuries that cause exquisite torture with every movement; but that trip must be finished, or in the latter event, fire must be lighted and camp of some kind made.

The beautiful marten stole gracing the shoulders of the elegantly dressed woman in Bond Street or on Broadway might, if it were able, tell a tale its owner little guesses.

At times the spirit or the northland, tiring of his heavy role, turns mountebank, and with sardonic humour he fashions mirages, travesties of the landscape they belie, and very baffling to one not acquainted with the topography of the district. Whole ridges of trees disappear from view, and across empty fields of ice a solid wall of forest presents itself, to melt into nothing, and be replaced perhaps by an expanse of open water which apparently bars further advance. It takes considerable steadiness of mind to march on into a section of landscape which you know not to be there, and so discredit the evidence of your senses.

Meanwhile this devil-turned-wizard conjures forests out of the ether, blots out mountains, and balances islands precariously one on another. A puerile occupation for an evil genius bent on destruction, yet men have been cajoled to death on bad ice by these tactics.

In a strange country, during the more vivid of these performances, it is as well to make camp, and leave the mummer to his clowning, until he allows the landscape to resume its normal contours.

After a more or less eventful visit to the "front," a companion and myself decided to desist from our efforts to relieve the stagnation of currency in the district, to return to the bush, and have a square meal.

My associate, not content with a few days' hilarity, had been looking too earnestly and too long on the wine when it was sixty-five over proof, and had tried to promote the health of the community by depriving it of its whiskey supply. The morning of the first day of the trip in was an epic of heroism on his part; and a good deal of the time he was not at all sure if his surroundings were real or the offspring of a slightly warped vision. I was not in a position to be of much assistance, having troubles of my own. But he kept on doggedly placing his feet one ahead of the other, until we arrived at the shores of a fair-sized lake.

Here a mirage was in progress. An island we well knew to be there was nowhere to be seen, and a dignified and solemn row of ancient trees, old enough probably to know better, were poised above the level of the surrounding scenery, head down.

My companion took a look at the manifestation, his eyes distended and his jaw dropped.

"Cripes," said he. "Do you see what I see?"

I replied that I thought I did. He shook his head.

"You don't see the half of it," he said. "This is the limit; I'm goin' back!"

Sometimes in winter a trail hidden by successive storms, or invisible in the darkness, has to be felt out step by step for miles at a time; and that at a speed little, if any less, than that attained to on good footing and during the daylight hours. The trail itself, if once passed over previously, is harder than the surrounding snow and a slight give of the shoe, slightly off on one side, is sensed, and the error rectified, without pause, at the next step. Thus a man and his outfit are enabled to pass dryshod over lakes that are often otherwise a sea of slush beneath the field of snow. A few steps into this and showshoes and toboggan become a mass of slush which immediately freezes, making progress impossible and involving the loss of an hour or more. This feat of feeling the way is common enough, but calls for intense concentration, and much resembles walking swiftly on a hidden tightrope; so much so, that a trapper will say with regard to a trip, that he went so many miles, of which he walked so much "on the tightrope." The strain attached to this form of exercise is such that on making a halt, one's frame is distinctly felt to relax. I have walked miles in this way, and then suddenly realized that my hands had been gripped tight all during the stretch in an effort, apparently, to hold the body free of the legs, as one who sits on eggs, dressed in his best, would do.

Under these conditions, the trail being most of the time invisible, a man travels to as much advantage in the night as in the daytime; more, in fact, as he is not constantly deceiving himself with fancied indications of the trail which land him into trouble.

As much travelling is done at night, almost, as in day; in summer to avoid the heavy winds of the daylight hours on large bodies of water, and in winter, because, owing to the length of the nights, much less wood is required for those who sleep out in daytime; also, the searing winds that generally go down with the sun, are avoided.

There is a peculiar, indescribable charm attached to night journeying that is handed down to some of us from the dawn of time; few can realize, without the experience, the feeling of wildness and barbaric freedom that possesses the soul of one who travels alone in the dark, out on the edge of the world; when anything may happen, beasts of all kinds are abroad, and flitting shapes appear and disappear, dimly seen by the light of the stars.

In a country where so little happens to break the monotony of wilderness travel, small occurrences, trivialities almost, become momentous occasions. The passage of a band of wolves at an unusual place, the distant sighting of an otter, a change of wind even. This is borne out in the nomenclature of sections of trail, and prominent features of the scenery. Such names as Hell's Gate, Steel River, Devil's Eddy, Smoky Falls, Lazy Beaver, Place-where-the-Devil-laughed, Dancing Portage, Hungry Hall, Lost Indian, are all apt reminders of the perhaps one outstanding incident that made history in that particular spot or region.

But the greatest thrill of all is that of suddenly finding strange footprints in a section where no signs of man, other than your own, have been seen for half a year. Fresh snowshoe tracks turning in, and going your way, perhaps. This opens up a wide field of speculation.

You undergo all the sensations experienced by Robinson Crusoe on his discovery of the well-known footprint. A man, one of your kind, and not long gone by; he slushed up the trail in one place, and it is not yet frozen!

A man, yes; but who? Frenchman? Indian? Assuredly not the latter, his tracks would be unmistakable. A wandering fur-buyer? The Mounted Police? Surely they are not going to be narrow-minded about that little affair last spring at Bisco. The Prince of Wales? Maybe; they say he is in Canada just now.

Anyhow this has got to be investigated. You quicken your steps, and two hours later you smell smoke, and suddenly come on a blazing fire, with a tea pail suspended over it. It is only Old Bill from the Wild Cat Hills; but anyway, Bill is a good old plug, and is just back up from "Canada," and he may have some news, or a letter.

Bill has no letters and less news, but he has a few choco-late bars, priceless treasures, which he shares, and a new brand of tobacco that would asphyxiate a horse, which he also endeavours to share. We eat and talk awhile, then Bill, who draws his own toboggan, gathers up his belongings, ducks into his tump line, and slipping with deft ankle movements into the bridles of an immense pair of trail breakers,★ shoes of an Indian rig, waves his hand, and is away. For Bill turns off here; he is leaving the Wild Cat Hills, and is going, footloose and free, to some far range as yet unexplored.

And as I stand and watch him go, I am lonesome a little, for the thought strikes me that Bill is old and may not come back. And so, bending forward against the creaking leather, snow flying in little puffs from his big snowshoes, he goes. Leaving behind him as he proceeds that winding, ever-lengthening, narrow rib-bon, the Trail, his one obsession for days to come, the only thing that connects him with his fellow man, and one that the first storm will obliterate.

★ Large snowshoes.

Down the hollow tunnels between snow-laden trees, over unmarked wastes, he picks his way by instinct; cynosure of all the hostile eyes that stare coldly out from shadowy recesses. Pushing doggedly on, across wind-lashed lakes, with their scurrying drift, and whirling, breathtaking snow-devils, past bald glistening mountains that stand guard at the portals of some mighty river. A moving speck, creeping across the face of the earth, he goes on to unknown destinations.

Day by day he penetrates deeper and deeper into the Kingdom of the Spirit of the North, where, jealous of such encroachment on his domain, with a thousand imps of mischief to do his bidding, master of all the powers of evil, the brooding Killer grimly bides his time; nor does he always wait in vain.

A small, red building overshadowed by a large canoe-shed, on the flat top of a rocky point; at the water's edge a dock at which float a number of canoes in various stages of loading. Men pass from the shed to the dock with bags of flour, sacks of beans, tents, blankets, boxes, and bundles. In the shade of the wide-topped jackpines, a knot of townspeople watch the busy scene, their eyes turned often to the door of the little red building. The laden men, too, often glance that way; all present wear an air of expectancy.

Presently the canoes are all loaded, the shed closed, and the men dispose themselves to wait. Some of these are attired in new mackinaw or khaki, and knee-boots; others, to whom, it is obvious, the proceedings are no novelty, wear the faded canvas clothing and the moccasins, or other heelless footwear, of the professional canoeman.

Soon the door of the diminutive office opens, and there steps out from it a man, weather-beaten, lean and wiry as a greyhound, dynamic energy apparent in every movement, indomitable will stamped on every feature. He closes the building as though for a long time; for not once again during five months will any of these men return to this spot, unless dismissed the Service, for this is the official Head Quarters of the Government Forest Rangers, the wiry man their Chief.

Seventy-five miles in is their distributing point, and from it these thirty men will successfully police from fire an area of ten thousand square miles. The Chief shoulders a heavy packsack, and steps quickly down to the dock with the lithe swing of an Indian. He glances appraisingly over his little band.

"Are we ready?" he asks.

It seems we are. He embarks in the rear canoe, for the trip ahead is long and arduous, and he must shepherd his men, unknown quantities many of them. Paddles are dipped, the veterans leading, and the flotilla is in motion. The bunched canoes string out, gain speed; the sun flashes on wet paddles, kneeling men sway to the stroke, and the canoes leap ahead in low undulations. The brigade is on its way, off on the Summer Trail.

The first objective is a long black point ahead, apparently the end of the lake. The point is reached, rounded, and another stretch of lake appears, with a similar point miles beyond. Hours of paddling, and no noticeable change in the scenery. A treadmill — but no stops.

Paddles, by pairs, click in unison with the regularity of clockwork; never a stroke is missed. Hours pass. The seasoned canoemen in front are setting a pace that never changes, never will change. They seem to have solved the problem of perpetual motion. The sun, a copper ball, burns its way across the sky, beating down on unshaded faces and bare forearms, and its reflected image on the glassy water stares into eyes puckered to mere slits against the scorching glare. The Chief, with his sterns-man, a supple, slant-eyed Cree, brings up the rear, watching his men, estimating their efficiency. Some parts of his patrol are difficult, and he must place his rangers judiciously.

Between two broken hills the lake narrows to a deep bay and finally comes to an end. Here a well-beaten, but not wide, path winds up a gully by carefully selected grades. Canoes are unloaded, and mountainous piles of baggage start up the ravine, as men assume their burdens and move off. This is the portage so long looked for as a change from the interminable paddling. And a change it certainly is. Everything, canoes and all, must be carried by manpower to the other side. Let us hope it is a short one. With our two hundred odd pounds apiece, by general consent conceded to be a "man's load," we commence the carry. An easy grade at first, but becoming rapidly more arduous as the two hundred and some pounds take their toll of nerve and muscle, with each successive upward step. Here the curse of Adam is fulfilled to the letter; sweat commences to pour into the eyes, down the body, dripping off the forearms. Vicious insects light and bite on contact. One hand is engaged in pulling forward and down on the top load to support the head, the other contains an axe or a pail of lard; so the flies stay until surfeited, and blood runs freely with the sweat. Up, and up, and then some. Surely this cannot go on much longer! But it does. Up on the crest, finally, where is a cool breeze; thank God for that; tear open the shirt and let it in.

Then down a declivity where the energy expended to keep from being rushed into uncontrollable speed, is apparently greater than the effort of climbing; the thought of a slip with that load is intolerable. Then a level spot, badly cluttered with boulders, and stones that move underfoot, where one walks with the precise steps of a cat, as a false step may mean a broken leg.

Men returning empty, carrying coiled tump lines, stand aside and give the trail to the burdened ones. No words are spoken on meeting; talking has become an effort, and the toilsome paddling of the forenoon now appears, by contrast, to have been little more than a light and healthful pastime.

At last, piles of bags and boxes lying in scattered heaps, but without confusion; the end, no doubt. You unload, and look around, and see no lake; only a continuation of that never-to-be-sufficiently-damned trail. This, then, is not the end, only a stage.★ How many more? True to the code you will not ask, but take what comes and like it; you coil your line and return. After all it was worth carrying that jag★★ if only to experience the feeling of comfort walking back without it. You step aside at intervals for heavily laden men; some of them have four hundred pounds and over. Incredible, but there are the bags — count them; a hundred of flour in each. These men trot, with short, choppy steps, but smoothly, evenly, without jar, whilst breath whistles through distended nostrils, and eyes devoid of expression stare glassily at the footing.

Several trips like this, then the canoes are taken. These, carried one to a man, do not stop at the stage, but, an easier load, seventy pounds perhaps, go on to the next stop, so that precious privilege, the rest walking back, will not be forfeited. Otherwise a stoppage would be necessary at the dump before again picking up a load, and delays are neither tolerated, nor expected; the sooner it is over the better; resting merely prolongs the agony. Stage after stage; stifling heat in a breathless scorching tunnel. Our hopes of a short portage have long ago faded entirely. Where is the end of this thing? Maybe there is no end.

And eventually every last piece and pound is dumped on the shores of a lake. Weary men make fire, cook, and wash the brassy film from their throats with hot tea. Hot tea on a broiling day! — yet the system calls for it. The lake is very small; not much respite here; load up, unload, and pack across again.

A new hand asks how many portages there are, and we hear it said that on this first leg of the journey there are fifteen more, and that the next one is called "Brandy" and admitted to be a bad

---

★ Portages are divided into convenient sections, and the dump at the end of each section is called a stage.
★★ Load.

one. We subsequently find this admission to be correct, but at the time, in view of our experiences on the last portage, we are all agog with interest as to what special features this alcoholic jaunt has in store.

We are not long in finding out. Almost a mile in length with five sharp grades arranged without regard for staging or symmetry, it has also a steep slope at the far end, which, being equal in sum to the aggregate of the hills so painfully climbed, at one fell swoop kicks your gains from beneath your feet, and lands you panting and half-dead back at the same level from which you started. So this is Brandy. She is, as we heard, a man-killer; and well named, for it is quite conceivable that more than one stricken man has found himself compelled to reach for his flask, before finally vanquishing this monster.

On the way back, after the first trip, we see the new man. He sits on a log with his head in his hands, exhausted, dejected. He can go no further. The Trail, ever on the watch, has weighed him in the balance, and he is found wanting. He will be sent back; for this is the Trail, where none may falter or linger, or evade the issue. For the time being he must do what he can, as to leave him is out of the question, but the weeding-out process has commenced.

On the third day we enter the pineries. Hills black with pine to the water's edge. Rock walls hundreds of feet in height and crowned with pine, falling sheer down into deep water. Pine, in mass formation, standing solemn, dignified, kings of all the forest; a sea of black sweeping tops swinging to the North; myriads of dark arms pointing one way, Northward, to journey's end; as though in prophetic spirit they see their doom approaching, and would flee before it to the last stronghold of the Red Gods. We are now entering the area for which this corps will be held responsible till late Fall, and two canoe crews receive their instructions, and leave the brigade taking each their separate way to a designated patrol district.

Indian signs now become frequent; teepee poles amongst the pine trees, in the glades, and on the beaches; caches raised high on scaffolds in sheltered spots; trail signs, marking a route; shoulder bones of moose hanging in pairs at campgrounds; bear skulls grinning out over the lake from prominent points. If you are stuck for tobacco you will find some in the empty brain box; but no bushman will take it; reprisals for vandalism of that kind may entail endless trouble. I once heard a white guide severely reprove a half-breed belonging to his party, who wishing to show contempt for such customs, and considering himself above them, took one of these skulls down and commenced to fill his pipe from it. The guide gave in no uncertain terms his opinion of the unsportsmanlike proceeding.

This is an Indian country; and at evening the double staccato beat of a drum swells and ebbs through the still air, faint but very clear, yet unaccountably indeterminate as to direction. A strangely stirring sound, giving an eerie quality to the surroundings. Those pines heard that sound three hundred years ago, when they were saplings; beneath these very trees the Iroquois war parties planned their devilish work, to a similar rhythm. We had thought these things were no longer done. The Cree is questioned, but he blinks owlishly, and has suddenly forgotten his English. The following day shows no sign of living Indians, but here and there is a grave with its birch-bark covering, and personal effects; always in a grove of red pines, and facing towards the sunset. Moose are seen every day now, and two men told off to fish when the evening halt is made, generally return in half an hour, or less, with enough fish for the entire party's meal.

Immense bodies of water many miles in length alternate with carries of from a hundred yards to three miles, so that there are stretches where we pray for a portage, and portages where we pray for a stretch. The pine-clad mountains begin to close in on the route, the water deepens, narrows, and commences to flow steadily.

We are now on the head of a mighty river, which drains all this region, and soon the portages become shorter, but more precipitous, and are flanked on one side or the other by a wicked rapids. Some of these can be run; but not all are experts, and the Chief will not allow valuable cargoes and, perhaps, useful lives to be sacrificed in order that some man of uncertain ability may try to qualify as a canoeman. Rocks that would rip the bottom from a canoe at a touch, lie in wait, invisible, just below the surface, but indications of their position are apparent only to the practiced eye. Eddies, that would engulf a pine tree, tug at the frail canoe essaying to drag it into the vortex. Treacherous cross-currents snatch viciously at the paddles; deceptive, smooth-looking, oily stretches break suddenly into six-foot pitches.

But there are amongst us some who have earned the right to follow their own judgment in such matters; these now take control of the situation. They are the "white water men," to whom the thunderous roar of a rapids, and the smell of spray flying in the face, are as the intoxication of strong drink. To such as these considerations of life and limb loom small compared with the maddening thrill of eluding and conquering the frenzied clawing and grasping of tons of hungry, rushing waters; yet coupled with this stern joy of battle is a skill and a professional pride that counts the wetting of a load, or the taking of too much water, an ineradicable disgrace.

None but those who have experienced it can guess the joyous daredeviltry of picking a precarious channel at racing speed between serried rows of jagged rocks, spiteful as shark's teeth. Few may know the feeling of savage exultation which possesses a man when the accumulated experience of years, with a split-second decision formed after a momentary glimpse through driven, blinding spume into some seething turmoil, and a perfect coordination between hand and eye, result in, perhaps, the one quick but effective thrust of the paddle or pole, that spells the difference between a successful run, and disaster. And as the canoe careens, and sidles, and plunges its way to safety, the pent-up emotions of its crew find expression in the whoops and shouts of the white canoemen, and the short, sharp yelps of the Indians, their answer to the challenge of the rapids. And the thundering waters drop back with a sullen growl, and a man may lean on his paddle, and look back and say, "Well, that was not too bad."

I know men who would camp a night at a bad rapids in order to have the sun in the right place for running, not able to resist picking up the gauntlet so arrogantly flung at their feet by some stretch of water that had already taken its toll of human life. But this hazardous pastime is not one to be entered upon lightly by those not knowing their danger, or who knowing it, overrate their own prowess. For a man well skilled in the game, with many years of hard apprenticeship to his credit, is sometimes called on to pay the extreme penalty; and a broken paddle, an unexpected obstruction, or sheer hard luck, may accomplish what the might of the river never could contrive.

Swept clear of his canoe, still living yet a dead man, he is whirled swiftly down; then comes the quick terrible realization of his awful extremity, that he is beyond aid, that this is the end. And the arches of the forest that have echoed to the shouts of triumph of those who run successfully, mockingly give back the cry of agony of the latest victim of that which knows no pity or remorse. A few swift seconds, and the black waters have thrown aside their plaything, limp and lifeless in the pool below, whilst the ring of trees around it stand all unheeding, or watch in silent apathy. And as if the act had been ordained from ages past, the silence of a thousand years resumes its sway; the pendulum of unmeasured time continues its sweep of the universe, and the soundless symphony of the infinite plays on.

★ ★ ★

Men react differently to the near approach of certain death. One, an Indian, laughed inordinately all during the last half-minute of his time on earth, and the ghastly bubbling gurgle as his mouth reached the level of the water, before it closed over his head for ever, will stay in my memory for many a day, as it doubtless will in the minds of all of us who had to stand helplessly by, and see him swept over a sixty-foot fall.

Another, also unable to swim, strangely, but undeniably, the usual thing with men who spend their lives in a canoe, after swamping in heavy water came to the surface with his hat on. Upon this hat he immediately clapped his hand, holding it in position and fighting for his life with one hand only, until he sank.

In another instance two men attempted to negotiate a dangerous place with a full load, in high water. The canoe filled, and, loaded down with traps, guns, flour, a stove, and other heavy articles, it immediately sank. One of the partners seized a bundle, which held him up for a few seconds only, when he disappeared, to remain under the ice all winter. The other was a powerful swimmer, and after losing much time and vitality in an effort, to rescue his companion, he commenced to fail in the icy water and made for land. Exhaustion was such, that, a short distance from shore, he gave up, allowing himself to sink. Not far below the surface his feet struck a rock, and he was able to retain his footing there, partly submerged, until sufficiently rested to make the remaining distance to safety.

Yet not always does the grim reaper stalk in the wake of misadventure which, if he be absent, is often in the nature of an entertainment for the lookers-on. A timely sense of humour has taken the sting from many a bitter misfortune, for out on the endless Trail, the line between tragedy and comedy is very finely drawn. A look, a word, anything that will crack a laugh in faces drawn with anxiety, no matter at whose expense, will often make a burlesque out of what would otherwise be an intolerable situation.

For instance, no one could ask for a more humorous and elevating exhibition than I myself once gave, before an interested audience of sixteen Fire Rangers. Upset by an unfortunate move, for which my partner and I were equally to blame, I swung out of the canoe as it capsized, keeping hold of the stern, and going down the rest of the swift water like the tail of a comet, amidst the sarcastic comment of the assembled Rangers. My bowsman was wearing heavy boots instead of moccasins, and in a kneeling position, the usual one in a canoe, his stiff footwear had become wedged beneath the thwart. He must have been almost a minute under the overturned canoe, unable to extricate himself, and in grave danger of drowning, when, with what little assistance I could give, he somehow got loose. Bewildered, he climbed onto the canoe, which being old and heavy, immediately sank, and me with it.

I am an indifferent swimmer, if any, and this was a dangerous eddy, and deep; there were no hand holds to speak of. So, although it rolled and twisted considerably in the cross current, I stayed with the canoe, on the chance that it would float up, as without it I would be a dead loss anyhow; and soon my head broke water again. The attentive concourse on the river bank, who were in nowise disturbed, evidently thinking we were giving an aquatic performance for their benefit to lighten the cares of a heavy day, were highly diverted, until my companion, on my return to the surface, swam ashore, where his condition apprised them of the true state of affairs. In a matter of seconds a canoe was racing towards me, whilst its occupants shouted encouragement. About this time I was in pretty bad shape, having taken much water, and my hold on the canoe was weakening; so I commenced to shout lustily, suggesting speed. To my horror, one of the men suddenly ceased paddling and commenced to laugh.

"Say," said he. "Why don't you stand up?"

And amidst the cheers and shouts of the appreciative assemblage, I stood up in about three feet of water. I had been floating with my legs out ahead of me, and had drifted backwards within a few yards of the shore.

Then there is the official whom I saw sitting in a canoe which had run aground and filled. Wet to the waist, he sat in the water with both feet elevated above the gunwales.

"What in hell you doin' there?" angrily demanded his assistant, who stood on the rock, submerged to the knees.

"Keeping my feet dry," replied the official with chattering teeth.

Many of the prospectors are old "desert rats" and plainsmen, used to horses and knowing but little about canoes. One such, not realizing the chances he was taking, attempted the negotiation of a difficult piece of fast water with the loaded canoe, whilst his companion crossed the portage. Unable to distinguish the channel, the prospector ran foul of a swift shallows; and, on getting out to lighten the load, he was swept off his feet and nearly carried away. The canoe swung sideways and filled, to the gunwales, and, with part of its contents, was salvaged only after an hour's hard work. An inventory was taken of the remaining goods, which were found to be thoroughly soaked. The man who had walked did not berate his crestfallen companion, who was responsible for the mishap, merely remarking disgustedly:

"We needn't have gone to all that trouble, we could have got that stuff just as wet letting it down on a rope."

The Height of Land is, for some reason, the breeding place of storms of a severity and suddenness that makes a familiarity with the signs preceding them imperative to those whose itineraries include lakes of any size. As one of the members of a heavily freighted brigade, caught in the centre of a lake forty-nine miles in length by one of these unexpected tempests, I once had this forcibly illustrated for me.

We were crossing at the narrowest stretch, a distance of fifteen miles, and were at about the centre, when, with very little warning, a gale sprang up which steadily increased until we were unable to ride it any longer. The waves had a twenty-four-mile sweep at us, yet we could have juggled our way to some bay that offered shelter, only for the fact that the lake being shallow, there was little buoyancy in the water, and the waves struck in rapid succession, with no sea-room between them. The canoes began to take water in quantities, and the danger of swamping was imminent, so we jettisoned the half of our valuable cargoes, and ran down wind to a small, bare rock island. Erecting tents was impossible without poles, so we bunched the canoes together and spread the tents over them. Here, with no wood, no brush, exposed to a continuous hurricane, we spent two days and a night. As the remains of our loads were the heavier packages that had been in the bottom of the canoes, and consisted in each case of flour, beans, and salt pork, all of which require cooking to be palatable, we came near to starving in the midst of plenty, and were mighty glad on the following night to make the mainland, and cook a few meals.

I have seen masses of water the height of a pine tree and ten yards across, spiralling and spinning across the centre of lakes at terrific speed in the spring of the year. With them a canoe has little chance. I once saw a point of heavy timber, perhaps thirty acres in extent, whipped, and lashed, and torn into nothing but a pile of roots and broken tree-stumps, in the space of fifteen seconds.

I saw a gap the width of a street, tearing itself at the speed of an express train through a hardwood forest, birch and maple trees, three feet through, being twisted around until they fell. Strange to say the few white pine escaped unscathed, standing around mournfully afterwards as though appraising the damage. In this instance there was a settlement near, in which a farmer claimed to have seen his pigpen, pigs and all, go sailing away into the unknown. On being asked how far the building was carried, he replied that he didn't know, but that it must have been quite far, because the pigs did not return for a week.

In a country of this description it is well to pitch camp, even if only for a night, with due regard for possible falling timber or cloud-bursts; in dealing with the unsleeping, subtle Enemy, ready to take advantage of the least error, it is well to overlook nothing.

A storm of this kind, at night, with nothing but a flimsy canvas tent between men and the elements, is a matter for some anxiety. The fierce rattle of the rain on the feeble shelter, the howling of the wind, the splintering crash of falling trees, which, should one fall on the tent, would crush every soul within it, make speech impossible. The blackness is intensified by each successive flash of lightning which sears its way between the rolling mass of thunder-heads, the air riven by the appalling impact between the heavenly artillery and the legions of silence. It is an orgy of sound; as though in very truth the wild women* on their winged steeds were racing madly through the upper air, screeching their war cries, and scattering wreck and desolation in their wake.

With the passing of the storm comes the low menacing murmur of some swollen stream, growing to a sullen roar as a yellow torrent of water overflows its bed, forcing its way through a ravine, sweeping all before it. That insistent muttering must not go unheeded, for there lies danger. Trees will be sucked into the flood; banks will be undermined, and tons of earth and boulders, and forest litter, will slide into the river channel, on occasion taking with them tents, canoes, complete outfits, and the human souls who deemed their feeble arrangements sufficient to cope with the elements.

Thus, with little preliminary, the Master of Destruction** ruthlessly eliminates those who so place themselves at his disposal; for at such times he scours the wilderness for victims, that he may gather in a rare harvest while the time is ripe.

* Valkyries.
** The brooding, relentless evil spirit of the Northland which every Indian believes haunts the northern fastnesses, with a view to the destruction of all travellers.

To those who dwell in the region that lies north of the Haut Terre, which heaves and surges, and plunges its way two thousand miles westward across the face of the continent, the settled portions of the Dominion are situated in another sphere. This is not surprising, when it is considered that a traveller may leave London and be in Montreal in less time than it takes many trappers to reach civilization from their hunting grounds. Most frontiersmen refer to all and any part of this vast Hinterland as the Keewaydin; a fitting name, of Indian origin, meaning the North-West Wind, also the place from which it comes. Only the populated areas are referred to as "Canada."

Canada, to many of them, is a remote place from whence come bags of flour and barrels of salt pork, men with pale skins, real money, and new khaki clothing; a land of yawning sawmills, and hustling crowds, where none may eat or sleep without price; and where, does a man but pause to gaze on the wonders all about him, he is requested to "move on," and so perforce must join the hurrying throng which seems so busy going nowhere, coming from nowhere.

A surge of loneliness sweeps over him as he gazes at the unfriendly faces that surround him, and he furtively assures himself that his return ticket is inside his hat-band, and wonders when is the next North-bound train. Supercilious bellboys accept his lavish gratuities, and openly deride him; fawning waiters place him at obscure and indifferently tended tables, marvel at the size of his tips, and smirk behind his back. For he is a marked man. His clothes are often old-fashioned and he lacks the assurance of the town-bred man. He has not the preoccupied stare of the city dweller; his gaze is beyond you, as at some distant prospect, his eyes have seen far into things that few men dream of. Some know him for what he is, but by far the greater part merely find him different, and immediately ostracize him.

He on whom the Trail has left its mark is not as the common run of men. Eyes wrinkled at the corners prove him one who habitually faces sun and wind. Fingers curved with the pressure of pole, paddle, and tump line; a restless glance that never stays for long on one object, the gaze of a bird or a wild thing, searching, searching; legs bowed a little from packing, and the lift and swing of wide snowshoes; an indescribable freedom of gait. These are the hallmarks by which you may know him.

There is another type; unwashed, unshaven, ragged individuals appear at the "steel" at intervals, generally men who being in for only a short time are able to stand that kind of thing for a limited period. They are a libel on the men they seek to emulate, wishing to give the impression that they are seasoned veterans, which they succeed in doing about as well as a soldier would if he appeared in public covered with blood and gaping wounds, or an actor if he walked the streets in motley.

Many, young on the trail, do some very remarkable feats, and impose on themselves undue hardship, refusing to make the best of things, and indulging in spectacular and altogether unnecessary heroisms. They go to the woods in the same spirit as some men go to war, as to a circus. But the carnival spirit soon wears off as they learn that sleeping on hard rocks when plenty of brush is handy, or walking in ice water without due cause, however brave a tale it makes in the telling, will never take a mile off the day's journey, nor add a single ounce to their efficiency.

The Trail, then, is not merely a connecting link between widely distant points, it becomes an idea, a symbol of self-sacrifice and deathless determination, an ideal to be lived up to, a creed from which none may falter. It obsesses a man to the utmost fibre of his being, the impelling force that drives him on to unrecorded feats, the uncompromising taskmaster whom none may gainsay; who quickens men's brains to shift, device, and stratagem, purging their bodies of sloth, and their minds of weak desires.

★ ★ ★

Stars paling in the East, breath that whistles through the nostrils like steam. Tug of the tump line, swing of the snowshoes; tracks in the snow, every one a story; hissing, slanting sheets of snow; swift rattle of snowshoes over an unseen trail in the dark. A strip of canvas, a long fire, and a roof of smoke. Silence.

Canoes gliding between palisades of rock. Teepees, smoke-dyed, on a smooth point amongst the red pines; inscrutable faces peering out. Two wooden crosses at a rapids. Dim trails. Tug of the tump line again: always. Old tea pails, worn snowshoes, hanging on limbs, their work is well done; throw them not down on the ground. Little fires by darkling streams. Slow wind of evening hovering in the treetops, passing on to nowhere. Gay, caparisoned clouds moving in review, under the setting sun. Fading day. Pictures forming and fading in glowing embers. Voices in the running waters, calling, calling. The lone cry of a loon from an unseen lake. Peace, contentment. This is the Trail.

> Tear down the tent and the shelter,
> Stars pale for the breaking of day,
> Far over the hills lies Canada,
> Let us be on our way.
> — TRAIL SONG

IV

THE STILL-HUNT

Deep in the jungle vast and dim,
That knew not a white man's feet,
I smelt the odour of sun-warmed fur,
Musky, savage and sweet.

Napoleon, so history informs us, said that an army travels on its stomach. He was right; Napoleon knew his stuff. More than that, this statement goes for Empires too, and the building of them, or any other line of human endeavour requiring a large expenditure of physical energy. The Bible itself is full of references as to how, when, and where its people ate.

On the Frontier eating a meal is not the ceremonial affair of politely restrained appetite and dainty selection seen in the best hotels and restaurants, but an honest-to-God shovelling in of fuel at a stopping-place, to enable the machinery to complete its journey, or its task. There the food supply is the most important consideration, and starvation is not merely going hungry for a few days, but becomes a fatal proposition. Civilization will not let you starve; the wilderness will, and glad of the opportunity.

Flour, beans, lard, tea, and a certain amount of sugar, with salt pork, may be transported in sufficient quantities to suffice for all winter, in a single canoe, for a single man.

But meat seems to be the only food, modern opinion to the contrary notwithstanding, which will supply the amount of energy needed to meet the climatic conditions, and successfully to withstand the constant hardship, which are two of the main features of existence in some parts of Northern Canada, and as much so today as ever they were in the early days. Without it the whole line of the offensive against the powers of the great white silence would perceptibly weaken; and meat boiled, fried, dried, smoked, or just plain frozen, is what this thin line of attack is moving up on.

This does not condone the indiscriminate slaughter of moose, deer, and other meat animals. Game protection is very strictly enforced in this country, and today the sportsman who comes out of the woods with his quota of trophies, while he leaves several hundred pounds of the best of meat to spoil in the woods, is counted guilty of a crime. The practice of supplying the crews of railroad construction and lumber camps with wild meat, fortunately not universal, is also to be much condemned. The companies, or contractors operating, are bearing the expense of boarding their crews, and the saving effected by the use of free meat is simply so much profit for the company, whose legitimate gains should not be so increased at the expense of the country, besides it does some honest tradesman out of his dues; and transportation facilities are no problem to this kind of pioneering.

It is no longer, as it was thirty years ago, a matter of seeing how much game one can kill to ascertain the number of different ways in which a stricken animal may hit the ground. Parts of this North country are swarming with game, but also, large areas of it are not. I have traversed regions a hundred miles in width where no track or other sign of animal life was to be seen save that of rabbits. The population of game animals, if evenly distributed, would not be as dense as it now appears to be, but there is enough meat in the North, in most places, to enable the pathfinders and the first fringe of scattering settlers, to live, and, if taken with discretion, not diminish the supply.

One sizeable moose will provide a man with meat for well over half the winter, and each settler family, with one moose per member, may, with due care, have the best of meat during all the cold months. With the coming of civilization and increased transportation facilities, hunting would no longer be necessary, and animals of all kinds could be preserved in perpetuity.

Pot-hunter is a term of reproach through all the length and breadth of the sporting world, as differentiating between the man who hunts for meat and the man who hunts for sport. But hunting to fill the pots of those families, who, as representatives of an entire people, are bravely struggling against adverse conditions and leading a life of deprivation and heavy labour, in their endeavour to bring some semblance of prosperity to a bleak and savage wilderness, is nothing to be held up to public scorn. These settlers and the trail-makers further afield are the people who are actually laying the foundation of an Empire overseas, subsisting for the most part on few enough of the necessaries of life; people to whom a large quantity of lard is as riches, and dried apples a luxury. Salt pork, which goes under the various euphonious titles of "Chicago Chicken," "Rattlesnake Pork" (on the supposition, based on the flavour, that the pigs it came from were fed on rattlesnakes), or just plain "sowbelly," whilst eatable to a hungry man, is no relish.

For these settlers to kill, subject to the liberal game laws of the different Provinces, an occasional moose to alleviate somewhat the monotony of beans and bannock to enable them to carry on cheerfully, is just as praiseworthy in principle as are the stupendous slaughters made by persons of high degree in Europe, where we may see recorded single bags of deer, bears, and wild boars, large enough to keep an able-bodied pioneer family in meat for five years. It is understood that these huge piles of meat are given to the poor, to hospitals, and other deserving institutions, which undoubtedly exonerates the men involved; so here, again, the much maligned pot gets in its nefarious work, without which such taking of animal life would be a shameful waste.

In the North, the failure of the fall moose hunt is as much of a catastrophe as the blighting of a wheat crop would be in more organized areas. Pot-hunting it is truly; but sport? Yes; the greatest sport in the world; the meat hunt of the Makers of a Nation.

Not so spectacular, this still-hunt, as were the great buffalo hunts of the emigrant trains crossing the plains, half a century ago, but every bit as much a part of the history of the development of the continent. As on today's frontier, the settler then was not as expert as his neighbour, the Indian, but by hook or by crook, he got his meat, and so does his successor today. An old-time buffalo hunt was an inspiring sight. The strings of light-riding savages on their painted ponies, probably the best irregular light mounted infantry the world has ever seen, naked to the waist, vying with each other in spectacular and hazardous stunts, exhibiting a skill in horsemanship never attained to by trained cavalry; the black sea of rolling humps, and bobbing heads, the billowing clouds of dust through which the fringe of wild, yelling horsemen were intermittently visible; the rumbling of innumerable hoofs, and, in the case of white men, the thudding of the heavy buffalo guns, combined to produce a volume of barbaric uproar, and a spectacle of wild confusion and savagery that had its duplicate in no part of the world.

The Indian and the settler killed, generally speaking, only enough for their needs. Then buffalo hides became of value, a dollar a piece or less. Immediately every man with the price of a camp outfit, a couple of wagons, a few horses and a gun, took to the buffalo country and, under pretence of clearing the plains for agricultural purposes, these animals were slaughtered without mercy. Right-minded people arose and condemned the perpetration of such a heinous crime as the destruction of an entire species to satisfy the greed of a few men. The United States Government, however, took no steps to prevent it, one official even suggesting placing a bounty on the buffalo, as it was understood that their destruction would settle once and for all the vexing and ever-present Indian problem.

It is worthy of note that at this time, Canada, with a large Indian population, had no such problem. The Blackfeet domiciled on both sides of the international boundary, whilst raiding trapper camps and committing depredations on the American side, respected the peace treaty they had made with Canada. This proves conclusively that a little tact and consideration could have accomplished with the Indians what bodies of armed troops could not.

Although no bounties were actually offered, the policy of destruction was carried out to the letter. The Indians, friendly or otherwise, took the warpath in defence of their ancient birthright; retaliatory tactics of the utmost cruelty were carried out against them, and some tribes were wiped almost out of existence. For several years, not many, the prairie became a shambles. The buffalo were eventually coralled in the state of Texas on one of their annual migrations, and one spring they failed to appear on the Canadian plains. The Indian problem was settled for all time.

A whole species of a useful and noble animal had been destroyed, and an entire race of intelligent and courageous people decimated and brought into subjection, in the space of a number of years that could be counted on the fingers of a man's two hands.

Allowing at a conservative estimate two hundred pounds of meat to each beast, and considering the semi-official computation of their number, which was around ten million head, it can easily be computed that two hundred million pounds of first-class meat, excepting the little that could have been eaten by the hunters themselves, was allowed to rot on the prairie. Add to this the greed and cruelty of the act, and the pitiable spectacle of the thousands of calves dying of neglect, or becoming a prey to wolves. This, however, is not the kind of Empire-building of which I like to speak, and serves as a very poor example of my subject. This hetacomb, too, was hardly a still-hunt.

It is not given to all to acquire skill in this most thrilling of sports. He who would become proficient at it must learn to move as a shadow, his actions smooth as oil, and his senses set to a hair-trigger touch; for the forest is argus-eyed, and of an unsleeping vigilance, and must always see him first.

Still-hunting is an art learned from the Indian, an accomplishment in which few white men excel, save only those who have spent many days in the lodges of those silent, thoughtful people, or consorted much with those who have. I can almost hear the howl of protest going up from a host of pseudo-bushmen, whose experience is confined to running moose down in deep snow, blundering on them in sections where they are numerous, or shooting them at the water's edge, which anybody can do. I repeat that the average white man is not a good still-hunter.

There are exceptions; famous guides, celebrated for their skill in "calling,"* crafty as the savage whose tricks they have acquired, men who have earned a reputation of never coming out without their moose, are to be met in bush communities in all parts of Canada; but they are as outstanding there as is a genius in a colony of artists. But all must take off their hats to the Indian. His own evasive, subtle mind fits him admirably to cope with the cunning and elusive nature of such animals as moose and deer. Indeed, it is probable that his type of mentality has been evolved by just such exercises during many generations, for the red man is primarily a hunter. Few but he are able, without snow, and in most cases even with it, to track and locate a moose without scaring the animal (in which case he is gone, and as impossible to overtake as a train would be), for no moose, unless bogged to the shoulders in snow, has ever been taken by tracking him down from behind. Not all are mentally fitted to enter into the intricacies of move and countermove, advance, circle, and retreat which must be studied in each case, or to guess the necessary allowance for the changing of a scarcely perceptible breath of wind.

Busy workers have not the time to acquire the knowledge that warns of too close an approach to a disadvantageous firing

* Moose can be called to a firing position by experts, in the right season.

position, nor have they, unless they live as close to Nature as their swarthy brethren, the instinct that evinces itself in the culminating achievement of knowing the exact position of the moose in relation to himself, before the last two or three steps are to be made that will expose the hunter, and give him his shot at a quarry that he has stalked for an hour. And all this without sight, sound, or indication of the presence of moose, excepting perhaps some week-old tracks and nibbled branches, and in a section, such as moose commonly resort to, where a man is lucky to be able to see ten feet ahead of him.

It takes no little skill also to enter a "yard" of moose, padded down with tracks as numerous as those of cows in a pasture, and make a specific set at one particular beast. Yet this is necessary; hit or miss, rambling tactics meeting with no more success than firing into the centre of a flock of ducks ever does. The least carelessness of approach, the rattle of cartridges in the pocket, the slapping of a twig on the clothing, or even too much mental concentration on the animal itself, causing uneasiness, will alike result in a sudden flurry and crackling of twigs and brush, the measured, rapidly diminishing thump of hoofs driven by legs working like piston-rods, the distant crash as some rotten tree gives way before the driving weight of flesh, bone, and muscle, and then utter silence. And like as not without a hair of the quarry having been seen.

The actual shooting is child's play. More moose are killed at fifty feet by good hunters, than at a hundred yards by good shots. A moose is not a hard target, and once seen, looms up amongst the undergrowth like the side of a barn. The difficult part is to get to see him. On the still-hunt the sum and substance of the hunter's efforts are to see the animal before it sees him; to closely approach a moose without his being aware of your presence is an impossible feat, as indeed it is with any other of these dwellers amongst the leaves. But like all the other types of deer, unless rendered frantic by the scent of man, his curiosity gets the better of him; he will stay until he gets a fleeting glimpse of what he is running away from. That is the hunter's only chance of success.

All animals that live in the wilderness are provided with a set of protective habits which the skilled hunter, having knowledge of them, turns to his advantage. Beaver, when ashore, post a guard; not much advantage there, you think. But standing upright as he does in some prominent position, he draws attention, where the working party in the woods would have escaped notice. Both beaver and otter plunge into the water if alarmed or caught in a trap (in this case a stone is provided which keeps them there, to drown). Foxes rely on their great speed and run in full view, offering excellent rifle practice. Deer contrive to keep a tree or some brush between their line of flight and their enemy, and the experienced hunter will immediately run to the clump of foliage and shoot unseen from behind it.

Moose feed downwind, watch closely behind them but neglect to a certain extent the ground ahead. When about to rest they form a loop in their trail, and lie hidden beside it, where they can keep an eye on it, manoeuvring to get the wind from their late feeding ground. These things we know, and act accordingly. We decide on the animal we want, and make a series of fifty-yard loops, knowing better than to follow directly in the tracks, the end of each arc striking his trail, which is a most tortuous affair winding in and out as he selects his feed. We do this with due regard for the wind, all along his line of travel, touching it every so often, until we overshoot where we suppose the trail ought to be. This shows — provided our calculations are correct, our direction good, and if we are lucky — that our moose is somewhere within that curve. It has now become a ticklish proposition.

We must not strike his tracks near where he is lying down (he cannot be said to sleep), for this is the very trap he has laid for us. If we go too far on our loop we may get on the windward side (I think that is the term; I am no sailor). Pie for the moose again. Probably he is even now watching us. To know when we are approaching that position between our game and the tell-tale current of air is where that hazard comes in which makes moose-hunting one of the most fascinating sports.

All around you the forest is grey, brown, and motionless. For hours past there has been visible no sign of life, nor apparently will there ever be. A dead, empty, silent world of wiry underbrush, dry leaves, and endless rows of trees. You stumble and on the instant the dun-coloured woods spring suddenly to life with a crash, as the slightly darker shadow you had mistaken for an upturned root takes on volition; and a monstrous black shape, with palmated horns stretched a man's length apart, hurtles through tangled thickets and over or through waist-high fallen timber, according to its resisting power. Almost prehistoric in appearance, weighing perhaps half a ton, with hanging black bell, massive forequarters, bristling mane, and flashing white flanks, this high-stepping pacer ascends the steep side of a knoll, and on the summit he stops, slowly swings the ponderous head, and deliberately, arrogantly looks you over. Swiftly he turns and is away, this time for good, stepping, not fast but with a tireless regularity, unchanging speed, and disregard for obstacles, that will carry him miles in the two hours that he will run.

And you suddenly realize that you have an undischarged rifle in your hands, and that your moose is now well on his way to Abitibi. And mixed with your disappointment, if you are a sportsman, is the alleviating thought that the noble creature still has his life and freedom, and that there are other days and other moose.

I know of no greater thrill than that, after two or three hours of careful stalking with all the chances against me, of sighting my game, alert, poised for that one move that means disap-pearance; and with this comes the sudden realization that in an infinitesimal period of time will come success or failure. The distance, and the probable position of a vital spot in relation to the parts that are visible, must be judged instantly, and simultaneously. The heavy breathing incidental to the exertion of moving noiselessly through a jungle of tangled undergrowth and among fallen timber must be controlled. And regardless of poor footing, whether balanced precariously on a tottering log or with bent back and twisted neck peering between upturned roots, that rifle must come swiftly forward and up. I pull — no, squeeze — the trigger, as certain earnest, uniformed souls informed me in the past, all in one sweeping motion; the wilderness awakes to the crash of the rifle, and the moose disappears. The report comes as a cataclysmic uproar after the abysmal silence, and aghast at the sacrilege, she startled blue jays and whiskey-jacks screech, and chatter, and whistle. I go forward with leaps and bounds, pumping in another cartridge, as moose rarely succumb to the first shot. But I find I do not need the extra bullet. There is nothing there to shoot. An animal larger than a horse has disappeared without a trace, save some twisted leaves and a few tracks which look damnably healthy. There is no blood, but I follow for a mile, maybe, in the hopes of a paunch wound, until the trail becomes too involved to follow.

I have failed. Disaster, no less. And I feel pretty flat, and inefficient, and empty-bellied.

Worst of all, I must go back to camp, and explain the miss to a critical and unsympathetic listener, who is just as hungry as I am, and in no shape to listen to reason. Experiences of that kind exercise a very chastening effect on the self-esteem; also it takes very few of them to satisfy any man's gambling instinct.

A big bull racing through close timber with a set of antlers fifty or sixty inches across is a sight worth travelling far to see. He will swing his head from side to side in avoidance of limbs, duck and sway as gracefully as a trained charger with a master-hand at the bridle, seeming to know by instinct spaces between trees where he may pass with his armament.

It is by observing a series of spots of this description that a man may estimate the size of the bull he is after.

The tracks of bull and cow are distinguishable by the difference in shape of the hoofs; the bull being stub-toed forward, and the cow being narrow-footed fore and aft. Also the bull swings his front feet out and back into line when running; this is plain to be seen with snow on the ground of any depth; furthermore the cow feeds on small trees by passing around them, the bull by straddling them and breaking them down. Tracking on bare ground is the acme of the finesse of the still-hunt, especially in a dry country; and tracking in winter is not always as simple as would appear. More than a little skill is sometimes required to determine whether the animal that made the tracks was going or coming. This is carried to the point, where, with two feet of snow over month-old tracks, visible in the first place only as dimples, an expert may, by digging out the snow with his hands, ascertain which way the moose was going; yet to the uninitiated tracks an hour old present an unsolvable problem as to direction, as, if the snow be deep, the tracks fill in immediately and show only as a series of long narrow slots having each two ends identical in appearance. The secret is this, that the rear edge of the hind leg leaves a sharper, narrower impression in the back end of the slot than does the more rounded forward side. This can be felt out only with the bare hands; a ten-minute occupation of heroic achievement, on a windy day on a bleak hillside, in a temperature of twenty-five below zero. Nevertheless a very useful accomplishment, as in the months of deep snow a herd may be yarded up a mile from tracks made earlier in the season.

But should the herd have travelled back and forth in the same tracks, as they invariably do, we have confusion again. In that case they must be followed either way to a considerable hill; here, if going downhill they separate, taking generous strides, or if uphill, short ones. Loose snow is thrown forward and out from the slots, and is an unfailing guide if visible, but an hour's sharp wind will eradicate that indication save to the trained eye.

Assuredly the hunt is no occupation for a pessimist, as he would most undoubtedly find a cloud to every silver lining.

There are many ways of killing moose, but most of them can be effected only at times of the year when it would be impossible to keep the meat, unless the party was large enough to use up the meat in a couple of days, or, as in the case of Indians, it could be properly smoked.

In the summer when they come down to water in the early morning and late evening, moose are easily approached with due care. They stand submerged to the belly, and dig up with the long protruding upper lip, the roots of water lilies, which much resemble elongated pineapples. Whilst eyes and ears are thus out of commission the canoeman will paddle swiftly in against the wind, until with a mighty splurge the huge head is raised, the water spraying from the wide antlers, running off the "pans" in miniature cataracts, when all movement in the canoes ceases, and they drift noiselessly like idle leaves, controlled by the paddles operated under water. The moose lowers his head again, and the canoes creep up closer now, more cautiously, care being taken not to allow the animal a broadside view. On one of the occasions when he raises his head the moose is bound to become aware of the danger, but by then the hunters have arrived within rifle shot of the shore; so, allowed to provide his own transportation to dry land, he is killed before he enters the bush.

In the mating season moose may be called down from the hills by one skilled in the art, and threshing in the underbush with an old discarded moose-horn will sometimes arouse the pugnacity of a reluctant bull; but when he comes it is as well to be prepared to shoot fast and straight.

Many sportsmen become afflicted with a peculiar malady known as buck-fever when confronted suddenly by the game they have sought so assiduously. The mental strain of senses keyed to the highest pitch, coupled with the quivering expectation of a showdown at any moment, is such that this "fever " induces them either to pump the magazine empty without firing a shot or forget to use the sights, or become totally incapable of pressing the trigger. Gentlemen of that temperament had better by far let fallen moose-horns lie when in the woods during the early part of October. They certainly are lacking in the *sang froid* of a prominent businessman I once guided on a hunt.

He was a man who liked a drink, and liked it at pretty regular intervals, when on his vacation. Included in the commissariat was a case of the best whiskey. Every morning when we started out a bottle was placed in the bow of the canoe and from it he gathered inspiration from time to time, becoming at moments completely intoxicated, as he averred, with the scenery. The agreement was that when the Scotch was gone the hunt was over, and, head or no, we were to return to town. It was not a good moose country. I had hunted all I knew how, and had raised nothing, and my professional reputation was at stake. The day of the last bottle arrived, and our game was still at large. As we started for the railroad I was in anything but a jubilant mood, when, on rounding a point, a large bull of fair spread stood facing us on the foreshore, at a distance of not over a hundred feet. I jammed my paddle into the sand-bar, effectually stopping the canoe, and almost whooped with joy; but my companion, who was pretty well lit by this time, gazed fixedly at the creature, now evidently making preparations to move off.

I urged an immediate shot. In response to my entreaties this human distillery seized his rifle and tried to line his sights. Failing, he tried again, and fumbled at the trigger, but the "scenery" was too strong for him. The animal, apparently fascinated by the performance, had paused, and was looking on. The man was about to make another attempt when he put the gun down, and raising his hand he addressed the moose.

"Wait a minute," said he.

Reaching down into the canoe he handed me over his shoulder not the rifle but the bottle, saying as he did so, "Let's have another drink first!"

After the first frosts bull moose are pugnaciously inclined towards all the world, and more than one man has been known to spend a night up a tree, whilst a moose ramped and raved at the foot of it till daylight. Whether these men were in any actual danger, or were scared stiff and afraid to take any chances, it is impossible to say, but I have always found that a hostile moose, if approached boldly down wind, so that he gets the man-scent, will move off, threateningly, but none the less finally. Although the person of a man may cause them to doubt their prowess, they will cheerfully attack horses and wagons, domestic bulls, and even railroad locomotives.

Bull moose are quite frequently found killed by trains at that time of the year, and they have been known to contest the right of way with an automobile, which had at last to be driven around them. A laden man seems to arouse their ire, as a government ranger, carrying a canoe across a portage once discovered.

It was his first trip over, and, no doubt attracted by the scratching sound caused by the canoe rubbing on brush as it was carried, this lord of the forest planted himself square in the middle of the portage, and refused to give the ranger the trail. The bush was too ragged to permit of a detour, so the harassed man, none too sure of what might occur, put down his canoe. The moose presently turned and walked up the trail slowly, and the man then picked up his canoe again, and followed. Gaining confidence, he touched his lordship on the rump with the prow of the canoe, to hasten progress; and then the fun commenced. The infuriated animal turned on him, this time with intent. He threw his canoe to the side, and ran at top speed down the portage, with the moose close behind. (It could be mentioned here, that those animals are at a distinct disadvantage on level going; had the ranger entered the bush, he would have been overtaken in twenty steps.)

At a steep cut-off he clutched a small tree, swung himself off the trail, and rolled down the declivity; the moose luckily, kept on going. After a while the ranger went back, inspected his canoe, which was intact, and put it out of sight, and it was as well that he did. He then returned to his belongings to find his friend standing guard over a torn and trampled pile of dunnage which he could in no way approach. He commenced to throw rocks at this white elephant, who, entering into the spirit of the game, rushed him up the trail again, he swinging off in the same place as before. This time he stayed there. The moose patrolled the portage all the hours of darkness, and the ranger spent the night without food or shelter.

A moose, should he definitely make up his mind to attack, could make short work of a man. They often kill one another, using their antlers for the purpose, but on lesser adversaries they use their front feet, rearing up and striking terrific blows. I once saw an old bull, supposedly feeble and an easy prey, driven out into shallow water by two wolves, where they attempted to hamstring him. He enticed them out into deeper water, and turning, literally tore one of them to pieces. Fear of wounding the moose prevented me from shooting the other, which escaped.

When enraged a bull moose is an awe-inspiring sight, with his flaring superstructure, rolling eyes, ears laid back, and top lip lifted in a kind of a snarl. Every hair on his back bristles up like a mane, and at such times he emits his challenging call — O-waugh! O-waugh!; a deep cavernous sound, with a wild, blood-stirring hint of savagery and power. This sound, like the howling of wolves, or the celebrated war-whoop when heard at a safe distance, or from a position of security, or perhaps in the latter case, at an exhibition, is not so very alarming. But, if alone and far from human habitation in some trackless waste, perhaps in the dark, with the certainty that you yourself are the object of the hue and cry, the effect on the nervous system is quite different, and is apt to cause a sudden rush of blood to the head, leaving the feet cold. The sounds, invested with that indescribable atavistic quality that only wild things can produce, under these conditions, are, to say the least, a little weakening.

Once, and once only, was I ever in any serious danger from the attack of a moose. On this occasion, needing meat, I was looking for moose tracks. Finding some indications, I had, after only a short still-hunt, come on to two of them, a cow and a well-grown calf, at the edge of a beaver pond. I shot the calf, which suited my requirements, it being yet warm weather, and the cow made two or three runs at me, but was easily scared away by a few shots fired in the air; I felt safe enough as I had in my pocket some spare cartridges, tied in a little buckskin bag to keep them from rattling.

Whilst skinning the kill I noticed a beaver swimming towards me, his curiosity aroused by the shooting probably, as I suppose that the crack of a rifle had never been heard before in all that region. The beaver was unprime, and the hide valueless, but, becoming interested in his movements, I sat down on the bank and watched him. Quite absorbed in my pastime I was suddenly startled by a slight crackling behind me, followed immediately by the hollow, coughing grunt of an angry bull moose. The sound was no novelty to me, but never before had it carried, to my ear, the note of menace that it now did. No thunderous bellowing roar of a lion could convey half the murderous intent expressed in the cold malevolence of that sound behind my back. It chilled me to the marrow, and the hair crept on my scalp. I jumped to my feet and whirled with a yell calculated to jar the horns off the creature's head, but which produced not the slightest effect. He stood facing me, every hair on his body erect, his eyes red with hate. He commenced rubbing his hocks together, sure signal of charge, and I smelt distinctly the sickening, musky odour these animals emit when about to fight.

Afraid to make a sudden movement, for fear of precipitating an attack, I reached stealthily for my rifle, jerked it to my hip, pumping as I did so, and fired; that is, I pulled the trigger, and almost before the answering click told me the gun was empty it flashed into my brain like an arrow from hell that I had emptied the magazine in driving away the cow.

But the spell was broken. The moose moved; so did I.

He had me between himself and the pond, with a margin of about ten feet in my favour. Once in the water, my chances I knew, would be poor; so I made pretty good time down the edge of it, and the moose ran parallel to me; we seemed to be pretty evenly matched for speed. At the end of the pond I turned, quickly jumped the creek, and made for a stretch of flat, steeply sloping rock, where I could not be cornered up; this was covered with a scattered growth of small jackpines, which, whilst not large enough to climb, offered dodging facilities. This move brought the moose directly behind me.

Still running, I got out my bag of cartridges, and pulled the string with my mouth: the knot jammed; I slackened my speed and tore at the bag with my teeth, ripping it, and spilling most of the cartridges. Ramming a shell into the breech I spun quickly round to find that the moose had stopped also, startled at my sudden move, and at about the same distance as before. I took quick aim, ready to shoot, but his rage was spent, and his former pugnacity gave way to uneasiness. I knew now that the danger was over, although I was obliged to sting him in the flank before I could get rid of him.

In the course of a hunt every detail liable to have a bearing on the situation must be noted; such as the roll of the land forming pockets where the wind may eddy; the direction of the different vagrant air currents, or a shift in the wind itself, must be tested for, generally by means of wetting a finger and holding it up, the side which the wind is coming from becoming immediately cool; or if there be snow, by throwing up handfuls and watching its drift.

Care must be taken that an approach is not made up a steep hill where your quarry will sight you before you can see enough of him to cover with your foresight; also that you do not stand out in prominent relief, in the full glare of the sun, or find yourself obliged to shoot into it.

I remember well seeing a much-needed buck saunter off into the bush in plain sight, owing to the fact that I faced the setting sun on a lake shore, and every time I raised my rifle the deer completely disappeared, swallowed up in the glare.

Trivial occurrences, that would appear to have no connection with the hunt whatever, may be of the utmost importance. The cawing of a few crows once led to a kill which was the realization of the dream of years to the sportsman I accompanied on the trip. It was in a burnt country, and my companion was unsuitably clad as to his feet in a pair of heavy, hard-soled boots, and in the dry, brittle ruck of the fire was making a terrific noise. We had heard that exciting, terrible sound, the clashing of huge antlers as two bulls fought to the death, about half a mile back; and we were now closely approaching our estimation of the position of this battle, which had ceased. I asked my companion to stand still for a moment so that we could listen awhile, and he unfortunately chose a brittle log to stand on, which gave way with a crash. Remarking meekly that he "made more noise standing still than some people did running," the unfortunate man urged me to try my luck alone.

Just at that moment we heard faintly a continuous, low sound, about two hundred yards to the south of us. This, after listening attentively, we made out to be the sound of crows, flocking together at some spot. This probably meant that some animal lay dead there, in all likelihood a moose, killed in a fight. My friend took courage on hearing the good news, and decided to see the thing through. As we listened, getting our bearings and testing the wind repeatedly, the sound changed to a scolding, and the birds seemed to scatter and take the air, as though disturbed. Better all the time; this argued a living moose, no doubt inspecting his victim, as they do periodically when victorious.

We laid our plan of approach and started away, and when we were within about twenty-five yards of the disturbance, the crows took flight, and we came suddenly out in plain view of a pool of water, in which lay a moose, very dead, and for a long time since, which it took no skill to determine. Seated in the water, feeding on the ill-smelling carcass, was about the biggest black bear I had seen for a long time, he being the cause of all the uproar.

Although it was not my hunt, the other man being for a moment spellbound, and with good reason, for it was a remarkable sight, I immediately shot the bear. On receiving the second bullet, he raced into an unburned patch of larches, where we eventually found him dead. This clump we circled, to find his point of egress, if any, as a wounded bear is apt to be dangerous, and we were as yet uncertain of his demise.

We had no more than half completed our detour when we heard that deep-throated gurgling cough that so thrills the hunter to the core of his being, and, it seemed, almost at our elbows. Turning we saw two big bulls looking down on us from the top of a knoll not fifteen yards away. Here this sportsman redeemed himself. The biggest bull did not offer him a very good target, but sensibly taking the smaller one that did, he dropped his moose neatly and cleanly with a well-placed bullet.

Some men are stricken with buck fever after the shooting is all over. One man, when I knocked down a badly wounded bull that would otherwise have suffered for hours and given us a long and useless chase, his gun empty, and thinking his game was escaping him, had been in despair. He became so excited on seeing the moose fall, and his trophy assured, that he started searching in all his pockets with fluttering hands, ejaculating disjointedly:

"You saved the day; you sure did. I appreciate that; believe me I do. I-I-yes sir, I must do something for you; something worthwhile, that you'll remember me by." Having at last located what he was searching for, he finally pulled out a gold cigarette-case, and opening it, he held it towards me. "Here," he said, "have a cigarette, you deserve it!"

I had no intention of accepting a gift offered in such circumstances, but his concluding words caused me to show some astonishment, and, noticing it, he suddenly became aware of the situation his excitement had tricked him into, and we both enjoyed a hearty laugh over the incident and I kept the cigarette to remember him by.

Being accustomed to hunting on the plains, where the game is in pockets, in gulleys, river bottoms, or in bluffs of poplar or willows, and thus standing partly located at the outset, and where it is more a matter of good shooting than good hunting, I found the still-hunt, as practised by the Northern Indians, an entirely different proposition. I know of no set of conditions to which the ancient simile of the needle in the haystack could be better applied.

My first experience was a good many years ago, with a young Ojibway, yet in his teens. He had all the quiet and confident bearing that goes with conscious ability, moved like a shadow, and addressed me not at all. From the outset he was in no hurry, spending much time listening to the wind above, and inspecting the ground below, both apparently inconsequent proceedings as there seemed to be no wind and the only visible tracks, to the reading of which I was no stranger, were old ones and plain to be seen. However, his tardiness suited me as, coming from a territory where walking is not popular, and with the slippery, stiff-soled moccasins of the plains Indian on my feet, I was quite well occupied keeping him in sight as it was, and sincerely hoped nothing would occur to increase his speed.

We proceeded in a fairly direct line of travel for maybe an hour, when on a sudden he stopped and, motioning me to come, showed me the fresh track of a cow moose. Our progress now became more circuitous and rambling, and he wandered apparently quite aimlessly around, listening meanwhile for a non-existent wind.

It was during the Fall of the year, and I found the wonderfully coloured woods a fairyland after the bare, brown prairie, and the dry harsh mountains protruding from blistering belts of sand. I was having a good time and, moose or no moose, the gyrations of my gnome-like and elusive companion intrigued me to the limit. Presently he stopped in a glade, and looked around, smiling with the air of one exhibiting a long-sought treasure. I also looked around, but did not smile, as I recognized the spot as the one at which he had discovered the moose track. I had been twisted often enough in my calculations in the wild lands to guess what that meant.

"Ki-onitchi-kataig, we are lost," I said.

He shook his head, and pointing to the moose track held up two fingers.

So that was it, he had in the circling discovered another moose. I had not seen him go through any motions indicative of a person discovering anything, moose or man, but supposed he must know what he was about. Maybe, I reflected, if we went around again, we could add another moose to the tally, and then surround them and make a general slaughter. The stripling now made some preparations. He took off his outside shirt and his hat, tying a folded handkerchief of indefinite colour around his bobbed hair. He hung his discarded clothing, with his blanket-cloth gun-case on a limb, and this mark of confidence in his ability to find the place again induced me also to remove and hang up my coat and hat; it seemed we must be about to hurry.

But my elfin guide stood motionless, apparently lost in thought, formulating his plans; and as he so stood, a study in black and tan, and faded buckskin, under the bronze dome of a giant birch tree, I thought that if only some great artist were there with skilful brush to commit to canvas the wondrous colour scheme, the shades, the shadows, the slanting streams of subdued light, the attitude of my primitive companion, wild, negligent, yet alert, furtive almost, like the creatures he was hunting, the masterpiece would result that could well be representative of a race, and of an epoch that will soon be with the things which are no longer, lost forever.

The moment passed and he moved on.

Our progress was now very slow. Twice I ascertained that we were covering short sections of our previous itinerary, backtracking in spots, making endless half-circles on a base line itself anything but straight.

On our left came a breath of sound, a slight rustle, and on the instant the boy sank into the woods like a hot knife through butter. Presently he returned, smiled his thin smile, and made the sign of a fox's tail. More half-circles. He commenced testing for the wind with a wet finger, and crumbling dry leaves in his hands allowed the dust to drift. The result was almost imperceptible. He seemed to gather some satisfactory information from the manoeuvre, however, as he nodded his head and went on.

Bars of sunlight hovered here and there as the trellised roof of leaves wavered and swayed, and in the more open spaces it filtered through, to lie in golden pools upon the forest floor. These he skirted stealthily, keeping in the gloom on their borders with that instinct of self-effacement which alike to the predatory or the furtive, spells success or safety.

He tested for wind more frequently now, on one occasion stopping and creeping backwards on his tracks, as though backing out of some sacred precinct that he had inadvertently entered. He circled out, and back into the same spot by another direction, a matter of yards only, and, selecting a spot in a wall of small evergreens, suddenly raised his rifle and fired.

At the same instant saw a patch of coarse hair resolve itself into a huge brown body, as a cow moose surged through the balsams, blood streaming from nose and mouth, to sink down within twenty feet.

The Ojibway blew the smoke out of his rifle.

"Meheu," he said, speaking for the first time. "It is done."

V

ON BEING LOST

Vainly walked he through the forest …
In the snow beheld no footprints,
In the ghastly gleaming forest
Fell, and could not rise from weakness,
Perished there from cold and hunger.
— Longfellow

Three years ago, on a night in spring, a man went down from his camp fifty yards to the river to get a pail of water and has never been seen since.

A year before the time of writing, in this district, a deer-hunter took an afternoon stroll and was discovered eleven days later, by one of a gang of twenty-five men who scoured the woods for him for twenty miles around.

In the first case the man strayed off the water-trail in the dark, and not arriving at the shack he attempted to correct his mistake and took a shortcut, only to arrive back to the river at another point. He again endeavoured to strike the camp but, angling too much to his right, missed it. So much was learned by the finding of the pail at the river bank, and by his tracks. After that he entered a country of burnt, bare rocks, and small patches of green swamp, and he is there yet.

The second man, having killed a deer, remained where he was, erected a shelter, and kept a fire. Beyond the mental strain incident to his adventure he was in good condition when found. Wherein lies the secret of the difference between being correctly and incorrectly lost.

The safest course, with night coming on, and being still astray, is for one to stop, make a fire, and as comfortable a camp as may

be, and wait for daylight, with the feeling of security that it brings
after the uncertainties and exaggerated forebodings of a long
night. Then, perhaps, bearings can be taken to better advantage,
and the sun may be shining, although it may now, after half a day
of extended and aimless ramblings, be impossible for the wanderer
to determine in which direction a start should be made.

Even so, he may strike for low land, and if his camp is not
situated on it he will have at least an idea where it should lie. The
inability of the average man to retain a record of his itinerary
to the rear, whilst he selects his route ahead, is responsible for
more loss of life in the woods than any other factor, excepting
perhaps fire. This is so well recognized that one of the Provinces
has passed a law prohibiting the killing of porcupines, except in
cases of emergency, they being the only animal that can be killed
by a starving man without weapons.

A man may start on a bright, sunshiny day, with all confidence,
to make his way to some as yet undiscovered lake or river, or to
look over a section of country, and find his trip going very satis-
factorily. Inviting glades, offering good travelling, open up in every
direction; gulleys lead on miraculously from one to another in just
the right directions; and an occasional glance at the sun, or the lie
of the land, affords all the indication of route necessary. The course
is smooth, the wheels are greased, and he slides merrily on his way.

Having lured him in so far with fair promise, the fickle landscape now decides to play one from the bottom of the deck.
The going becomes thicker during the next half-hour, and the
ground inclined to be swampy, with quite a few mosquitoes present. The interest aroused by these features induces a slight relax-
ing of concentration, and during such period of preoccupation
the sun guilefully seizes on this as the psychological moment at
which to disappear. The travelling becomes worse, much worse.
Dwarf tamarac,* spruce, and cedar have now superseded the

* American larch.

more generous and tractable hardwoods, and standing close-packed, with interlaced limbs, they form an entanglement from the feet up, through which a man is hard put to it to force a passage. Overhead is an impenetrable mass of twisted branches, through which the perspiring man vainly endeavours to get a glimpse of the sun, only to discover that it is gone. From the high ground further back he has seen a ridge of hardwood across the swamp, perhaps a mile away or more, where the footing will be good; so he presses on for this. He fights his way through the tangled growth for hours, it seems, and appears to be no nearer the slope of deciduous timber than he ever was. He now, wisely, decides to eat and think it over; so making a fire, and infusing his tea with swamp water, he builds himself a meal.

After this, and a smoke, being now refreshed, he goes forward with renewed energy and zeal. This, in time, wears off; there is no improvement in the going, he seems to arrive nowhere, and would be much cheered by the sight of a familiar landmark. This, however, is not forthcoming; but presently he smells smoke. Wondering who but one in his own predicament would make a fire in such a jungle, he trails up the smoke, finding an odd footprint to encourage him; he will at least see a man, who may know the district. He arrives at the fire, and no one is there, but there are tracks leading away which he commences to follow, on the run. All at once he notices something oddly familiar in the shape of a spruce top he is climbing over, and with sudden misgiving he sets his moccasined foot into one of the stranger's footprints, to find that they fit perfectly; the tracks are his own. He has been tracking himself down to his own fireplace!

Mixed with the feeling of affront at the scurvy trick that is making a laughing-stock of him for all the forest, is more than a hint of uneasiness, and, taking careful observations, he starts out anew, this time more slowly and coolly. An hour finds him back at the long-dead fire. With a sudden burst of speed in what he hopes is the right direction, he puts this now thoroughly distasteful piece of scenery behind him, tearing and ripping his way through this endless maze, that seems somehow to cover all Northern Canada. He frequently maps out his line of march with a stick in the mud, and spends much time in abstruse calculations; but it is only a matter of time till he returns, torn, exasperated, scarcely believing his eyes, to this hub of the wheel on which he is being spun so helplessly.

And on him dawns, with sickening certainty, the indisputable fact that he is lost. He becomes a little panicky, for this begins to be serious.

He appears to be unable to get away from this spot, as though held by a powerful magnet which allows him to wander at will just so far out, drawing him inexorably back at intervals. He is caught in the grip of the endless circle, which from being a mere geometrical figure, has now become an engine which may well encompass his destruction. As these thoughts pass swiftly, fear enters his heart. If wise, he will now get him a quantity of boughs, and construct a lean-to, gather a pile of wood, and pass the night in comfort, hoping for the reappearance of the sun in the morning. Or he may blindly obey the almost uncontrollable impulse of the lost, to run madly, tearing through underbrush regardless of clothing and skin, so as to get as far from the hateful spot as possible, and go on, and on, and on — to nowhere. He will almost inevitably take the wrong direction, at last breaking away from that deadly circle, in which case his speed only serves to plunge him deeper and deeper into a wilderness that stretches to the Arctic Sea. Darkness finds him exhausted, and almost incapable of making camp, and when the sun rises the next morning, his calculations, if he has any, are so involved, that he knows not whether to travel facing the sun, with his back to it, or across it.

He may be later stumbled upon, by the merest accident, by some member of a search party, or by his partner, if the latter is a skillful tracker; or again, he may find his way to a large body of water and wait to be picked up by some Indian or other passerby. This within a reasonable distance of civilization. If far in the woods he will wander hopelessly on, sometimes in circles, at times within measurable distance of his camp, past spots with which he is familiar, but is no longer in a condition to recognize. The singing of the birds becomes a mockery in his ears; they, and everything around him, are carrying on as usual, each in its own accustomed manner of living, and yet he, the lord of creation, is the only creature present who is utterly and completely subjugated by his surroundings.

Hunger gnaws his vitals, and hot waves of blood surge through his brain, leaving him weak and dizzy. Still he must keep on, always; he may yet strike some trapper's cabin or Indian encampment; even his deserted fireplace, once so odious, now appears in the light of a haven of refuge.

As the hours pass swiftly on, and the setting of another sun finds him no nearer safety, his mind becomes obsessed by strange fancies; the grey whiskey-jacks, trail companions on more fortunate trips, flickering across his line of vision like disembodied spirits, whispering together as they watch him, become birds of evil omen, sent to mock him with their whistling. Luminous rotting stumps, glowing in the darkness with ghostly phosphorescence, seem like the figments of a disordered dream; and a grey owl, floating soundlessly on muffled wings, has all the semblance of an apparition with yellow, gleaming eyes. The little distant red spots, like fire, that every tired man sees at night, are to him real enough to cause him to chase them for long distances in the falling dusk, spending his waning strength, and undergoing the added mental torture of disappointment. The whole world of trees, and shadows, and dark labyrinth becomes a place of phantasma and fevered imaginings, and his soul becomes possessed by a shuddering dread that no known danger of ordinary woods travel could account for. The sepulchral glow of the moon transforms the midnight forest into an inferno of ghostly light, pregnant with unnameable supernatural possibilities.

As he grows weaker he becomes the victim of hallucinations, and is beset by a form of insanity, the "madness of the woods," in which the dim arches become peopled with flitting shapes and formless apparitions. Gargoyle faces leer and grimace at him from out the shadows; Indians appear, stare momentarily beyond him as though he were invisible, to disappear again, eluding his frantic efforts to attract their attention. Acquaintances stand beckoning in the distance who, when he approaches, retreat yet further, and beckon again, finally fading to nothingness, or walking callously out of sight. And he shouts frenziedly that they may stop and wait for him, at which the woods become suddenly deserted, and his voice echoes hollowly through the endless, empty ramifications, which have now assumed the appearance of a tomb.

And there hangs over him as he blindly staggers onward, a Presence, an evil loathsome thing, which, as though to mark him as its own, envelops him with its shadow; following him like a hideous vampire, or some foul, carrion bird, waiting but for the moment when he will drop, watching with a terrible smile. For the ghoul that sits enthroned behind the ramparts of the North, holds always in his hand the strands of his entanglements, sleeping not at all, lest, of those who stumble unawares within them, there should one escape.

For another day, perhaps two, or even three, he stumbles on; muttering, at times raving; falling, getting up, only to fall again; crawling at last in that resistless urge of the lost to keep on while there is yet life; and always just ahead dangles the will-o'-the-wisp of hope, never fulfilled.

And if ever found, his bones will indicate his dying posture as that of a creeping man.

In Northern Quebec, during one of the mining rushes which are yet in progress, a prospector came out to the railroad to report his partner lost. This had happened six weeks before his arrival at the "front." He had spared no effort, and had used every means that mortal man could devise to recover his companion, but without avail. As this had happened in a territory that could only be reached by something over two hundred and fifty miles of a rough and difficult route, which it would take at least two weeks to cover, it was considered useless to make any further attempt, as the man had no doubt been long dead.

The prospector, however, had his doubts. Both men were experienced bushmen, although perhaps not gifted with that sense of direction which not even all Indians possess. Being no tenderfoot, the missing man would not be likely to make any further false moves after the initial one of getting lost, and this thought had kept alive a spark of hope.

For two weeks the bereft man could not get his friend out of his mind; often he dreamed of him. After one of these dreams, more vivid than the rest, in which he saw his partner crawling, in the last extremity, along the sandy beach on the shores of a shallow lake, he decided to revisit the ground, having been lucky in his prospecting, by means of an airplane. In a few hours he was hovering over the scene of the mishap.

Nearly every lake in the district was visited for signs of life, but none of them answered the description of the dream lake. Eventually the pilot, fearing to run out of gasoline, advised a return. Influenced by his vision, as indeed he had been in deciding to make the trip, the miner asked the aviator to fly low over a cluster of lakes about twenty miles from the original camp site, one of them being plainly shallow, and having sand beaches down one side.

And, as they passed over the sheet of water, they saw a creeping thing, moving slowly along on the beach, stopping, and moving on. At that distance it could have been a bear, or a wolf hunting for food, and they were about to swing off to the south and civilization when they decided to make one last attempt and investigate.

Three minutes later the two men were confronted by an evidence of human endurance almost past belief. Practically naked, his body and face bloated with the bites of mosquitoes he no longer had the strength to fight, his two month's beard clotted with blood and filled with a writhing mass of black flies, emaciated to the last degree, the missing man, for it was he, was even yet far from dead.

But, after sixty-two days of suffering such as few men are called on to endure, this man who would not die could no longer reason. He stared dully at his rescuers, and would have passed on, creeping on hands and knees. And he was headed North, going further and further away from the possibility of rescue with every painful step.

Very gently he was carried, still feebly resisting, to the waiting plane, and in two hours was in safety.

Later the rescued man told how, confused by the non-appearance of the sun for several days, he had wandered in circles from which he could not break away, until he commenced to follow lake shores, and the banks of rivers, expecting them to lead him to some body of water that he knew.

On the reappearance of the sun, after about a week, he was so far gone as to become possessed by the idea that it was rising and setting in the wrong places, and travelled, accordingly, north instead of south, continuing in that direction long after he had ceased consciously to influence his wanderings. For food he had dammed small streams and set a weir of sticks in a pool below, easily catching the fish left in the drained creek bed. During the weeks of the sucker run, he fared not too badly, as suckers are a sizeable fish of two or three pounds weight, and fish, even if raw, will support life. Later this run ceased, and the suckers returned to deep water. He was then obliged to subsist on roots and an occasional partridge killed with a stone, until he became too weak to throw at them.

He next set rabbit snares of spruce root, most of which the rabbits ate; so he rubbed balsam gum on them, which rabbits do not like, and occasionally was lucky. Soon, however, he lacked the strength to accomplish these things, and from that on lived almost entirely on the inside bark of birch trees. So far north there are miles of country where birch trees will not grow, so he was often without even that inadequate diet. At last he was crawling not over a couple of hundred yards a day, if his last day's tracks were any indication. To travel six or eight days without food is an ordeal few survive, and only those who have undergone starvation, coupled with the labour of travelling when in a weakened condition, can have any idea of what this man went through.

His mind a blank, at times losing sight of the object of his progress, daily he crept further and further away from safety. And there is no doubt that insanity would eventually have accomplished what starvation apparently could not.

This "madness of the woods" that drives men to destruction, when a little calm thinking and observation would have saved the day, attacks alike the weak-willed and the strong, the city man and the bush-whacker, when, after a certain length of time, they find themselves unable to break away from the invisible power that seems to hold them within a definite restricted area from which they cannot get away, or else lures them deeper and deeper into the wilderness. Men old on the trail recognize the symptoms and combat them before their reasoning powers become so warped that they are no longer to be relied on.

This peripatetic obsession causes men to have strange thoughts. Under its influence they will doubt the efficiency of a compass, will argue against the known facts, fail to recognize places with which they are perfectly familiar.

One lumberjack foreman who became twisted in his calculations, struck a strange road, followed it, and arrived at a camp, and not till he entered it and recognized some of the men, did he realize that the camp was his own. Some men lost for long periods, and having been lucky enough to kill sufficient game to live on, although alive and well seem to lose their reasoning powers entirely. At the sight of men they will run, and are with difficulty caught, and with staring eyes and wild struggles try to free themselves and escape.

Only those who, relying on no compass, spend long years of wandering in the unmarked wastes of a wild country, acquire the knack, or rather the science, of travelling by the blind signs of the wilderness. Ordinary woodsmen of the lumberjack type, whose work seldom calls them off a logging road, are as easily lost as a townsman. Timber cruisers, engineers, and surveyors are all compass men. Their type of work makes necessary the continuous use of this instrument, and they do little travelling without it.

It is only amongst men of the trapper or prospector type that we find developed that instinctive sense of direction, which is a priceless gift to those who possess it.

Travelling in an unpeopled wilderness calls for an intense concentration on the trail behind, a due regard for the country ahead and a memory that recalls every turn made, and that can recognize a ridge, gulley, or stream crossed previously and at another place. Swinging off the route to avoid swamps, and other deviations must be accomplished without losing sight of the one general direction, meanwhile the trail unrolls behind like a ball of yarn, one end of which is at the camp and the other in your hand.

If the sun is out it is an infallible guide, provided proper allowance is made for its movement. In returning by the same route no attempt is made to cover the same ground, unless convenient, so long as creeks, ridges, flats, and other features are recognized as they occur, and provided you remember at about what angle you traversed them. Every man has a tendency to work too much to either left or right, and knowing that, he must work against it.

The tops of pine trees on the crest of ridges point uniformly northeast; in level bush, if open to the wind, the undergrowth has a "set" to it which can sometimes be detected. The bark is thicker and the rings in the timber closer together on the north re times when my failure to apply the lessons so painstakingly taught me, if known, would be the cause of much disappointment and terse but apt comment spoken through the blue smoke-haze in certain shadowy lodges, beneath the sombre spruces.

As late as four years ago I was guilty of a piece of bad judgment, or several of them, that left a considerable blot on my record, already none too spotless, and came near to settling for all time my earthly problems. The occasion was one on which it became necessary, owing to the destruction of a hunting ground by fire, to move several hundred miles to the north, and, in so doing, I failed to make the necessary allowance for changed climatic conditions. This resulted in my arriving behind the season, and finding the trading post out of many things, and its stock, much depleted, consisting mainly of culled or damaged goods remaining after the Indians, now long departed for their hunting grounds, had taken their pick. Amongst these leftovers was a one and only pair of moose-hide mitts, too small to be of much use. Having at that time no hides of my own, these I was obliged to take; the initial mistake and one for which, later, I dearly paid.

I was able to locate a ground with the assistance of the post manager and a very inaccurate map, and had a bad two weeks getting in with my stuff, fighting ice and snowstorms all the way, a matter of seventy miles or more. The trapping was fair, but the ground, being small, was soon hunted out, necessitating long trips into the interior in search of fur.

There had been much soft weather after the preliminary cold snap, and I started out on an exploration trip on a wet, soggy day, on which dragging and lifting the slushed snowshoes was a heavy enough labour. I perspired profusely, and on leaving the chain of lakes on which my cabin was situated for the overland trip to other waters, I hung up my outside shirt and leggings and proceeded without them, a piece of foolishness bordering on the criminal.

side of trees in exposed places. Do not forget that water always runs downhill; moose and deer tracks in March are mostly found on a southern exposure; the snow of the last storm is generally banked on the side of the trees opposite from the direction of the wind it came with, which you will, of course, have noted; and the general trend, or "lie" of the country in all Northern Canada is northeast and southwest. Taking an average on all this data, some pretty accurate travelling can be done.

These are some of the indications by which Indians travel, nor have they any God-given superiority over other men in this respect. Only intensive training and habits of acute observation bring them to the pitch of excellence to which they often attain. One generation out of their environment and the faculty is as dead as it is in most white men. There is as much difference between travelling by compass and picking a trail by a study of details such as were just mentioned, as there is between a problem in mathematics and a work of art.

A compass calls for progression in straight lines, over all obstacles, or if around them by offsetting so many paces and recovering that distance, the obstruction once passed; a purely mechanical process. Little advantage can be taken of the lie of the land, and a man is more or less fettered in his movements.

There are highly important operations and improvements taking place all along the frontier which would be almost impossible without this device and very accurate results are obtained by its use in mapping out the country; but for ordinary travelling purposes he is freer who uses the sun, the wind, the roll of mountains and the sweep of the earth's surface as his guides, and from them he imbibes a moiety of that sixth sense which warns of danger and miscalculation, so that a species of instinct is evolved — whereby a man may be said to feel that he is wrong — almost as infallible, and more flexible of application than any instrument can be, and to it a man may turn when all else fails. This is developed to a remarkable degree in some individuals.

Of all the snares which Nature has set to entangle the footsteps of the unwary the most effective is the perfidious shortcut. Men well tried in woodcraft succumb to its specious beguilements in the endeavour to save a few hours and corresponding miles. I firmly believe there never yet was a shortcut that did not have an impassable swamp, an unscalable mountain, or an impenetrable jungle situated somewhere about its middle, causing detours, the sum of which amount to more than the length of the original trail. This is so well recognized that the mere mention of the word "shortcut" will raise a smile in any camp. Often an old trail that seems to have been well used long ago, after leading you on for miles in the hopes of arriving somewhere eventually, will degenerate into a deer path, then to a rabbit runway, and finally disappear down a hole, under a root.

After many years in the woods with the most efficient instructors at the work that a man could well have, I find that I cannot yet relax my vigilance, either of thought or eye, for very many minutes before I become involved in a series of errors that would speedily land me into the orbit of the endless circle. I find it impossible to hold any kind of connected conversation and travel to advantage. In the dark especially, if the mind slips a cog and loses one or more of the filaments of the invisible thread, it is impossible to recover them, and nothing then remains but to stop, make fire, and wait for daylight.

My first experience in this line was far from heroic. I remember well my initial trial trip with an Indian friend who had volunteered for the difficult task of transforming an indifferent plainsman into some kind of a woodsman. We sat on a high rocky knoll on which were a few burnt pines, on one of which we had hung up the packsack. All around us were other knolls with burnt stubs scattered over them. The lower ground between them was covered with a

heavy second growth of small birch and poplars, wi. My task was to leave the hill on which we were sea and climb another, identical in appearance, even to . distant about three hundred yards. Nothing, I consi well be easier, even without the sun which I had to hel

I descended the slope and struck through the small its foot, and soon found that I was entangled above, below all sides by a clawing, clutching mass of twisted and wiry growth, through which I threshed with mighty struggles. about twenty minutes I saw the welcome shine of bare rock was glad enough to get into the open again. I climbed the kn and there, to my astonishment, sat my friend and mentor at foot of one of the chicos,★ calmly smoking, and apparently n having turned a hair in his swift trip through the jungle.

I owned myself beaten, remarking that he must have made pretty good time to have arrived at the spot ahead of me. He looked mildly surprised, and replied that he had not arrived at any place, not having as yet moved. I hardly believed him until I saw the packsack where I myself had hung it, and my humiliation was complete when I realized that I had walked right down into that flat and turned round and walked right out again.

This was my first acquaintance with the charming endless circle. It was not my last, and even today it sneaks alongside of me through the forest like a spinning lariat, hopefully waiting for the day when I shall place my foot within. And these days I hold that imaginary ball of twine very tightly in one hand, whilst scrutinizing the landscape ahead with a view to my proposed route, and I fight flies with the other.

My tutors have turned me out, so they consider, a finished product, and in certain circumstances I am able to contrive, devise, and stand from under with the best of them; yet even today there

★ A dry standing tree of a good size. "Chico" is of French origin, and is now a recognized word in bush phraseology.

It soon commenced to snow heavily, and so continued for the rest of the day; a wet, heavy fall which in my half-clothed condition, quickly wetted me to the skin. With that lack of common sense for which some people are remarkable, I carried on obstinately. Late that afternoon I found beaver. Not waiting to set any traps, as a cessation of movement, and dabbling elbow deep in ice water meant a clammy chill which I was in no mood to endure, I made fire and drank tea, and thus fortified, commenced the return trip.

All went well for the first few miles. The sky cleared, and it turned colder, which, whilst it froze my outer clothing, made it windproof, and lightened the heavy going considerably, the snow no longer clogging my snowshoes. The moon would rise shortly and everything was coming my way. I anticipated an easy journey home; I had found beaver of a potential value amounting to some hundreds of dollars, and a little wetting damped my spirits not at all.

The fact that I was probably two hundred miles directly north of my accustomed range, and in a country of severe and sudden storms and erratic changes in temperature, did not enter into my calculations.

My outbound route had been very circuitous, and at a point where I thought it would be to my advantage I attempted the old, oft-tried, and justly notorious expedient of a shortcut in the dark. On such a night, calm, clear, and frosty, nothing could possibly go wrong, and I expected to strike my own tracks in a patch of timber near the lake where my clothing was, and so on home. Half an hour from that time, in my wet condition, I became chilled with the now rapidly increasing cold, and was again obliged to make fire in a small gulley, where I waited the coming of the moon.

A chill wind arose, whistling bleakly over the deserted solitude, and I shivered over my fire, seemingly unable to get warm. The eastern sky lightened, and soon the ragged outline of the pointed spruce stood darkly silhouetted against the great moon, now creeping up over the ridge, and commencing to flood the little valley with a lambent glow. The uncertain illumination lent an appearance of illusive unreality to the surroundings which affected me strangely, and I began to have some misgivings as to the advisability of going further that night.

As the pale disc cleared the hills the shadows shortened and I made out to see a small sluggish stream, picking its somnolent way amongst snow-covered hummocks of moss and scattered clumps of larches. The prospect was not inviting, so not waiting to dry my mitts and moccasins, I prepared myself for a fast trip to my clothes, and abandoned my fire; two more mistakes either one of which, under the circumstances, was sufficient for my undoing.

I examined the creek and having ascertained the direction of its flow, decided to go downstream, as long as its direction suited me; and turning my back on my sheltered nook, with its abundance of dry wood and friendly twinkling fire, I started on a very memorable journey. And at my elbow, as I walked, there sounded a still, small voice which said plainly and insistently, "Do not go; stay by the fire; there you are safe; do not go"; the voice, so often disregarded, of discretion, making a last bid to stay the tragedy of errors now about to be consummated.

The going was bad. There was not enough snow to level the inequalities of the ground, and the floor of the gulley was plentifully bestrewn with broken rock piles, studded with large hummocks, and pitted with holes; and, the moon only serving in this instance to increase the shadow cast by these obstacles, I stumbled and fell repeatedly, arising from each fall chilled to the bone.

Presently the stream meandered off to the right, out of my projected line of travel, and the sides of the ravine fell away into low undulations, which flattened out and eventually disappeared altogether. I realized that I was on the borders of one of those immense muskegs with which this North Country abounds. I pressed on my way, hoping that I would soon emerge into a belt of timber, which in that region would indicate the proximity of a lake, but none was to be seen save a small clump of spruce to my right and far ahead; and on all sides the white, endless fields of snow lay stretched in dreary monotony.

The moon, having become hazy whilst I was yet at the fire, was now circled by a band of rainbow hue, and before long became completely obscured; a storm threatened and soon became imminent. A low moaning sound could be heard to the north, increasing every minute, and I bitterly regretted leaving my late campground; but, as there was yet enough light to distinguish the details of the scenery, such as they were, with that fatuous optimism that has driven many a man out over the edge of the Great Beyond, I cast behind me the last atom of discretion and pushed forward with all possible speed.

Suddenly, with the whistling and screaming of a myriad hell-bound demons, the blizzard struck, sweeping down from the north in a choking, blinding wall of snow and zero hurricane, lashing the surface of the muskeg into a whirling, frenzied mass of hissing snow-devils, sticking to my frozen and inadequate clothing in a coat of white, and effectually blotting out every vestige of the landscape.

Staggered by the first onslaught, I quickly recovered and, realizing the seriousness of the situation, I took a firm grip on my reasoning powers, whilst my mind subconsciously searched the screeching ether for some indication of direction.

In the open the wind eddied and rushed in from every side, and no bearings could be taken from it, but I thought I could detect above the other sounds of the tempest, the deeper roar of wind in the block of timber, now distant about half a mile. With this as a guide I continued on my journey, my objective now the shelter of the grove in question.

Bent almost double, gasping for breath, my clothing caked with frozen snow, becoming rapidly exhausted, I knew that, dressed as I was, I could not long survive in such a storm.

The insistent barrier of the wind became a menace, a tangible, vindictive influence bent on my destruction. All the power and spite of the hurricane seemed centred on my person with the intention of holding me back, delaying me until my numbed limbs refused further duty, driving me down, down in between the snow mounds, where, shrieking with triumph, it would overwhelm me with a whirling mass of white, and soon nothing would remain save the roar of the wind, the scurrying drift, and the endless, empty waste of snow.

Coupled with this cheerful reflection was the thought that perhaps, after all, my senses were deceived concerning the supposed position of that bluff of timber, and this spurred me on to renewed speed, if such a word could be applied to my groping progress. My arms became numb to the elbow, and my legs to the knee. My eyelids repeatedly stuck together with rime which I rubbed off with frozen mitts; and I stumbled on, knowing I must never fall.

The wind seemed to redouble its fury, and the wall of resistance that it opposed to my efforts seemed more and more a malicious attempt to detain me until I no longer had the strength to fight it. So that it became a personal issue between the tempest and myself; it with all the howling fury of unleashed omnipotent power, and I with all the hate, and bitterness and determination its buffeting had aroused in me.

How long this continued I do not know, but suffice it that in time I heard with certainty the roar of wind-tossed treetops, and soon a black wall of forest rose up before me, and I knew that I now had a fighting chance. I quickly skirted a section of the belt of evergreens, looking up in an endeavour to find a bare pole protruding through the black tops, indicating a dry tree, but could distinguish nothing. Entering the grove I quickly chipped various trees, tasting the chips for dry wood; every one stuck to my lips, showing them to be green and impossible to start a fire with. A deadly fear entered my heart; supposing there was no dry wood, what then?

I commenced a frantic but methodical search, tapping boles with my axe for the ring of dry timber, but without avail.

Meanwhile the cold was biting deeper and deeper, and I was well aware that any wood found after the lapse of another twenty minutes would be useless, as I should by that time be unable to light a fire.

In a kind of a panic I ran out into the open, and, the storm having abated somewhat, I saw, to my unspeakable relief, a tall dry tamarac standing no great distance away, and hidden from me till then.

I attacked it furiously with my axe and now found that my wet mitts had frozen into such a shape that it was almost impossible to chop. I made several strokes, and the axe twisted in my grip and no more than dinged the tamarac, hardest of dry woods.

Once a glancing blow struck my foot, shearing through moccasin and blanket sock, drawing blood. Eventually the axe flew out of my numbed hands entirely and I lost precious seconds recovering it. There was only one alternative; I must chop barehanded. This I did, felling the tree, and continuing cutting it up until my fingers began to freeze. And then I found that my mitts, already too small, had so shrunken with the frost that now, hard as iron, *I could not put them on again.*

I stood for a moment, as the deadly import of this entered my brain with damning finality. I was confronted with the stark staring fact that I could no longer use my hands; and around my feet the snow was stained with an ever-widening patch of blood. I was as near to death as mortal man may be and yet live.

The storm had passed. The Northern Lights commenced their flickering dance. The landscape had now assumed an appearance of hypocritical solemnity; the moon also appeared, to lend the proper air of sanctimonious propriety fitting to the occasion, and the capering corpses* in the northern hemisphere mocked with their grotesque gyrations my abortive movements.

I marvelled somewhat that in this present day and age of achievement, with civilization at its peak, I should be beyond its help, dying in a way, and owing to conditions long supposed to be out of date. I got a slight "kick" out of the notion, and thus exhilarated suddenly decided that this was no time and no place to die. I intended to be no spectacle for a gallery of ghouls, nor did I propose to submit dumbly to the decrees of one whom I had yet to meet — The Devil of the North forsooth, with all his power and his might!

I laughed aloud, for I had a trump card; two of them, in fact, one up each sleeve; he should not freeze my hands, and so destroy me. I decided that I would freeze my hands myself. And so I did, cutting up and splitting, until my hands became bereft of power and feeling, fully believing that I had lost my fingers to save my life.

I made a fire. The agony of it as the circulation made its way through the seared flesh; and the fear of a horrible death by blood-poisoning, or a useless existence without hands! For a man finds these things hard to accept with the calmness expected of him, and I am perhaps of softer mould than some.

Gibbering madmen have before now dragged their hideous deformities out to the haunts of man to exhibit them as payment exacted for lesser follies than I had committed that night. My fingers were frozen and my foot cut to the bone, but not badly enough to cause permanent injury, although I could hunt no more that winter.

I later found that the muskeg skirted the lake, and the next morning as I moved out I discovered that the clump of spruce that I had originally intended to pass by was an offshoot of the forest that I was looking for, and that I had spent the night, half-frozen, within a rifle-shot of my discarded clothes.

* Indian name of the Northern Lights, "Dance of the Dead Men."

So I am still in doubt as to whether that blizzard was intended to destroy me, or if it was not merely one of those rough, but friendly attempts to set us on the right road, that we sometimes suffer at the hands of our friends.

VI

THE FALL OF THE LEAF

Now the Four-Way Lodge is open,
Now the Hunting Winds are loose.

Much has been written concerning the beauties and the joys of spring. Poets have glorified that time of flowers, and budding leaves, and frisking lambs in every language. I have, however, formed the opinion, after observing a good many of them, that spring is a time of the year to be regarded as something to look back on, or forward to, but not to enjoy. In the snow countries it is a season of floods, wet feet, bad trails, transportation difficulties, and shortage of supplies.

Easter is a favourite season for breaking ice, and carrying canoes on snowshoes over portages flooded with slush; whilst the weather is a nightmare of wet snowstorms and chill rains, or, if warm and clear the resultant thaw produces torrents of melted snow water and shaky ice. By the time these conditions mend equipment has been damaged far more than by the wear and tear of a whole year of honest travel. Men's patience is worn to a frazzle, and the seeds of a wasting sickness are often laid in the system of those who perforce must sleep out in the rain or not sleep at all.

Here, spring is a time of the year when the marriage market is weak, bootleggers' receipts are high, and those of the Church very low. I think the habitants★ have a saint whose specialty it is to care

★ French-Canadian settlers.

for travellers at this season. I should much like to meet him, and discuss the matter quietly as between gentlemen, without witnesses.

Rarely do we hear favourably, in poetry or in prose, of that season called by some the "death of the year," and too often looked forward to with misgiving as the precursor of dread Winter, the Fall. To those who may view its splendours in a forest untouched by the hand of man, autumn means much more than just the transition between the closing of summer and the coming of winter. In a country composed, as Canada is, largely of wild lands it means above all the opening of the hunting season, with the breaking of the monotony of civilized life, and all the freedom for the indulging of primitive instincts that goes with it.

It is a time of painted forests decked out in all the gay panoply of Indian Summer, of blue haze which lends enchantment to distant prospects, and of hills robed in flaring tints, which, in spite of their brilliance, merge and blend to form the inimitable colour scheme which, once every year, heralds the sad but wondrous spectacle of the falling of the leaves. Motionless days of landscapes bathed in waiting silence; the composed and breathing calm of an immense congregation attending the passing of a beloved one, waiting reverently until the last rites have been completed; for this is the farewell of the leaves to the forest which they have for a time adorned. Their task performed, with brave colours flying they go down in obedience to the immutable law of forest life, later to nourish the parent stem that gave them birth. And in the settled hush that precedes their passing, even the march of time itself seems halted, that there may be no unseemly haste in their disposal, whose life has been so short.

In the endless spruce forests of the High North, much of the beauty of Fall is lost, and passing suddenly out of the gloomy evergreens onto a rare ridge of birch and poplar, with their copper and bronze effects, is like stepping out of a cave into a capacious, many-pillared antechamber draped in cloth of gold. It is only in the hardwood forests of beech, maple, and giant black birch yet remaining in certain areas, that the full beauty of the Fall of the Leaf can be appreciated. It was once my fortune to make a trip at this season, in a reserved area of some three thousand square miles in extent, in the heart of the strong woods country, below the Ottawa River. A lovely region it was, and is, of peaceful, rock-girdled lakes, deep, clear, and teeming with trout; and of rich forests of immense trees reaching in a smooth billowing tide in every direction. Here was not the horrific sepulchral gloom of the goblin-haunted spruce country, nor the crowded formation of hostile array. The trees, huge of trunk and massive of high-flung limb, stood decorously apart, affording passage for several men abreast; and the dimness was rather that of some enchanted palace seen only in a dream, and in which chords of stately music could be expected to resound at any moment.

The wide and spreading tops met overhead to form a leafy canopy that was a blaze of prismatic colour, as though the lofty pillars supported a roof of stained glass, through which the sunlight filtered here and there, shedding a dim but mellow glow upon the forest floor.

Between the well-ordered files one walked without obstruction, and in momentary expectation of a fleeting view of some living creature, of the many who dwelt herein. Every step opened up new vistas through the open woodland, the level bottom of which was relieved by terraces edged with small firs that loomed up blackly in the riot of colour, and occasional smooth white boulders which stood crowned by grey and hoary beeches with gnarled limbs, and serpentine, protruding roots, standing like effigies or statues carved from blocks of marble in some old castle garden. There the figure of a man was belittled, dwarfed to insignificant proportions, by the grandeur, and the vast and looming bulk of the objects by which he was surrounded.

At intervals the dimness was brightened, at about twice the height of a man, by the bright tinted foliage of dogwood, and moose-maple saplings. The gloom made the stems invisible at a little distance, and where the shafts of sunlight struck them, these gay clusters appeared like Japanese lanterns of every imaginable shape and hue, suspended in mid-air to light these ancient halls far some carnival or revel. In the wider spaces between the smooth grey hardwoods, stood the bodies of huge white pine, fluted red-brown columns upwards of six feet across, rearing their bulk up through the roof of leaves, to be shut off completely from further view; yet raising their gigantic proportions another half a hundred feet above the sea of forest, to the great plumed heads that bowed to the eastward each and every one, as though each morning they would salute the rising sun.

Although in the dimness of the ancient forest no breeze stirred the leaves of the young maples, far above, the air was never still. And through the dark masses of the noble sweeping tops of the pine trees, a steady wind played in a deep, prolonged and wavering note, as of the plucked strings of an unseen distant harp; gently humming like the low notes of an organ played softly, dying away to a whisper; swelling again in diapason through the vast transept of the temple of silence, the unceasing waves of sound echoing and resounding across the immeasurable sweep of the universe.

No moose were to be seen in this region, but every once in so often, a group of deer leaped out of sight, with sharp whistles, and spectacular display of white tails.

The air was filled with the low sound of falling leaves, as they made their hesitant way to earth, adding little by little to a variegated carpet already ankle deep. And as they came spinning, floating, and spiralling down like golden snowflakes, the sound of their continuous, subdued, rustling transformed the stately forest into a shadowed whispering gallery, in which it seemed as though the ancient trees would tell in muted accents the age-old secrets of days gone by, did one but have the ears to understand.

★ ★ ★

To the forest dwellers, autumn, with its sounds, its smells, its tang, which like good wine, sends the blood coursing and tingling through the veins, with its urge to be up and doing, and the zest and savour of its brittle air, is more than a season; it has become a national institution.

The signs of its coming are eagerly noted by all in whom one drop yet remains of the blood of long gone savage ancestors. Over the whole of North America the first frosts, where they occur, are a signal for the overhauling of weapons of all kinds, and the assembling of implements of the chase. Men step lighter, as with kindling eye they seem to emulate the hustle, the bustle, and the preparation of all living creatures in response to the stirring call of this magic season. For now the Hunting Winds are loosed to course at will along the highways of the forest, stirring the indolent to action, and quickening the impulses with their heady bouquet.

Now the Four-Way Lodge is open, and out from its portals pour the spirits of all the mighty hunters of the Long Forgotten Days, to range again the ancient hunting-grounds. And when a chill wisp of a breeze sweeps down into the forest, and scooping up a handful of leaves, spins them around for a moment in a madly whirling eddy, and of a sudden lets them drop, many will say that it is the shade of some departed hunter who dances a ghostly measure to the tune of the hunting winds.

The woods are full of crisp rustlings, as small beasts scamper over frosted, crackling leaves, intent on the completion of self-appointed tasks. The surface of the waters is broken by clusters of ducks and waterfowl of all kinds, noisily congregated for the fall migration. Along the shoreline, ever-widening V's forge silently ahead, as beaver and muskrats, alert, ready to sink soundlessly out of sight on the least alarm, conduct their various operations. Porcupines amble along trustfully in the open, regardless of danger; and, partly owing to their bristling armour and greatly owing to the luck of fools, generally escape unscathed. Back in the hills any number of bears are breaking off boughs and shredding birch-bark, to line dens that a man could be well satisfied to sleep in.

In the blaze of the declining sun the hills seem crested with fire, as the level rays strike the scarlet of the maples on the ridges. The russet of the whispering sedge-grasses on the river-flats and marshlands and the yellow of the wild hay in the beaver meadows, take on a metallic sheen, like burnished golden filigree, in which is set some placid sheet of water, reflecting on its glassy surface an inverted, flaming forest, and the hue of the evening sky, pink with its promise of frost, as the short day draws to its close.

The light mists of evening that begin to rise in the fen-lands are permeated with the aromatic scent of dried cherry leaves, and the spicy odour of the sage. With the near approach of darkness everything that had life is in movement, preparing for the great change soon to come, and the air is full of subdued sound, barely audible but insistent, as a myriad creatures of every size and species comb the face of the earth for the wherewithal to pass the winter, now so close upon them.

Slight noises in the distance have a startling penetration in the thin and buoyant air, and the passage of a squirrel over the dry leaves creates a disturbance out of all proportion to his size. Swift creatures, no longer silent-footed, rattle noisily across the brittle carpet on important errands. The crackle of brush, the sharp, alarmed whistle of a deer, and the whirring flight of a family of partridges, herald the approach of some creature larger than common, and a bull moose, in all the savage splendour of bristling mane and wide-spread antlers, stalks out beyond the tree-line onto the strip of grasses that border the lake, and calls his challenge, bidding defiance to all the world. His summons unanswered, he threshes mightily in the tall reeds, twisting and tearing saplings with deep grunts and hollow rattling of horns, in the futile rage of his unfulfilled desire for combat. Shortly he stops to listen, and, seeming to detect some dissonance in the scheme of his surroundings, he becomes uneasy, and retires, though with hesitation. And then, reason enough for the moose's trepidation, there comes stealing in from the south a low-set, slim canoe, loaded to the gunwales, slipping silently along, propelled by the deft, light strokes of the practiced canoeman.

And on the instant all sound ceases, and silence falls, abruptly as the sudden quenching of a light.

The light craft skirts the shore amidst the idly floating leaves, and its progress is as soundless as theirs, yet no movement rewards the vigilance of the man kneeling in its stern; the policy of proscription declared against this arch-enemy of all living creatures, this pariah of the society of the woods, could not be more completely carried out were he some noisome pestilence stalking through the kingdom of the wild.

The canoe lands at an open point of jack-pines and the man unloads, erects his tent with a few swift movements, and soon the glimmer of his camp fire lights the now rapidly falling dusk, and its smoke hangs in banks and wisps over the water, edging the wreaths of mist with blue.

Darkness settles and the fire dies. The stars, large and far apart, seem almost within reach, and the blade of the low-hung moon lies on its back just clear of the needle-pointed spruce that crown an eminence. And overhead the long wavering lines of wild geese pass at frequent intervals from the north with discordant clamour, as they retreat before an enemy with whom they have already been in action, and whose further advance is now imminent.

And as the night wears on and the moon sinks behind the hill, the population of the woods recommences its interrupted labours.

Small, earnest forest people in unnumbered multitudes race back and forth from cache to cache. The faintly discernible sounds of the daylight hours increase in volume during the stillness of the night, and are punctuated by distinguishable noises that much intrigue the curiosity of the listener; the distant screaming of a rabbit being prepared for cold storage by some successful butcher; the "plop," and rustle, and scratch, as muskrats, like little gnomes, with short swift runs and hops work feverishly at their harvesting; the thumps and thuds, draggings and scrapings, and the low murmur of voices, as the gangs in the beaver-works labour prodigiously to complete their preparations....

But as daylight commenced to show in the east, these noises gradually ceased and day broke over an empty forest devoid of life or sound, save for a small flock of black ducks at their morning toilet and a porcupine, who had been appeasing his insatiable appetite for leather with a tump line, forgotten outside the tent on the point.

There was some slight commotion within the tent and a stream of smoke issued from the long, narrow stove pipe projecting from it. The porcupine, interested in this new development, stared stupidly at the smoke for a while, then, taking a few last bites out of the canoe gunwale in passing, lumbered off with the consciousness of a good night's work well done.

At this juncture the man emerged from the tent, and the sight of the ruined tump line evoked a string of caustic remarks, arranged with the alliterative proficiency of one well versed in the art. The porcupine listened in pained surprise for a moment, and withdrew tactfully further into the timber; and, with a preliminary four-foot jump, the black ducks took the air and, circling the shoreline once, hit for the south.

The man viewed the angry-looking sunrise with misgiving. Wasting but little time on his hasty breakfast, he soon loaded up and headed for the north. The ice rimming the shores of his landing place had had to be broken with a pole to get the canoe into the water, and the rime that had settled on the beaver hay was heavy enough to show the passage, during the night, of a fox. These signs increased his apprehension, for he had also heard the all-night passage of the wild geese. Well he knew the penalty he might pay for having, in his ambition, penetrated so far before settling for the winter. He was caught in a network of small waters soon to be frozen, and tie him up for the Fall hunt. The special devil to whom is allotted the control of the legions of Winter, might wantonly loose them on a waiting world at any moment that his whim suggested. Soon he would throw up his ramparts and entanglements, effectually blocking all attempts at progress, sealing all hands into whatever neck-of-the-woods they were caught in, until winter was sufficiently advanced to release them. For this particular devil is well skilled at his game. Not his, as yet, a barrage of heavy storms, deep snow, and zero wind. Coarse work, that, so early in the bout; anyhow, these men seemed to weather well on such stuff. Better, at first, a little display of skill, the deft touch of the artist; snow enough to cause a burdened man to slip on a sidehill, ice enough to cajole him out onto the water to try conclusions, and then to fail with a canoe badly scratched and cut; cold enough to freeze the one bag of much treasured potatoes, but not sufficient to make good ice.

Thus Ka-peboan-ka, keeper of Keewayedin, the North-West Wind, rewards the effrontery of those who deem their small goings and comings should enter into the calculations of the Red Gods.

The man's prognostications seemed about to prove only too true. Before noon of that day, ragged strips of grey clouds tore across a leaden sky, to the accompaniment of a shrill whining storm-wind that ripped the last leaves from the hardwoods, where they had hung but tenuously for days, ready to drop at the first volley of the advancing hosts of winter. And all Nature stood by in hole, and den, and matted evergreen covert, or builded house, waiting for that moment against which all had prepared for forty days or more: excepting man. He, the most intelligent and gifted of living creatures, alone was not ready. Abroad with a heavy out-fit and unprepared, of all things having life he was to be the sole victim of the cataclysm now about to occur.

In two days a devastating change had come over the land-scape. Gone from the uplands was the wonderfully blended colour scheme. There only remained a few garish patches of red splotched here and there, like dabs of paint scattered at random on a grey canvas, and only serving to accentuate the stark nakedness of the bare limbs through which the wind whistled and thrummed. Gone was the carnival note of the gay hanging lanterns of the dogwoods, as they stood now extinguished, in the empty halls of their revel. Before the chilling blast clouds of dead leaves eddied and volleyed down the roofless naves, flying at times in whirling masses high above the crest of the forest. And slanting, hissing down from the North, sifting through the naked limbs of the hardwoods, there rattled onto the fallen leaves a few hard flakes of the first snow. And Ka-peboan-ka, the old, the mischievous, the boisterous, having gloated long enough over his all-too-effective work, rubbed his hands gleefully, and entered the lists for the final bout with the crimson and brown youth,* whose warm smile was fast fading as he weakened, this time to fall and rise no more.

And Ka-peboan-ka threw over his body his white mantle, and danced a whirlwind dance of triumph, till the air about him became filled with flying snowflakes. And countless leagues of grey and purple landscape petrified and turned slowly white, as he blew his whistling blasts of icy breath into the four corners of the earth. In the morning the sun rose glittering but without warmth on a world blanketed beneath a heavy pall of snow.

Winter was on.

* Indian personification of Indian Summer.

VII

THE TALE
OF THE BEAVER PEOPLE

Of all beasts he learned the language
Learned their names and all their secrets
How the beavers built their lodges.
                          — LONGFELLOW

On the shores of a nameless lake I crouched and shivered in the wet sage-brush. It was breaking day; the smell of the dawn was in the air, and a Clammy mist enveloped the land, through which, in spots, individual trees showed as shadows, faintly, if near at hand. Further than that nothing was visible.

Low, mysterious noises came to my ear, and as the light waxed stronger these became louder, so as to be distinguishable; the leap of a fish; the quacking of a couple of ducks in a reed-bed; the staccato, nervous tapping of a woodpecker; a distant hollow crash in the depth of the forest; a slight rustle in the bushes behind me as a weasel peered out with extended neck, to vanish suddenly, appearing instantaneously ten feet away almost before his disappearance had been registered by the eye.

The mist commenced to rise, and a current of air stirred the poplar leaves to a light fluttering. The ducks became partly visible, and seen through the vapour they seemed to float on air, and to be of inordinate size.

I shivered some more.

Under the influence of the slight breeze the fog billowed slowly back exposing the little sheet of water; the wavering line of the hills on the far shore appeared and disappeared within its folds, and the crest the ridges seemed to float on its surface like long, low islands. To the East was clear of fog and the streaks of clouds that hung there, as I watched, turned slowly pink. Not ten feet away, on a log, a muskrat rubbed himself dry with vigorous strokes, and as he scrubbed mightily I could hear his little gusts of breath in the thin air. A flock of whistlers volleyed overhead with bullet velocity, circled the pond, and lit on the water with a slithering splash; a kingfisher dived like an emerald streak at the rise of a speckled trout, and, missing his stroke, flew with a chattering laugh to a dry limb. And at the discordant sound came the first notes of the plaintive song of the Canada bird, a haunting melody that ceases in full flight, the remainder of the song tantalizingly left unsung as though the singer had become suddenly weary: a prelude in minor cadence. And from all around, and across the pond, these broken melodies burst out in answering lament, while the burden of song was taken up by one after another trilling voice. There poured out the rippling lilt of the American robin, suggestive of the clear purling of running water; the three deep golden notes of some unknown songster, the first three chords of an obbligato plucked from the strings of a bass viol. Others, now indistinguishable for very volume, joined in as the slowly rising sun rolled up the curtain of the mist on the grand overture conducted by the Master Musician, that is the coming of day, in the unspoiled reaches of the northern wilds.

I drew the blanket-case off my rifle and pumped a shell into the breech. I was there with a purpose: for the time was that of the spring hunt, and this was a beaver-pond. Two deer appeared in the reeds in a little bay, necks craned, nostrils working as they essayed with delicate senses to detect the flaw in the perfectly balanced structure of the surroundings which I constituted. I did not need them; and moreover, did they take flight with hoarse whistles and noisy leapings all living creatures within earshot would be immediately absorbed by the landscape, and my hunt ended. But I am an old hand at the game, and, having chosen a position with that end in view, was not to be seen, heard, or smelled.

Yet the scene around me had its influence, and a guilty feeling possessed me as I realized that of all present in that place of peace and clean content, I was the only profane thing, an ogre lurking to destroy. The half-grown ferns and evergreen sedge grasses through which the early breeze whispered, would, if I had my way, soon be smeared with the blood of some animal, who was viewing, perhaps with feelings akin to my own, the dawning of another day; to be his last. Strange thoughts, maybe, coming from a trapper, one whose trade it is to kill; but be it known to you that he who lives much alone within the portals of the temple of Nature learns to think, and deeply, of things which seldom come within the scope of ordinary life. Much killing brings in time, no longer triumph, but a revulsion of feeling.

I have seen old hunters, with their hair silvered by the passage of many winters, who, on killing a deer would stroke the dead muzzle with every appearance of regret. Indians frequently address an animal they are about to kill in terms of apology for the act. However, be that as it may, with the passing of the mist from the face of the mountains, I saw a large beaver swimming a short distance away. This was my game; gone were my scruples, and my humane ideas fled like leaves before the wind. Giving the searching call of these animals, I cocked my rifle and waited.

At the call he stopped, raising himself in the water to sniff; and on the summons being repeated he swam directly towards me, into the very jaws of destruction. At about fifteen feet I had a good view of him as he slowed down, trying to catch some indication of a possible companion, and the beautiful dark fur apprised me of a hide that would well repay my early morning sortie. The beaver regarded me steadily, again raising himself to catch an expected scent, and not getting it he turned lazily to swim away. He was at my mercy, and I had his head snugly set between the forks of my rear sight, when my heart contracted at the thought of taking life on such a morning. The creature was happy, glad to be in God's good sunlight, free after a winter of darkness to breathe the pure air of the dawn. He had the right to live here, even as I had, yea, even a greater claim, for he was there before me.

I conquered my momentary weakness; for, after all a light pressure on the trigger, a crashing impact, would save him many days of useless labour. Yet I hesitated, and as I finally laid my rifle down, he sank without a ripple, out of sight. And I became suddenly conscious of the paeans of praise and triumph of the feathered choir about me, temporarily unheard in my lust to kill; and it seemed as though all Nature sang in benediction of an act which had kept inviolate a sanctuary, and saved a perfect hour from desecration.

I went home to my cabin and ate my breakfast with greater satisfaction than the most expertly accomplished kill had ever given me; and, call it what you will, weakness, vacillation, or the first glimmerings of conscience in a life hitherto devoted to the shedding of blood, since the later experiences I have had with these animals I look back on the incident with no regret.

At one time beaver were to the north what gold was to the west. In the early mining camps gold was the only medium of exchange; and from time immemorial at the northern trading posts a beaver hide was the only currency which remained always at par, and by its unchanging value, all other furs were judged. It took so many other hides to equal a beaver skin; and its value was one dollar. Counters were threaded on a string, each worth a dollar, and called "beaver," and as the hunter sold his fur its equivalent in "beaver" counters was pushed along the string. No money changed hands. So many discs were replaced in settlement of the hunting-debt, and as the trapper bought his provisions the remaining "beaver" were run back down again, one by one, a dollar at a time, until they were all back where they belonged, and the trade completed.

They usually went back down the string a good deal faster than they came up, and the story is told of the hunter with two bales of fur who thus paid his debt, spoke twice, and owed a hundred dollars. Although pelts were cheap provisions were not. I have spoken with men, not such very old men either, who traded marten, now selling as high as forty dollars, at the rate of four to a beaver, or twenty-five cents each.

A hunter must have had to bring in a stupendous amount of fur to buy even the barest necessities, when we consider the prices that even today obtain at many of the distant posts; a twenty-five pound bag of flour, $5.00; salt pork, $1.00 a pound; tea, $3.00 a pound; candles, 25 c. each; sugar, 50 c. a pound; 5 lb. pail of lard, $4.50; a pair of trousers, $25.00; and so on. The oft-told tale of piling beaver hides to the height of the muzzle of a gun in order to purchase the weapon, although frequently denied, is perfectly true. Many old Indians living today possess guns they bought that way. It is not so generally known that some unscrupulous traders increased the price by lengthening the barrels, necessitating the cutting off of a length with a file before the weapon could be used.

Although beaver do not exist today in sufficient quantities to constitute a hunt, up till ten years ago they were the chief means of subsistence of an army of white hunters, and thousands of Indians. Since their practical extermination the Northern Ojibways are in want, and many of the bands have had to be rationed by the Government to prevent their actual starvation.

The first, and for over a hundred years, the only business in which Canada was engaged was the fur trade, of which the beaver was the mainstay; and its history affords one of the most romantic phases in the development of the North American Continent.

The specimens of beaver pelts exhibited to Charles of England influenced him to grant the famous Hudson Bay Company's Charter, apportioning to them probably the largest land grant ever awarded any one concern. Attracted by the rich spoils of the trade, other companies sprang up. Jealousies ensued, and pitched battles between the trappers of rival factions were a common occurrence. Men fought, murdered, starved and froze to death, took perilous trips into unknown wildernesses, and braved the horrors of Indian warfare, lured on by the rich returns of the beaver trade. Men foreswore one another, cheated, murdered, robbed, and lied to gain possession of bales of these pelts, which could not have been more ardently fought for had each hair on them been composed of gold.

The Indians, meanwhile, incensed at the wholesale slaughter of their sacred animal, inflamed by the sight of large bands of men fighting for something that belonged to none of them, took pay from either side, and swooped down on outgoing caravans, annihilating them utterly, and burning peltries valued at hundreds of thousands of dollars. Often, glad of a chance to strike a blow at the beaver man, the common enemy, they showed a proper regard for symmetry by also destroying the other party that had hired them, thus restoring the balance of Nature. Ghastly torturing and other diabolical atrocities, incident to the massacre of trappers in their winter camps, discouraged hunting, and crippled the trade for a period; but with the entire extinction of the buffalo the Indian himself was obliged to turn and help destroy his ancient friends in order to live. Betrayed by their protectors the beaver did not long survive, and soon they were no more seen in the land wherein they had dwelt so long.

Profiting by this lesson, forty years later, most of the Provinces on the Canadian side of the line declared a closed season on beaver, of indefinite duration. Thus protected they gradually increased until at the outbreak of the World War they were as numerous in the Eastern Provinces as they ever had been in the West. I am not an old man, but I have seen the day when the forest streams and lakes of Northern Ontario and Quebec were peopled by millions of these animals. Every creek and pond had its colony of the Beaver People. And then once again, and for the last time, this harassed and devoted animal was subjected to a persecution that it is hard to credit could be possible in these enlightened days of preservation and conservation. The beaver season was thrown open and the hunt was on.

Men, who could well have made their living in other ways, quit their regular occupations and took the trail. It was the story of the buffalo over again. In this case instead of an expensive outfit of horses and wagons, only a cheap licence, a few traps, some provisions, and a canoe were needed, opening up widely the field to all and sundry.

The woods were full of trappers. Their snowshoe trails formed a network of destruction over all the face of the wilderness, into the farthest recesses of the north. Trails were broken out to civilization, packed hard as a rock by long strings of toboggans and sleighs drawn by wolf-dogs, and loaded with skins; trails over which passed thousands and thousands of beaver hides on their way to the market. Beaver houses were dynamited by those whose intelligence could not grasp the niceties of beaver trapping, or who had not the hardihood to stand the immersion of bare arms in ice water during zero weather; for the setting of beaver traps in mid-winter is no occupation for one with tender hands or a taste for tea-fights. Dams were broken after the freeze-up, and sometimes the entire defences, feed house, and dam were destroyed, and those beaver not captured froze to death or starved in their ruined works, whilst all around was death, and ruin, and destruction.

Relentless spring hunters killed the mother beavers, allowing the little ones to starve, which, apart from the brutality of the act, destroyed all chances of replenishment. Unskillful methods allowed undrowned beaver to twist out of traps, leaving in the jaws some shattered bone and a length of sinew, condemning the maimed creatures to do all their work with one or both front feet cut off; equivalent in its effect to cutting off the hands of a man.

I once saw a beaver with both front feet and one hind foot cut off in this way. He had been doing his pitiful best to collect materials for his building. He was quite far from the water and unable to escape me, and although it was late summer and the hide of no value, I put him out of misery with a well-placed bullet.

Clean trapping became a thing of the past, and unsportsmanlike methods were used such as removing the raft of feed so that the beaver must take bait or starve; and the spring pole, a contrivance which jerks the unfortunate animal into the air, to hang for hours by one foot just clear of the water, to die in prolonged agony from thirst. To inflict such torture on this almost human animal is a revolting crime which few regular white hunters and no Indian will stoop to.

I remember once, on stopping to make camp, hearing a sound like the moaning of a child a few yards away, and I rushed to the spot with all possible speed, knowing bear traps to be out in the district. I found a beaver suspended in this manner, jammed into the crotch of a limb, held there by the spring pole, and moaning feebly. I took it down, and found it to be a female heavy with young, and in a dying condition; my attempts at resuscitation were without avail, and shortly after three Jives passed into the discard.

The Government of Ontario imposed a limit on the number to be killed, and attempted, futilely, to enforce it; but means were found to evade this ruling, and men whose allowance called for ten hides came out with a hundred. There is some sorcery in a beaver hide akin to that which a nugget of gold is credited with possessing, and the atmosphere of the trade in these skins is permeated with all the romance and the evil, the rapacity and adventurous glamour, attendant on a gold rush. Other fur, more easily caught, more valuable perhaps, may increase beyond all bounds, and attract no attention save that of the professional trapper, but at the word "beaver," every man on the frontier springs to attention, every ear is cocked. The lifting of the embargo in Ontario precipitated a rush, which whilst not so concentrated, was very little, if any, less than that of '98 to the Yukon. Fleets, flotillas, and brigades of canoes were strung out over the surface of the lakes in a region of many thousand square miles, dropping off individually here and there into chosen territories, and emerging with spectacular hunts unknown in earlier days. The plots and counter-plots, the intrigues and evasions connected with the tricks of the trade, resembled the diplomatic ramifications of a nation at war.

History repeated itself. Fatal quarrels over hunting grounds were not unknown, and men otherwise honest, bitten by the bug of greed and the prospect of easy money, stooped to unheard-of acts of depravity for the sake of a few hides.

Meanwhile the trappers reaped a harvest, but not for long. Beaver in whole sections disappeared and eyes were turned on the Indian countries. The red men, as before, looked on, but this time with alarm. Unable any longer to fight for this animal, which, whilst no longer sacred was their very means of existence, they were compelled to join in the destruction, and ruin their own hunting grounds before others got ahead of them and took everything. For ten years the slaughter went on, and then beaver became scarce.

The part-time hunter, out for a quick fortune, left the woods full of poison baits, and polluted with piles of carcasses, and returned to his regular occupation. The Indian hunting grounds and those of the regular white trappers had been invaded and depleted of game. The immense number of dog-teams in use necessitated the killing of large numbers of moose for feed, and they also began to be scarce. Professional hunters, both red and white, even if only to protect their own interests, take only a certain proportion of the fur, and trapping grounds are maintained in perpetuity. The invaders had taken everything.

Today, in the greater part of the vast wilderness of Northern Canada, beaver are almost extinct; they are fast going the way of the buffalo. But their houses, their dams, and all their works will long remain as a reproach and a heavy indictment against the shameful waste perpetrated by man, in his exploitation of the wild lands and the dwellers therein. Few people know, or perhaps care, how close we are to losing most of the links with the pioneer days of old; the beaver is one of the few remaining reminders of that past Canadian history of which we are justly proud, and he is entitled to some small niche in the hall of fame. He has earned the right to our protection whilst we yet have the power to exercise it, and if we fail him it will not be long before he is beyond our jurisdiction for all time.

The system that has depleted the fur resources of Canada to a point almost of annihilation, is uncontrolled competitive hunting and trapping by transient white trappers.

The carefully farmed hunting territories of the Indians and the resident white trappers (the latter being greatly in the minority, and having in most cases a proprietary interest in the preservation of fur and game, playing the game much as the Indian played it) were, from 1915 on, invaded by hordes of get-rich-quick vandals who, caring for nothing much but the immediate profits, swept like the scourge they were across the face of northern Canada.

These men were in no way professional hunters; their places were in the ranks of other industries, where they should have stayed. The Indian and the dyed-in-the-wool genuine woodsmen, unsuited by a long life under wilderness conditions to another occupation, and unable to make such a revolutionary change in their manner of living, now find themselves without the means of subsistence.

Misinformed and apparently not greatly interested provincial governments aided and abetted this destructive and unwarranted encroachment on the rights of their native populations who were dependent entirely on the proceeds of the chase, by gathering a rich if temporary harvest in licences, royalties, etc. A few futile laws were passed, of which the main incentive of enforcement often seemed to be the collection of fines rather than prevention. Money alone can never adequately pay the people of Canada for the loss of their wildlife, from either the commercial, or recreational, or the sentimental point of view.

We read of the man who opened up the goose to get all the golden eggs at once, and the resultant depression in the golden-egg market that followed. The two cases are similar.

We blame the United States for their short-sighted policy in permitting the slaughter of the buffalo as a means of solving the Indian problem of that time, yet we have allowed, for a paltry consideration in dollars and cents, and greatly owing to our criminal negligence in acquainting ourselves with the self-evident facts of the case, the almost entire destruction of our once numerous fur-bearing and game animals. Nor did this policy settle any Indian problem, there being none at the time, but it created one that is daily becoming more serious. The white man's burden will soon be no idle dream, and will have to be assumed with what cheerful resignation you can muster.

We must not fail to remember that we are still our brother's keeper, and having carelessly allowed this same brother to be robbed of his rights and very means of existence (solemnly agreed by treaty to be inalienable and perpetual, whereby he was a self-supporting producer, a contributor to the wealth of the country and an unofficial game warden and conservationist whose knowledge of wildlife would have been invaluable) we must now support him. And this will complete his downfall by the degrading "dole" system.

At a meeting I attended lately, it was stated by a competent authority that there were more trappers in the woods during this last two years than ever before. The fact that they paid for their licences does not in any way compensate either the natives or the country at large for the loss in wildlife consequent on this wholesale slaughter.

The only remedy would seem to be the removal from the woods of all white trappers except those who could prove that they had no alternative occupation, had followed trapping for a livelihood previous to 1914 (thus eliminating the draft evaders and others who hid in the woods during the war) and returned men of the voluntary enlistment class. It is not perhaps generally known that the draft evaders in some sections constitute the majority of the more destructive element in the woods today. Forced to earn a livelihood by some means in their seclusion, and fur being high at the time, they learned to trap in a kind of way. They constitute a grave menace to our fur and game resources, as their unskillful methods make necessary wholesale destruction on all sides in order to obtain a percentage of the fur, leaving in their path a shambles of unfound bodies, many of them poisoned, or crippled animals, which, unable to cope with the severe conditions thus imposed on them, eventually die in misery and starvation.

Regulations should be drawn up with due regard for conditions governing the various districts, these to be ascertained from genuine woodsmen and the more prominent and responsible men of native communities. Suggestions from such sources would have obviated a good deal of faulty legislation. Those entrusted with the making of our game laws seem never to become acquainted with the true facts until it is almost too late, following the progress of affairs about a lap behind.

Regulations, once made, should be rigorously enforced, and penalties should include fines and imprisonment, as many illegal trappers put by the amount of a possible fine as a part of their ordinary expenses.

There is another point of view to be considered. If the depletion of our game animals goes on much longer at the present rate, specimens of wildlife will soon be seen only in zoos and menageries.

How much more elevating and instructive is it to get a glimpse — however fleeting — of an animal in its native haunts than the lengthy contemplation of poor melancholy captives eking out a thwarted existence under unnatural conditions? Fur farms may perpetuate the fur industry eventually unless the ruinous policy of selling, for large and immediate profits, breeding animals to foreign markets is continued. But these semi-domesticated denatured specimens will never represent to the true lover of Nature the wild beauty and freedom of the dwellers in the Silent Places, nor will they ever repopulate the dreary empty wastes that will be all that are left to us when the remaining Little Brethren have been immolated on the altars of Greed and Ignorance, and the priceless heritage of both the Indian and the white man destroyed for all time.

In wanderings during the last five years, extending between, and including, the Districts of Algoma in the Province of Ontario and Misstassini in the Province of Quebec, and covering an itinerary of perhaps two thousand miles, I have seen not over a dozen signs of beaver. I was so struck by this evidence of the practical extinction of our national animal, that my journey, originally undertaken with the intention of finding a hunting ground, became more of a crusade, conducted with the object of discovering a small colony of beaver not claimed by some other hunter, the motive being no longer to trap, but to preserve them.

I have been fortunate enough to discover two small families. With them, and a few hand-raised specimens in my possession, I am attempting the somewhat hopeless task of repopulating a district otherwise denuded of game. It is a little saddening to see on every hand the deserted works, the broken dams, and the empty houses, monuments to the thwarted industry of an animal which played such an important part in the history of the Dominion.

Did the public have by any chance the opportunity of studying this little beast who seems almost able to think, possesses a power of speech in which little but the articulation of words is lacking, and a capacity for suffering possible only to a high grade of intelligence, popular opinion would demand the declaration of a close season of indefinite duration over the whole Dominion.

Did the Provinces collaborate on any such scheme, there would be no sale for beaver skins, and the only source of supply being thus closed, poaching would be profitless. Even from a materialistic point of view this would be of great benefit, as after a long, it is to be feared a very long, period a carefully regulated beaver hunt could be arranged that would be a source of revenue of some account.

It is generally conceded that the beaver was by far the most interesting and intelligent of all the creatures that at one time abounded in the vast wilderness of forest, plain, and mountain that was Canada before the Coming of the white man.

Although in the north they are now reduced to a few individuals and small families scattered thinly in certain inaccessible districts, there has been established for many years, a game reserve of about three thousand square miles, where these and all other animals indigenous to the region are as numerous as they were fifty years ago. I refer to the Algonquin Provincial Park in Ontario. This game sanctuary is guarded in the strictest manner by a very competent staff of Rangers, and it is a saying in the region that it would be easier to get away with murder than to escape the consequences of killing a beaver in their patrol area.

This little worker of the wild has been much honoured. He ranks with the maple leaf as representative of the Dominion, and has won a place as one of Canada's national emblems, by the example he gives of industry, adaptability, and dogged perseverance; attributes well worthy of emulation by those who undertake to wrest a living from the untamed soil of a new country. He is the Imperialist of the animal world. He maintains a home and hearth, and from it he sends out every year a pair of emigrants who search far and wide for new fields to conquer; who explore, discover, occupy, and improve, to the benefit of all concerned.

The Indian, who lived by the killing of animals, held his hand when it came to the beaver. Bloody wars were waged on his behalf by his red-skinned protectors, until the improvements of civilization raised economic difficulties only to be met by the sale of beaver skins, with starvation as the alternative.

The red men considered them as themselves and dignified their Little Talking Brothers with the name of The Beaver People, and even in these degenerate days of traders, whiskey, and lost tradition, there are yet old men amongst the nations who will not sit to a table where beaver meat is served, while those who now eat him and sell his hide will allow no dog to eat his bones, and the remains feet, tail, bones, and entrails, are carefully committed to the element from which they came, the water.

It would seem that by evolution or some other process, these creatures have developed a degree of mental ability superior to that of any other living animal, with the possible exception of the elephant.

Most animals blindly follow an instinct and a set of habits, and react without mental effort to certain inhibitions and desires. In the case of the beaver, these purely animal attributes are supplemented by a sagacity which so resembles the workings of the human mind that it is quite generally believed, by those who know most about them, that they are endowed to a certain extent with reasoning powers. The fact that they build dams and houses, and collect feed is sometimes quoted as evidence of this; but muskrats also erect cabins and store food in much the same manner. Yet where do you find any other creature but man who can fall a tree in a desired direction, selecting only those which can conveniently be brought to the ground? For rarely do we find trees lodged or hung up by full-grown beaver; the smaller ones are responsible for most of the lodged trees. Instinct causes them to build their dams in the form of an arc, but by what means do they gain the knowledge that causes them to arrange that curve in a concave or a convex formation, according to the water-pressure?

Some tame beaver objected strongly to the window in my winter camp, and were everlastingly endeavouring to push up to it articles of all kinds, evidently thinking it was an opening, which it is their nature to close up. That was to be expected. But they overstepped the bounds of natural impulse, and entered the realm of calculation, when they dragged firewood over, and piled it under the window until they had reached its level, and on this improvised scaffold they eventually accomplished their purpose, completely covering the window with piled-up bedding. Whenever the door was open they tried every means of barricading the opening, but found they could never get the aperture filled. One day I returned with a pail of water in each hand to find the door closed, having to set down my pails to open it. I went in, and my curiosity aroused, watched the performance. As soon as I was clear, one of the beaver started to push on some sacking he had collected at the foot of the door, and slowly but surely closed it. And this he often did from then on. Instinct? Maybe.

Their general system of working is similar in most cases, and the methods used are the same. However, in the bush no two places are alike, and it requires no little ingenuity on the part of a man to adapt himself to the varying circumstances, yet the beaver can adjust himself to a multiplicity of different conditions, and is able to overcome all the difficulties arising, meeting his problems much in the way a man would.

In the accompanying sketch on page 193 will be seen a lake A, representing a pond well-known to me on which there was a beaver family. There was much feed at the place marked Z on the further bank of the river B, but none on the lake, which had been very shallow, but was dammed at X. Between the spot on the river marked Z and the lake was a distance of two hundred yards. The problem was to get the feed across to the pond. The river route was too far, and to draw it such a distance in a country bristling with dangers was not to be considered, so the beaver dug a canal towards the river. Now this stream had run swiftly two miles or more before it reached the point Z, therefore, naturally at that place would be much lower than the level of the lake. On the completion of the canal C the lake would consequently be drained. This the beaver were well aware of, and to avoid this contingency, the channel was dug as far as D, discontinued for a few yards, and continued on to the river, leaving a wall, which being further heightened, prevented the escape of their precious water.

Thus they could float their timber in ease the full distance, with the exception of one short portage. A problem not easily solved.

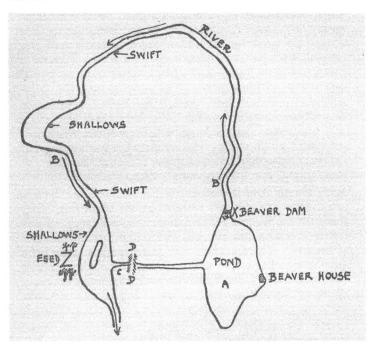

Grey Owl's drawing of a beaver dam.

Their strength is phenomenal and they can draw a stick which, in proportion, a man could not shift with his hands; and to move it sideways they will go to each extremity alternately, poise the end over their head and throw it an appreciable distance. I have seen two small beaver struggling down a runway with a poplar log, heaviest of soft woods, of such a size that only the top of their backs and heads were visible above it.

Shooting them when they are so engaged, a common practice, somehow seems to me in these latter days, like firing from ambush on children at play, or shooting poor harmless labourers at work in the fields.

The beaver is a home-loving beast and will travel far overland, around the shores of lakes and up streams, searching for a suitable place to build. Once settled where there is enough feed, and good opportunities to construct a dam, a family is liable to stay in that immediate district for many years. The young, at the age of two years, leave home, and separating, pick each a mate from another family, build themselves a house and dam, and settle down to housekeeping; staying together for life, a period of perhaps fifteen years. At the end of the third year they attain full growth, being then three feet and a half long with the tail, and weighing about thirty-five pounds. In the spring the mother has her young, the male making a separate house for them and keeping the dam in repair. The last year's kittens leave the pond, going always downstream, and wander around all summer, returning about August to assist in the work of getting ready for the winter. The first part of these preparations is to build a dam, low to begin with, and being made higher as needed. The main object of this structure is to give a good depth of water, in which feed may be kept all winter without freezing, and heavy green sticks are often piled on top of the raft of supplies, which is generally attached to the house, in order to sink it as much as possible. Also by this means the water is flooded back into the timber they intend to fall, enabling them to work close to the water and facilitating escape from danger.

Much has been said concerning the timber they are supposed to spoil in this way, but the shores of a lake are hardly ever low enough to allow any more than the first narrow fringe of trees close to the water to be drowned, and that is generally of little value commercially.

The immense amount of work that is put into a dam must be seen to be realized. Some of these are eight feet high, a hundred yards long, and six feet through at the base, tapering up to a scant foot at the water level. Pits are dug near the ends from which are carried the materials to prevent seepage, and a judicious admixture of large stones adds the necessary stiffening at the water-lines. Canals are channelled out, trees felled near them, neatly limbed, cut up, and all but the heavier portions drawn to the water and floated away. The heightened water facilitates this operation and besides thus fulfilling his own purpose, the beaver is performing a service for man that, too late, is now being recognized.

Many a useful shortcut on a circuitous canoe route, effecting a saving of hours, and even days, a matter of the greatest importance in the proper policing of the valuable forests against fire, has become impracticable since the beaver were removed, as the dams fell out of repair, and streams became too shallow for navigation by canoes.

The house alone is a monument of concentrated effort. The entrance is under water, and on a foundation raised to the water level, and heightened as the water rises, sticks of every kind are stacked criss-cross in a dome-shaped pile some eight feet high and from ten to twenty-five feet in width at the base. These materials are placed without regard to interior accommodation, the interstices filled with soil, and the centre is cut out from the inside, all hands chewing away at the interlaced sticks until there is room enough in the interior for a space around the waterhole for a feeding place, and for a platform near the walls for sleeping quarters. The beds are made of long shavings, thin as paper, which they tear off sticks; each beaver has his bed and keeps his place.

Pieces of feed are cut off the raft outside under the ice, and peeled in the house, the discarded sticks being carried out through a branch in the main entrance, as are the beds on becoming too soggy. Should the water sink below the level of the feeding place the loss is at once detected, and the dam inspected and repaired. Thus they are easy to catch by making a small break in the dam and setting a trap in the aperture. On discovering the break they will immediately set to work to repair it without loss of time, and get into the trap. When it closes on them they jump at once into deep water and, a large stone having been attached to the trap, they stay there and drown, taking about twenty minutes to die; a poor reward for a lifetime of useful industry.

Late in the Fall the house is well plastered with mud, and it is by observing the time of this operation that it is possible to forecast the near approach of the freeze-up.

And it is the contemplation of this diligence and perseverance, this courageous surmounting of all difficulties at no matter what cost in labour, that has, with other considerations, earned the beaver, as far as I am concerned, immunity for all time. I cannot see that my vaunted superiority as a man entitles me to disregard the lesson that he teaches, and profiting thereby, I do not feel that I have any longer the right to destroy the worker or his works performed with such devotion.

Many years have I builded, and hewed, and banked, and laboriously carried in my supplies in readiness for the winter, and all around me the Beaver People were doing the same thing by much the same methods, little knowing that their work was all for nought, and that they were doomed beforehand never to enjoy the comfort they well earned with such slavish labour.

I recollect how once I sat eating a lunch at an open fire on the shores of a beautiful little mountain lake, and beside me, in the sunlight, lay the body of a fine big beaver I had just caught. I well remember, too, the feeling of regret that possessed me for the first time, as I watched the wind playing in the dead beaver's hair, as it had done when he had been happy, sunning himself on the shores of his pond, so soon to become a dirty swamp, now that he was taken.

In spite of his clever devices for protection, the beaver, by the very nature of his work signs his own death warrant. The evidences of his wisdom and industry, for which he is so lauded, have been after all, only signposts on the road to extinction. Everywhere his bright new stumps show up. His graded trails, where they enter the water, form ideal sets for traps and he can be laid in wait for and shot in his canals. Even with six feet of snow blanketing the winter forest, it can be easily discovered whether a beaver-house is occupied or not, by digging some snow off the top of the house and exposing the large hollow space melted by the exhalations from within. The store of feed so carefully put by, may prove his undoing, and he be caught near it by a skillfully placed trap. Surely he merits a better fate than this, that he should drown miserably three feet from his companions and his empty bed, whilst his body lies there until claimed by the hunter, later to pass, on the toboggan on its way to the hungry maw of the city, the home he worked so hard to build, the quiet and peace of the little pond that knew him and that he loved so well.

This then is the tale of the Beaver People, a tale that is almost told. Soon all that will remain of this once numerous clan of little brethren of the waste places will be their representative in his place of honour on the flag of Canada. After all an empty mockery, for, although held up to symbolize the Spirit of Industry of a people, that same people has allowed him to be done to death on every hand, and by every means. Once a priceless exhibit displayed for a king's approval, the object of the devotion of an entire race, and wielding the balance of power over a large continent, he is now a fugitive. Unable to follow his wonted occupation, lest his work show his presence, scarcely he dares to eat except in secrecy, lest he bring retribution swift and terrible for a careless move. Lurking in holes and corners, in muddy ponds and deep unpenetrable swamps, he dodges the traps, snares, spring poles, nets, and every imaginable device set to encompass his destruction, to wipe him off the face of the earth.

Playful and good-natured, persevering and patient, the scattered remnants of the beaver colonies carry on, futilely working out their destiny until such time as they too will fall a victim to the greed of man. And so they will pass from sight as if they had never been, leaving a gap in the cycle of wilderness life that cannot be filled. They will vanish into the past out of which they came, beyond the long-forgotten days, from whence, if we let them go, they can never be recalled.

VIII

THE ALTAR OF MAMMON

And the smoke rose slowly, slowly
Through the tranquil air of morning
…
Ever rising, rising, rising
Till it broke against the heaven
And rolled outward all around it.
                    — LONGFELLOW

Away back around 1870 or maybe 1880, for Indians pay little attention to dates, a large war party of Sioux and Blackfeet Indians from the Western plains penetrated as far east as North-Western Ontario. Some of the more vivid incidents connected with their arrival so impressed the Crees of that district that, from then on, they kept a permanent guard on an eminence, in order that, in the event of a return visit, they might be prepared to welcome their guests in a suitable manner.

The mountain became known as Sioux Lookout, a name it, together with the town at its foot, retains to this day, and the lookout is still a lookout, not for hostiles, but for that far more deadly enemy, fire.

When the marauders returned home from their barbering expedition, they referred to Canada, with Indian aptitude, as the Land of the Red Sunset; and the suitability of the name is as apparent now at the setting of the sun on nearly every summer day as it was then. In the summer months the sun goes down daily a blood-red ball, seen through a pall of smoke at varying distances, painted in garish hue by the vapour emanating from the destruction of one of Canada's most valuable assets, her timberlands.

As a woman's hair is — or was — her chief adornment, so Canada's crowning glory is her forests, or what remains of them.

With her timber gone, the potential wealth of the Dominion would be halved, and her industries cut down by one-third; yet the forest is being daily offered up for a burnt sacrifice to the false gods of greed and waste, and the birthright of future generations is being squandered by its trustees. Not only is the interest, the merchantable timber arriving at maturity, being used up faster than it accumulates, but the capital, the main body of the forest, is fast disappearing. Year by year for three-quarters of a century, this useless and costly destruction has been going on for five months out of every year; sometimes in widely separated districts, at others in a seething wall of flame that stretches clear across the greater part of Canada.

This is no exaggeration; in large cities such as Montreal, Toronto, and Ottawa the sun has been noticeably darkened on more than one occasion by the smoke of fires two hundred miles away. Whole towns such as Haileybury, Liskeard, Cochrane, and many others, have been swept off the face of the earth. Mining camps such as Porcupine and Golden City have been burnt with loss of life running into three figures. In the latter case, I happened to be in the district, and at a distance of twenty miles I distinctly heard the roar of the flames, little knowing the holocaust that was taking place. The smoke was such that it was impossible to see a quarter of a mile on the lakes, and all travelling had to be suspended except by those familiar with the country. A shortage of canoes compelled hundreds of people to enter the lake by which the town was situated, where they extended in a living chain, holding hands to support each other, dipping their bodies from time to time under the surface to wet their clothes. Many of these were suffocated by smoke, those near the shore were badly scorched, and some were drowned. Relief trains sent up to the end of the steel were got through with difficulty, being on occasion derailed by the twisted metals, and in the tank of one locomotive that could be driven no further on account of the heat, a man was later found scalded to death.

I assisted in the work of recovering some of the bodies scattered through the charred forest, prospectors caught far from water by the sudden rush of fire; they mostly in crouching positions, with the hands held over the face, sights terrible to see. This particular fire travelled, in spots, at an estimated speed of forty miles an hour, creating a hurricane of its own, and during the short time of its duration, laid waste an area as large as the South of England.

When it is considered that catastrophes such as these can be, and mostly are, caused by a carelessly discarded cigarette or match, unextinguished camp fires, or some other simple and preventable cause, and that useful lives and valuable timber, running into untold sums, can be destroyed by the criminal neglect of one individual, it is not very hard to see that fire protection in Canada has become a matter of the gravest importance.

No longer is the settler in danger of massacre, although in some districts wolves menace his stock, but in what is known as the "backwoods," which includes all that region of half-cleared farms on the fringe of the forest proper, his life and property are in danger from forest fires as never before.

The Governments of the various provinces keep in the woods, during the danger period, forces of men equipped with every contrivance that could possibly be brought to bear on fires at such distances from vehicular transportation. In days now happily gone by, Fire Ranging was more or less of a farce. By the patronage system, then in vogue, men were often appointed to the staff of the Service who by trade were entirely unsuited to the position. In those days the way a man cast his vote was considered of more importance than the service he could give in the field, and those who had the responsibility of seeing the work done, or were genuinely interested, were hampered by the vote-peddlers. The rank and file consisted mostly of college students out to make enough money to see them through their winter courses; estimable fellows, all of them, but just as much out of place in their new environment as an Indian or a trapper would have been had he gone to their colleges and tried to assume the *rôle* of professor. Most of them were unused to a canoe, the only means of transportation, excepting for the little knowledge they might have picked up at summer resorts or at a boating club. The time that should have been spent patrolling the beat was expended in futile endeavours to do their own cooking, keep from getting lost, and generally take care of themselves; and many of them unfortunately looked on the expedition as a frolic, or else a chance to get a few lessons in woodcraft, and be paid for it.

Meanwhile Canada was burning up.

Some of the chiefs and their assistants were highly efficient men, who took their responsibilities very much to heart; and there were a few men of undoubted ability salted through the heterogeneous mass of inefficiency, but they were not common; and alone these men could do little. So, every spring, there was the elevating exhibition of ten or a dozen canoes starting out on an expedition intended to protect the most valuable, and at the same time the most perishable asset that particular Province owned, with a good two-thirds of its personnel now dipping a paddle in the water for the first time in their lives. And so the procession wobbled and weaved along the route, herded on its unwilling way by a harassed, discouraged, and vitriolic Chief, who tore his hair, and raved and pleaded at every portage. He was held answerable for the proper distribution of his men by a certain date, and in the ease I have in mind he got them there, God knows how.

In one instance a young man who had passed, on an Ontario Reserve, what must have been a most uncomfortable summer between the flies, the loneliness, and a very exaggerated fear of wild beasts, on his return home caused to be published in a Toronto newspaper an account of his experiences. Among other things he related how an inhuman and relentless Chief had banished him and his partner to a remote and "very undeveloped" district, where they were frequently lost, and at one time were obliged to lock themselves in, while a ferocious lynx of large size laid siege to their camp for an entire day. As further evidence of the Chief's brutality he stated that some rangers who had been discharged had been obliged to find their way out without a guide! It is to be supposed that they found the lack of a footman also very distressing at times. This was about eighteen years ago, and although, apparently, taken seriously at the time the story would not be published in these days, except as a joke, as it is well known that there are no authentic accounts of lynx, unless in a trap, ever attacking a man, and the Forest Ranger of today is certainly in no need of a guide. But this gives an idea of the protection that one of Canada's most heavily forested regions was getting up to a not so very distant date.

This has all been changed. The firefighting machinery is now one of the most efficient and highly organized branches of the government service. Only men of known ability are employed. Districts where much travelling is done are patrolled by airplanes, which are also used for transporting firefighting apparatus to places to which it would be otherwise impossible to move it. Steel towers, hauled in sections by dog-teams during the winter, are erected on commanding situations and connected by telephone, and in them sentinels are posted every day of summer. Portages are kept in first-class condition, and shortcuts established, so that gangs of men and equipment may be rushed to the scene of a fire in the shortest possible time. Professional woodsmen and Indians are kept on the payroll for the express purpose of discovering blocks of valuable timber, and opening up routes to them.

A hundred miles each side of the railroad, in wild districts, is protected in the most intensive manner; beyond that the type of man who is responsible for most of the fires is rarely found. Those who have sufficient experience to enable them to penetrate farther than the Rangers go, will neither intentionally nor carelessly set a fire.

In case of fire a government ranger of the lowest rank has power, in emergency, to call to his aid all the able-bodied men he needs, employed or otherwise, and he takes charge of the situation, although paradoxically they receive more wages for the duration of the fire than he does. All this comes a little late, but something may be saved.

The numerous lumber camps situated on the fringe between civilization and the true wilderness have long been known for their hospitality, their generosity to Indians, and the readiness of their crews to assist in cases of distressed travellers, and in the event of fire. No man need go hungry or want for a bed when passing through the lumbering districts, and weary trappers have rested in them for days, regaling themselves with cooking such as only the old-time camp cooks know how to put up, free of any charge.

Most of the companies are honest in their dealings with timber on Crown lands, but unfortunately some of these concerns have passed out of the hands of the big-hearted lumber kings, and under a new regime fail to keep up the traditions. There are a number of them now being operated by foreign amalgamations with huge sums of money behind them, and having no special interest in the country, their only concern being to get what can be got whilst the getting is good. They employ labour certainly, as long as it lasts, even as the beaver supported a large population for a time and are gone now. The two cases are parallel.

The white pine, king of all the Forest, at one time the mainstay of the lumber industry, is now only existent in a few remote districts, or in reserves set aside by a wise government. But the pine is hard to save. Politics have still a little to say, for it is a profitable tree, and many are the hungry eyes turned on the rolling dark green forest of the reserved lands. Certain unscrupulous lumber companies, of foreign origin, have been the cause of fires designed to scorch large areas of timber on Crown lands. Burnt timber must be immediately sold or it will become a total loss. The burning of an old lumber camp, and the sacrifice of some logging gear in the fire establishes innocence on the part of the company, and they come into possession of a nice, juicy cut of timber which rightly belongs to the public. The money is paid over but the pine is none the less gone.

I remember once visiting a lumber camp belonging to a foreign company, to obtain details of a fire that had taken place on their cuttings. Somehow or another it did not transpire what my business at the camp was, but we, the camp bosses and myself, fell into an argument as to whether the timber on a certain lake in the Forest Reserve would ever be cut. They declared that it surely would, and I stoutly maintained that it would not.

"The Government won't sell," I finished triumphantly.

"They'll sell if it burns, won't they," said one of the bosses with a knowing wink, not knowing what I represented. Two summers later a large block of timber adjacent to the lake was burnt and the district for miles around has passed into the hands of its enemies.

A letter appeared not long ago in a prominent newspaper in a Canadian City, in which it was pointed out that the reports being circulated concerning the alleged shortage of pine were hurting the lumber industry. It will be far worse hurt when the pine are gone, which will be before very long, and most of the old white pine companies are even now turning their attention to pulp, which, whilst not quite so profitable, employs as much labour, the main issue. It were better so than that the people of Canada should be robbed of the pleasure of having at least one or two National Parks in a state of Nature, if they serve only the purpose of a monument to the forest that is gone, a memento of the Canada that-was in the days of the Last Frontier. Let us, before it is too late, learn a lesson from the tale of the beaver and the buffalo. The forest is a beaten enemy to whom we can well afford to be generous.

Too many regard the wilderness as only a place of wild animals and wilder men, and cluttered with a growth that must somehow be got rid of. Yet it is, to those who know its ways, a living, breathing reality, and has a soul that may be understood, and it may yet occur to some, that part of the duty of those who destroy it for the general good is to preserve at least a memory of it and its inhabitants, and what they stood for.

The question of reforestation immediately crops up.

I feel that the planting of a few acres of seedlings to compensate for the destruction of thousands of square miles of virgin timber, whilst a worthy thought, and one that should be extensively carried out, seems much like placing two cents in the bank after having squandered a million. Let us keep on with the good work by all means, but why not at the same time devise means to save a little of what we have?

This reforestation may salve the consciences of those who would ruthlessly sell or cut the last pine tree, but by the time the seedlings arrive at maturity, a matter of a hundred and fifty years or more, the rabble of all nations will occupy so much territory that the trees will have no room to grow.

No one seems to have thought of ascertaining just how long a soil impoverished by being systematically denuded of its natural fertilizer, by the removal of all mature timber, will reproduce a forest worthy of the name. In these domestic woodlands there will fall no logs to rot and nourish the trees growing to take their places, especially in the unproductive barrens to which the interests of practical forestry have been relegated by the somewhat overzealous land-hunters.

We have already today examples of this depreciation in "land-power" in some of the great wheat-growing areas of the West. The ruinous "scratch-the-land-and-reap-a-fortune" policy of the propagandists of settlement schemes in the past has been followed only too closely; and, insufficiently fertilized, the soil, having given all it had, is beginning to run out.

There are today in Canada large concerns that in the guise of a benevolent interest in Wildlife, and under cover of a wordy forest preservation campaign (of which reforestation, *not* conservation, is the keynote), are amalgamating in order to gain possession of practically all of Canada's remaining forests.

And, let us be warned, they are succeeding handsomely.

Enormous areas are already beyond the jurisdiction of the people. As a sop to public opinion the benefits of reforestation are dwelt on, not as a contributing factor in silviculture (and a very necessary one it is), but as a substitute for the timber they wish to remove. According to those interested the forests will burn, fall down, decay, or rot on the stump if they are not cut immediately, and in return they will plant comparatively infinitesimal areas with tiny trees, to replace the fast disappearing forests on which they are fattening.

So we have the highly diverting spectacle of one man, standing in the midst of ten million acres of stumps and arid desolation, planting with a shovel a little tree ten inches high, to be the cornerstone of a new and synthetic forest, urged on to the deed by a deputation of smug and smiling profiteers, who do not really care if the tree matures or not — unless their descendants are to be engaged in the lumbering business.

How have the mighty fallen, and will continue to fall!

Even the policy of girdling* the hardwood species where they are not useful as firebreaks, woods whose beautiful fall colouring and grateful shade are a tradition in Canada, has been advocated to allow the growth of more easily merchantable species in their place at some future date. The virtual drying-up of springs, lakes, creeks and even fair-sized rivers consequent on this wholesale removal of forest growth, we hear nothing about.

Even an Act of Parliament to preserve a few hundred square miles of Canada's natural scenery intact for the benefit of the

---

* Removing a ring of bark entirely around a tree, on which it dies.

people, has to be fought through a number of sessions before it can wrest from destruction beauty spots of inestimable value to the nation, the benefits of which will accrue to the greater number and for all time, not only temporarily to an individual or a company.

And until the politics in which the issue is obscured are kept out of the matter and replaced by public-spirited altruism and a genuine forest conservation policy, the will of the people will be overridden, and the forest will continue to fall before the hosts of the God of Mammon, until the last tree is laid in the dust.

No punishment can be severe enough to atone for the deliberate or careless setting of fire, and how little this is realized even today is illustrated by the decision, handed down, of a magistrate in a middle-sized town, when a man charged with having a bottle of whiskey in his possession during a prohibition wave was fined two hundred dollars, and another guilty of setting fire, and destroying several thousand dollars' worth of timber, paid only ten dollars and costs.

I may seem to overemphasize this point, and perhaps could be accused of speaking too strongly, but if you had seen, as I have, noble forests reduced in a few hours to arid deserts sparsely dotted with the twisted, tortured skeletons of what once were trees, things of living beauty, (or if you are very practically minded, things of high value), excuse could no doubt be found for my zeal.

I know a little lake, called by the Indians the Place of Calling Waters, a blue gem, circled, as I once saw it, by a yellow beach of sand, and set in a valley of ancient spruce and birches. In the middle distance a dark pine stood out in silhouette, with its twisted arms thrown out against the Western sky, and the haze of evening dimmed the bristling outline of the wooded mountains.

It is different now. The glade is cut and the lake polluted. The giant pine no longer flaunts his banner-like limbs in the face of the burning sun, and the mountain has become a pile of sterile rocks, covered with a skeleton forest of burnt rampikes, whose harsh outlines no haze can ever soften. And the cause? A "Hunky"* colony.

Beauty spots such as this little Lake of Calling Waters, groves redolent with the clean smell of the leaves, carpeted in Spring with a myriad flowers, must soon be laid waste and trampled underfoot by the unsavoury hordes of Southern Europe, and their silence broken by a babel of uncouth tongues.

A frenzied and misdirected immigration policy, *encouraged by the demands of a wage-cutting type of employer by no means rare, and promoted by shipping and transportation companies whose only interest is to collect fares*, is fast filling up Canada with a polyglot jamboree of languages, among which English is by no means the predominating feature. The unskilled labour market in Canada is glutted. Every city has its unemployment problem. Prosperity there is, but not enough to provide a livelihood for the adult male population of all Europe.

The United States found it hard to absorb the immense quantities of immigrants landing on her shores, and was obliged to institute the quota, a wise act. There is room in Canada for some of the surplus population of the British Isles, and employment for them, but, at the present rate of increase from other sources, the population will soon, if it does not already, exceed the supply of labour that the country has to offer. Later, when the harm has been done, measures similar to those now in use on the other side of the line may have to be adopted, and the Briton, arriving here and finding the country overstocked, will naturally ask "Where do we go from here?"

The Southeastern European will work for less wages than the "white" races, and has therefore to a very large extent supplanted the old-time, happy-go-lucky lumberjack of song and story. This is

---

* Bohunk, a term applied to S.E. Europeans. They are rated as of the lowest grade of intelligence by U.S. Government standards. It is known that they frequently cause fires deliberately, in order to obtain employment fighting them.

to say nothing of other occupations he has seized on and monop-
olized, for no one will work with him.

He lowers the standard of living by existing under conditions
that the English-speaking and French-Canadian nationalities would
not tolerate, and in order to live the cheaper, in places where he
boards himself will kill every living creature from a whiskey-jack
up, to eke out his niggardly diet.

The "Bohunk" or "Bolshie" is seldom seen without a homemade cigarette, hanging from his lower lip, which he will carelessly
spit out into the inflammable forest litter. For days perhaps the dry
muck will smoulder along, until a breeze springs up and fans the
"smudge" into a blaze which leaps quickly from one resinous tree
to another, till the whole forest is in flames.

This type herds together in communities where the whole
output of his labour is just sufficient to support life, and generally in sections where the timber he cuts and destroys is worth
infinitely more than his contribution to the wealth of the country.

At the present time, in some sections, timber as a national
asset is worthy of far more consideration than the attempts at
agriculture carried on in the same area. Forest regions of the
backwoods, of the semi-cultivated type, abound with deserted
farms, which, having run out owing to poor soil, serve no purpose save that of creating a fire hazard when overgrown with
wild hay.

I venture to say, and I am upheld in this by recent findings
of expert silviculturists, that a large percentage of the land now
under so-called cultivation in forest regions, would be of far
greater value under timber, and should never have been opened
for settlement in the first place.

Agricultural overproduction has, in some parts of the country, reached such a pitch that many farmers are feeding the
best of grain to their cattle and pigs as being a more profitable
method of disposal than selling it, whilst as an example of market prices, they must sell eggs at 5 and 10 cents a dozen and

butter at 15 cents a pound, as against 40 cents and 35 cents in former times. Many farmers with large holdings are mortgaged to the hilt. These are cold facts and will bear investigation; and although those who are engaged in the emigrant trade (for so it can well be called) may not agree with these statements, bankers and others doing business in these areas will.

And yet with a worldwide business depression in full swing, and an unemployment tally of many thousands to account for, we allow transportation concerns to issue flamboyant literature far and wide with a view to attracting to these shores boatloads of unwanted foreign-born "settlers." A period of readjustment and retrenchment, followed up by properly balanced and strictly enforced immigration legislation, will be necessary before any influx of unskilled, ignorant peasantry can be looked on with equanimity by the citizens of this Dominion.

The forest-fire menace in Canada is very real, yet the continued carelessness of unintelligent vandals, who get into the country simply because they have so much money, can't speak English, and do not happen to have consumption or a wooden leg, is destroying as much, if not more, valuable timber than is cut for useful purposes. Hundreds of square miles of the finest forests now remaining on the American Continent, trees that were old when Wolfe stormed the citadel at Quebec, will be carelessly burnt every summer to provide a Roman holiday for an alien race. It would not be fair to blame the "Hunky" for all the fires, but with less of him the fire risk would be much reduced.

As an example of the spirit of some of these foreigners who, in certain districts, infest our forest countries, I will give an experience of my own. It fell to my lot to be passing a lumber crew just as a fire, of which they themselves were the originators, entered the green bush adjacent to their cuttings and was fast eating its way into the Government Reserve. As a Ranger it became my duty to take charge of the situation and I was obliged to call on the entire crew of two camps, some eighty or ninety men all told. When they assembled I saw at a glance that every man-jack was a Bohonk.

My troops were useless from the start. They shambled along with hands in pockets, or unwillingly holding shovels or axes, babbling and cackling in their own language. I caught more than one covert glance and sneering inflection cast my way and looked for trouble. I distributed them as best I could, an operation which much resembled that of lining up a herd of pigs on a skating rink, and turned them loose on the fire.

While passing along the edge of the burn, noting the wind, direction the fire was taking, locating water and such things, I noticed the two foremen, Germans, (good solid citizens they were too), two French cooks and some choreboys working like demons at a spot otherwise deserted. The foremen should have been foreing, the cooks cooking and the choreboys choring, but it transpired that the Bolsheviek had deserted in a body and had taken the bush, hiding out from the distasteful job, and these men had turned out to fight the fire alone.

"The Soviet sons-of-dogs," swore one German. "Wait till I get them birds into the big timber!"

I routed out all the slackers I could find, and passed up and down the entire fighting-line, wheedling, threatening, and cursing, until at last I became so exasperated that I threw the light axe I carried at one of the most impudent of them, close enough to startle him, where it stuck into a cedar with a good solid "chuck," an Indian trick, and hitherto used only as a pastime. This created some impression, and by brandishing the axe, and a fluent use of all the profanity I could invent, better results were obtained.

And this was the spirit with which these men, aspiring to become citizens of a new and progressive country, met an emergency that was destroying their very means of livelihood, and for which they themselves were responsible.

I fail to see what right men such as these have to a share in the unearned increment of Canada, whilst the English-speaking and French-Canadian workers are shouldered aside to make room for them. It will keep Canada busy absorbing the British population she is getting, a people who would have the interests of the country at heart, without having to divide up their birthright among a clamouring multitude of undesirables, who should never have gotten past the immigration barriers.

For a woodsman to revisit a country that he once knew as virgin and find it has been destroyed by fire is like coming home and finding the house burnt. Trappers and Indians rarely set fire; if they did their occupation would be soon gone. No man will burn his own property, and the proprietary feeling of these people towards their stamping grounds is very real. Most of them are the best unofficial Fire Rangers we have.

It is a serious misfortune, nay, a catastrophe of sweeping proportions, for a trapper to be burnt out, or see his territory going up in smoke. I know whereof I speak, having had the distress of seeing the greater portion of a well-loved and familiar landscape destroyed by a fire in the space of forty-eight hours, I myself and several others barely escaping with our lives, and this necessitated my moving out of the district entirely. I was in the Fire Service at the time, and on going out to the village for provisions was detained by the Chief as smoke had been observed in a district with which he knew me to be familiar. That same evening an Indian, having paddled fifty miles without stopping, save for portages, came in and reported the exact location of the fire, which had come from somewhere south and west, and was fast eating its way into my hunting ground.

The next day a gang of hastily hired rangers and Indians started for the scene of the trouble. The main route was very circuitous, and more than once my fortunate knowledge of the presence of beaver enabled us to make use of several shortcuts, the dams being in good condition, and the shallow creeks, otherwise unnavigable, being well flooded. With these things in our favour we arrived within ten miles of our objective late on the first day and we began to hear the roar of the fire. That night, as we camped, sparks and large flakes of dead ashes fell into the tenting ground, and the sky was lit up by the terrible, but beautiful and vivid glare of a sea of flames. Much delayed by numerous portages, it was not until noon the next day that we were within measurable distance of the conflagration, which was a "hum-dinger." There was a considerable mountain between us and the fire, and along the foot of this we tugged and hauled heavily loaded canoes up a shallow river, plugged with old fallen timber. Sparks, brands, and burning birch bark fell about us unheeded. Sweating white men cursed and heaved, and passed scathing remarks on the owner of the country who did not keep his rivers in shape — myself. Patient, silent Indians juggled canoes and their loads with marvelous dexterity from one point of least resistance to another. Men of four nations waded in mud to the knees, broke paddles, and ripped canvas from canoe-bottoms, unreprimanded by an eloquent and forceful Chief.

At his desire I described a short route to the fire area, and he swiftly made his plans and disposed his forces. My allotted sector, with two Crees, was the mountain, at the foot of which a couple of men made camp. Once up the mountain, from which we had a plain view of the camp, we separated, each taking a different direction, in order to get three observation angles on the fire from the eminence. Once alone, and in a fever of anxiety concerning my possible losses, I plunged ahead at full speed, angling towards the greatest volume of sound. I must mention here, that being used to moccasins, I was much hampered by a pair of stiff hard-soled larrigans which I had donned for firefighting purposes, and in which at times I was at some pains to keep on my feet.

I was suddenly startled by the sight of a bear which lumbered by me, bound for the river. A rabbit raced almost between my legs, then another and another. The roar had become deafening, and the heat almost unbearable, and I strained every muscle to attain the western, or far, crest of the mountain, before it became untenable for my purpose. I saw another galloping rabbit, and noticed curiously that it was passing from the left, when it should have been coming head on. A partridge flew, again from my left, struck a tree, and fell to the ground, scorched, blinded, and gasping. It I killed in mercy.

Just then I detected a sharper undertone of sound underlying the deeper heavy roar ahead of me, and on looking to the left and behind me, towards the line of flight of the bird, from whence it seemed to come, I saw the thin crackling line of a ground-fire creeping swiftly towards me like a molten carpet, now within a hundred yards of me, and backed at no great distance by a seething wall of flames. The fire had met me more than halfway, and had thrown out a flanking party. I was neatly trapped.

I turned and incontinently fled, making for the widest part of the V of flames, as the main conflagration had now caught up. And here is where my hard-soled 'packs* came in. Unused to boots, I found I could not run on the slippery jack-pine needles without losing time, and it took all of whatever willpower I may possess to tone my movements down to a swift walk, and curb my desire to race, and scramble, and tear my way regardless of boots, direction or anything else, just run — run. The flames were now on three sides of me, and my clothes were becoming brittle. Fortunately the intense heat kept the smoke up so that if I could keep my distance I was in no danger of suffocation; the danger lay in a very probable enveloping movement by the enemy.

I saw some harrowing sights. Dumb creatures endeavouring to save their lives from the one element against which all are helpless, some succeeding, others not. I saw tiny partridges in huddled groups, some lying on their backs with leaves in their

---

* Shoepacks, also larrigans; an oil-tanned moccasin of heavy leather, sometimes having a boot-like sole.

claws, beneath which they deemed themselves invisible, realizing that there was danger somewhere, and using the only protection that they knew. And — I know of no greater love that a mother can have than this — I saw the hen bird sitting dumbly by, unable to herd the little creatures to safety, waiting to burn with them.

The smoke darkened the brightness of noonday, but the cavern of flames lit up the immediate surroundings with a dull red glow. I was keeping ahead of the fire but my direction began to be a matter of doubt. "Follow the animals," I kept thinking; but all that could had gone by, and now there were no more. I forced back my terrible fear. I caught myself saying, "You can't make me run, you — you can't make me run," and there I was running and slipping and stumbling in my deadly footwear; and with a jerk I slowed, or rather accelerated, to my swiftest walk.

More partridges, eyeing me dumbly from low limbs, and the chicks huddled beneath: oh the pity of it! Two more rabbits: follow them, follow them, fast! A small muskeg showed up; I raced for it expecting a pond: there was none. Past the muskeg and on. The growth of small cypress that cluttered the forest here became very thick. Surrounded by smoke, now commencing to billow down with the back-draught of the fire, my brain reeling with the heat, with the horror of what was too probably to be my funeral pyre driving me on, I scrambled desperately ahead, with no thought but to keep the advancing flanks of the destroyer behind me.

My feet seemed leaden, and my head a shell, light and empty, as I squirmed with desperate contortions to force a way through the continuous barrier, like a cane-brake, of small trees. I could no longer keep any specific direction, but knew I must now be far past the camp. I thought momentarily of my two companions; I had long since passed the area they had been assigned to. And then, breaking at length through the last of the barrier of saplings, I burst out on to the eastern brow of the mountain. Fire goes but slowly down a hill, so I took time to breathe, and looking down could see the camp; and from its proximity I knew that my ordeal by fire had not lasted over twenty minutes, if that, though I would have sworn that it had occupied an hour.

The campground itself was a scene of the utmost confusion. Tents were being pulled down by main force and jammed into canoes, sometimes poles and all; pots, blankets, baggage, and equipment of all kinds, seemed, at that distance, to be picked up in quantities and dumped onto the nearest craft.

I descended the mountain, the fire commencing to creep over its edge, and found waiting for me with a canoe one of the Crees who had gone up with me. He had seen me coming out on the summit, expecting me there as he watched the course of the fire. He grinned and spoke in English:

"Hot like hell, eh?"

"Some," I replied soberly, as I felt the split and scorched back of my canvas shirt.

On the river just above the camp was a live beaver-dam, and it came as a timely assistance in aiding us to make our getaway, deepening the river so that we reached without loss of time a mile and a half portage leading inland to a large lake. This, one of my main trails, was in good shape, and we moved over it at nothing less than a trot. To check the fire was impossible without a change of wind, and in any case reinforcements were necessary.

The Chief and one man commenced the return trip to get help, and from what I saw of the river afterwards, and judging by the two men's description, the first part of the journey must have been something in the nature of running the gauntlet. The fire had crossed the river for most of its length in the interim, and was yet burning on both sides in many places. The aftermath of a fire is often as dangerous as the element itself, as trees, tottering on burnt-out stumps or severed roots, fall without warning. On the section of the stream where the logjams were, necessitating delays, these men were in danger of being killed or injured at any minute, as trees fell without warning across the river, and into it. On the lower reaches the fire was still burning, but here the water was fortunately deeper, and when some blaze hotter than common was encountered, the men crouched, half-submerged under the overturned canoe, which lying with its gunwales completely under water, afforded an airtight shelter as long as the canvas should last, or until the blaze died down. They told of a big bull moose with scorched hair and staring eyes, that fell exhausted into the water, and lay there sucking air into the tortured lungs in great gasps, paying no more attention to the canoe than had it been a floating chip. I saw on those waters dozens, no less, of small birds of all kinds floating dead along the river banks and young things such as half-fledged waterfowl, tiny squirrels, and odd humming-birds, that had made the water only to drown or die of suffocation; a pitiful sight.

Moose we found dead — by the smell, a week later — that for some unexplainable reason had died within reach of water, but no bears, although these latter were making full use of the banquet all ready cooked and served for their convenience.

My camp and complete outfit were saved, but my heart was saddened by the thought of the terrible loss of life amongst my poor beasts, and the destruction of the noble jack-pine forest in which I had roamed so long.

Amongst the Indians on this expedition there was an old man, a conjurer, whose name means "The Little Child." He was the oldest man in the party, and the leadership of this "little child" in matters of bush technique was tacitly accepted by all. This ancient carried a drum. He took charge of the Indians in a very effective manner, but did no work. The Chief had noticed this, and had asked me to speak for him concerning the matter, and the following conversation ensued:

"Little Child, why do you not work, as the others are doing."

"Because," replied Little Child, "I am here for another purpose."

"But," said the Chief, "I thought you were here to fight fire."

Little Child shook his head, and speaking gently, as to one who is mentally deficient, said:

"You do not understand. I am not here to fight that fire; I am here to put it out!"

The two ideas being synonymous in the executive's long experience, he found this a little puzzling.

"What do you mean by that?" he asked.

"Wait and see," replied the Indian.

Knowing better than to give direct orders to one of his race the Chief went on his way; but I waited, and I saw. What actually happened was remarkable enough. The weather had been hot, the sun shining without intermission for many days, and there was every sign of these conditions lasting indefinitely. This made our work the harder. Nevertheless, the next day Little Child deserted the party, taking his drum. As he left he said to me:

"I am now going to put out the fire. Two days, maybe three; wait and see!"

He secreted himself a mile away on a hill, and during two evenings and the whole of two nights we heard that drum, with never a break in its rhythm; tum-tum, tum-tum, tum-tum, tum-tum; the double staccato beat of the conjuror. The nights were very calm, and we heard, thinly, the high-pitched undulations of a three- or four-note chant continuously repeated. Incessantly, without change it came and went, swelled and flattened to a prolonged minor note, and commenced again; until some of the white men, who were not used to that kind of thing, began to feel uneasy as to what it could mean. The Crees and Ojibways lapsed into a listless apathy, but none the less, each one of them could have posed for a statue intended to portray intense attention. At noon of the third day Little Child came down, put his drum into a gaily decorated case, and demanded something to eat. He had not broken his fast during three days. After he had eaten he said:

"I will now sleep. Tonight it will rain; tomorrow there will be no fire. Meheu! It is finished."

Some time after midnight all hands awoke to a torrential downpour that streamed over the dried earth and under tents, to soak up through groundsheets and blankets; but we cared not, our work was done; the fire was out.

And Little Child had made a reputation as being either a magician of satanic abilities, or the best weather-prophet in Eastern North America.

IX

THE HOUSE OF MCGINNIS

On the sunny banks of it,
Thoughtful little creatures sit.
— STEVENSON

A loud thud, a crash, the tinkle of broken glass, then silence. A sound as of a handsaw being run at great speed by an expert, a bumping, dragging noise and a vicious rattling; then another crash; more silence.

"And what," asked my guest as we neared the camp, "is that; an earthquake?"

"That," I answered, with some misgiving, "is the beaver, the ones you are coming to see!"

We entered the cabin, and the scene within was something to be remembered, the devastation resembling that left in the wake of a young whirlwind. The table was down, and the utensils it had held had disappeared; a four-foot stick of wood protruded through a shattered window, and below the one that remained a quantity of wood had been piled, affording facilities for the effective use of a battering ram. The washstand had been dissected and neatly piled in the bunk from which the blankets had been removed, these being included in a miscellany of articles such as dishes, moccasins, and so forth, with which the stove was barricaded. With hurried apologies to my visitor I assessed the damage, but beyond the disarrangements just mentioned, there was no serious harm done; that is, so far, no lives had been lost. I had been away two days, being delayed by soft weather, which, with its exhilarating effect on these animals, accounted for the delirious attack on my humble fixtures.

There was no sign of the raiders, they having retreated to their house at the presence of a stranger; but later they appeared and were introduced, and again retired, hopping and capering like little round gnomes, taking with them the peace offerings of chocolate and apples which they accepted, after considerable diplomatic manoeuvring, from my companion.

McGinty and McGinnis, having put their house in order, were receiving from five to half past, the guest providing the luncheon.

After open water on until early in June, the spring hunt is in full swing on the frontier, and towards the end of that period the young beaver are born. The mother, who lives at this time in a separate lodge built and tended by the male or buck beaver, being generally larger than the rest of the family is much sought after. She is easily caught close to the house, and drowns at the entrance, whilst the kittens within listen in terror to her frantic struggles to escape. Crying continuously in child-like wails, they wait in vain for the big kindly brown body that is supporting their feeble existence, till the thin little voices are stilled, and two pitifully small bundles of fur cease to move, and lie in the house to rot.

A neighbouring hunter once came to me and asked if I would come and remove a live beaver from a trap from which the drowning-stone had come loose. After several hours' travelling we arrived at the spot, when my companion refused to go to the trap, saying he could not bring himself to inflict any further torture on the suffering creature.

"Wait till you see," he told me.

I went to the place he described, and this is what I saw.

The beaver, a large female, moaning with pain, was shaking the trap that was firmly clamped on one front foot, and with the other she held close to her breast, nursing it, a small kitten beaver, who, poor little fellow, little knew how close he was to having his last meal.

I liberated her as gently as possible, and she made no effort to bite me.

With a sharp blow of my axe I severed the crushed and useless paw, when, parched with thirst, she immediately commenced to drink the blood which flowed from the wound as though it had been water. She then made slowly and painfully for the lake, only to return for the young one, who had become intensely interested in my footwear and was with difficulty prevailed on to enter the water. My companion approved of my action, although he had lost a valuable hide; he had seen the young one there, he said, and his heart had turned to water. This experience gave me some food for thought, and had its effect in hastening a decision I later arrived at, to quit the beaver hunt altogether.

Since that occurrence I have been the means of saving several pairs of small lives by following the carcass-strewn trails of the spring hunters, keeping the little fellows for about a year, after which period they get too reckless with the furniture to be any further entertained as guests.

Only those who have had the opportunity of studying living specimens over an extended period can obtain any idea of the almost human mentality of these likeable little creatures. Destructive they are, and their activities have much the same effect on the camp that two small animated sawmills running loose would have. They resemble somewhat an army tank, being built on much the same lines, and progressing in a similar manner, over or through anything that is in the way. After the first six months they can sink themselves through a six inch log at a remarkable speed, biting lengthways with the grain of the wood for three or four inches, cutting the cross section at each end and pulling out the chip.

They roam around the camp, and, with no evil intent but apparently from just sheer joy of living, take large slices out of table-legs, and chairs, and nice long splinters out of the walls, and their progress is marked by little piles and strings of chips. This in the fore part of the evening. After "lights out" the more serious work commences, such as the removal of deerskin rugs, the transferring of firewood from behind the stove into the middle of the floor, or the improvement of some waterproof footwear by the addition of a little openwork on the soles. They will gnaw a hole in a box of groceries to investigate, and are very fond of toilet soap, one brand in particular preferred, owing, no doubt, to the flavour incident to its school-girl complexion-giving qualities.

In winter they will not leave the camp and I sink a small bath tub in the floor for them, as they need water constantly. They make a practice of lying in the tub eating their sticks and birch tops, later climbing into the bunk to dry themselves. To accomplish this they sit upright and squeeze and scrub the entire body. The water never penetrates beyond the guard hairs into the fur, but I suppose half a pint is no exaggeration of the amount of water one of them will squeeze out of his coat.

Tiring of this performance, I once removed the bench by which they climbed into the bunk and prepared for a good night's rest at last. I had got so used to the continuous racket they created all night, between the drying-off periods, that, like the sailor who hired a man to throw pails of water against the walls of his house all night while on shore, I could not sleep so well without the familiar sounds, and during the night I awoke to an ominous silence. With a premonition of evil I lit the lamp and on taking stock saw one of my much-prized Hudson Bay blankets hanging over the edge of the bunk, and cut into an assortment of fantastic patterns, the result of their efforts to climb into the bed. The regularity of the designs startled me, and I began to wonder if I had gone suddenly insane, as nothing short of human agency, it seemed, could have cut those loops and triangles so symmetrically. Closer examination showed that the effect had been produced by their gathering the blanket in bunches with their forepaws, and cutting out a few pieces from the pucker, with more or less pleasing results.

Apparently realizing, by the tone of certain carelessly worded remarks which I allowed to escape me, that they had gone a little too far this time, the guilty parties had tactfully retired to their trench under the wall, awaiting developments. This excavation they had made themselves. In building the camp I had made an aperture in the bottom log, and constructed outside it, at great trouble, what was, I considered, a pretty good imitation of a beaver house. The first night in they had inspected my work, found it unsuitable, and proceeded to block up the entrance with sacking. They then commenced operations under the bunk, cutting a hole in the floor for the purpose, and digging out the soil. This dirt they trundled up from the depths, pushing it ahead of them, walking with the hind feet only, the forepaws and chin being used to hold the mass together. Whilst thus engaged they rather resembled automatic wheelbarrows. They brought up, on each journey, perhaps the full of a two-quart measure apiece of earth, which was painstakingly spread on the floor as it accumulated; as the tunnel was dug out for about six feet beyond the wall, there was quite an amount of dirt brought into the shack, and there were times when I, also, was quite busy with a shovel. They took my interference in good part, hopping and capering about my feet in their clumsy way, much as I imagine elephants would gambol. They eventually got pretty well organized, one sleeping and the other working in shifts of two or three hours each.

After about a week of this a large mound of earth was eventually patted down smooth and solid near the water supply, and operations apparently brought to a satisfactory conclusion; so I considered that we should all now take a good rest. But the beaver is not a restful animal. Doubtless they had been warned by those advertisements that remind us that those "soft foods are ruining our teeth," for anything that offered resistance enough was bitten, the harder the better. Anything that gave good tooth-holds was hauled, and everything that could be pushed was pushed high, west, and sideways. Quantities of birch-bark were carried into the bunk and shredded, this contribution to the sleeping accommodation supposedly entitling them to a share of the blankets. They apparently took notice that I put wood into the stove at intervals, and in a spirit, no doubt, of co-operation, at times they piled various articles against the stove. Once when I had been out for a short time, I returned to find the camp full of smoke, and a pillow, a deerskin rug, and a map of some value to me, piled around the stove, and all badly scorched. Eventually I was obliged to erect a wire screen for safety.

It is remarkable that in spite of the orgy of destruction that went on for the first two weeks in camp, the door, an easy target, was not molested, and nothing was cut that would occasion an air leak into the camp. It is their nature to bank up against the intrusion of cold, and any loose materials that they could gather would be piled along the foot of the door, where there was a certain amount of draught. They barred the door so effectually on one occasion that I had to remove a window to enter the cabin.

Some mornings, at daylight, I would awaken to find one on each side of me sleeping, lying on their backs snoring like any human. At intervals during sleep they sharpen their teeth in readiness for the next onslaught. When working, if the teeth do not seem to be in good shape, they pause for half a minute or so and sharpen them, repeating this until they are suited. The skull is fitted with a longitudinal slot which allows for the necessary motion of the jaws, and the resultant grinding is much like the whetting of an axe. The sound of an axe or knife being filed struck them with terror, and they would drop everything and run to me for protection, evidently thinking the noise came from some large animal whetting its teeth.

Beaver are the most persevering creatures I know of, man not excepted, and any job which they undertake is never abandoned until completed or proved impossible. They conduct their operations with all the serious intentness and economy of movement of trained artisans, and at the conclusion of each stage, small adjustments are made, and little pats and pushes given, either expressing satisfaction with the work or testing its solidity, I know not which.

These queer little people are also good housekeepers. Branches brought in for their feed are immediately seized on and piled to one side of the entrance to their abode. After feeding on pancakes or bread pudding, which they dearly love, the dish is pushed away into some far corner, along with the peeled sticks and other used portions of feed. Their beds, consisting of sacks, which they tear to shreds, mixed with shredded birch-bark and long, very fine shavings cut from the floor, after being used for a period, are brought out and scattered on the floor, apparently to dry, and taken in again after a couple of days. They spend long periods on their toilet. One of the toes of the webbed hind feet is jointed so as to bend in any direction, and is fitted with a kind of double claw; with this they comb their entire coat.

They seem capable of great affection, which they show by grasping my clothing with their strong forepaws, very hands in function, pushing their heads into some corner of my somewhat angular personality, bleating and whimpering. At times they clamour for attention, and if taken notice of they shake their heads from side to side, rolling on their backs with squeals of joy. If left alone for as long as twenty-four hours, on my return they are very subdued until I talk to them, when they at once commence their uncouth gambols and their queer wrestling.

They conduct these wrestling matches — for they can be called nothing else — by rising on their hind feet, supported by the tail, while the forepaws are locked in neck and underarm holds, looking like dancers. In this position they strain and push, each striving to overcome the other, until one begins to give way, walking backwards, still erect, pushed by his adversary. Then, perhaps by the judicious use of his tail, he recovers, prevails, and the walk commences in the opposite direction. They go at this for all they are worth, and the changes in the expression of their voices, according to the luck they are having, are remarkably plain. This performance resembles a violently aggressive foxtrot about as closely as it does anything else, and is continued until one or the other allows his tail to double under him and is bowled overt protesting loudly.

One peculiarity they have is that, when hungry, they do not fawn as most domestic animals do, but complain loudly, standing on their hind legs and grasping at the dish. If the food is withheld they scold shrilly, beating the air with their forepaws. Also, if in their work they fail in some object such as the placing of a stick, they jerk the limbs and head violently and show every sign of irritation, resuming the attempt with an impetuous violence that either makes or breaks. But as a rule they are very tractable, and after feeding will follow one all over the camp, and at times are rather a nuisance in their desire to be taken up and petted.

The male beaver has, to a certain extent, the protective instinct that dogs possess, but not of course so highly developed. I had no knowledge of this until one day I happened to be resting on my blankets on the floor after a trip — a common custom in the woods — and lying with his head on my shoulder was a six months old buck beaver. An Indian friend came in, and busied himself in some way that brought him close to my head, on the opposite side from my furry chum. Immediately the latter crossed over and stationed himself between the man's feet and my person. My friend found it necessary to pass around me, and the beaver made a quick shortcut across my face, and again took post between us. Noticing this, and thinking it might be coincidence, my companion returned to his former position, and the beaver returned also, again using my face for a runway, blowing and hissing his disapproval. It is the more remarkable in that the man was a frequent visitor, and on the best of terms with both animals, playing with them by the hour during my absence.

Another time I received a visit from a passing hunter, and on his entrance, the female beaver, always more docile than her mate, must needs go over and make an inspection of the newcomer. The male also went towards him, with every sign of disapproval, and on the stranger stooping to pat the other, reached out with his hand-like forepaw, and endeavoured to pluck her away.

Beaver are far from being the dumb creatures that most animals are. While working they are continually murmuring and muttering, even if alone, and if some distance apart occasionally signal their position by short, sharp cries. It is very rarely that speaking to them does not elicit some kind of answer.

They have a large range of distinctly different sounds. The emotions of rage, sorrow, fear, joy, and contentment are expressed quite differently, and are easily recognized after a short period of observation. Often when a conversation is being carried on they will join in with their vocal gymnastics, and the resemblance to the human voice is almost uncanny to those not accustomed to hearing it, and has been partly the cause of their undoing, as they are a very easy animal to imitate. When in trouble they whimper in the most dolorous fashion, and become altogether disconsolate. They have an imitative faculty of a sort, as any kind of bustle or quick moving around results in a like activity on their part, entailing a good deal of unnecessary gathering and pushing and dragging.

In common with most animals when tamed, beaver will answer to a name. In Canada an Irishman is known as "a Mick," and the Indian word for beaver, Ahmik, is identical in pronunciation. So I gave them Irish names, of which the two most notable were McGinty and McGinnis, names they got to know very well, and they were suitable in more ways than one, as they both had peppery tempers, and would fight at the drop of the hat anything or anybody, regardless of size, always excepting each other or myself.

My camp became known as "The House of McGinnis," although McGinty, whimsical, mischievous as a flock of monkeys, being the female was really the boss of the place; and although I am deficient in the art of making the best mousetraps, all the world hereabouts has made a beaten path to my door on their account.

In the spring they become very restless, and nothing short of confinement in a wire pen will hold them. If allowed to go they will travel far and wide; they do not forget their old home, but will return after three or four weeks, and feed all around the camp, using it as a headquarters and eventually settling in the vicinity.

I turned the two Mc's loose last spring and they made themselves a small house and a dam on a pond in a little valley back of a mountain called the Elephant, and would come when called and enter the cabin, which practice they have continued till the present time. They would always answer at intervals all the way down the lake, a not loud but very clear and penetrating sound, much like two notes of a violin sounded together, which changed to the "hoo! hoo!" of welcome as they landed. They have ventriloquial powers, as have some other creatures in the forest country, and at times it was impossible to tell the direction from which they were coming. This no doubt is a protection against the prying ears of certain beasts with a taste for beaver meat.

Domesticated beaver will under no circumstances bite a human being, and if annoyed they will hold a finger between their dangerous teeth, exerting only just so much pressure, screeching with rage meanwhile. At a sharp exclamation they will release their hold. They are no mean adversaries in a fight, striking a series of quick raking blows with the heavy pointed claws of the front feet, and they have been known to kill dogs with one slashing bite of their razor-edged teeth, aimed always at the throat.

In the wild state they mate for life, and in captivity they show the same fidelity to the hand that reared them. They are a "one-man dog," accepting neither food nor favour from strangers, puffing and blowing their dissatisfaction at the near approach of one they do not know; yet this little beast, with the mind of a man and the ways of a child, can work his way very deeply into the affections of those who get to know him, and I have been offered sums of money out of all proportion to their actual value, but cannot bring myself to sell them into captivity.

It is a remarkable fact that the hand-raised beaver do not, to my knowledge, associate with their own kind, building for themselves within a short distance of others, but never on the same pond.

It is indeed difficult to guess what mental processes take place back of the bright beady eyes in those thick skulls. It is hard to doubt that they are governed by something more than instinct, as they sit and ponder, seeming to deliberate before making some move. But undoubtedly this same instinct is very strong, as, turned loose at the age of a year, and with no experience, they conduct their affairs with the efficiency, though lacking for a time the ingenuity, of their wild brethren; but it leaves much to be accounted for.

Indians become much attached to them as pets, and refer to them as "Little Indians." I know of a young girl who had a much-loved pair of young beaver, that once in their daily swim were swept away on the spring flood, and were unable to return, as their habit generally was. It was at a time of year when the deep snow lining the creek beds was underlaid by a foot or so of icy water, and snowshoes would not bear up. Yet this child negotiated several miles of streamland under these conditions, through the tangled growth of willows and alders, crawling on her hands and knees for long distances over the hollow snowbanks. In spite of this device to distribute her weight, she broke through repeatedly and waded in the icy slush, only, on overtaking them, to find her little friends unable to make shore. She was overtaken by her people, who found it no easy task to dissuade her from further useless exposure, and she was obliged to return to the camp without her pets, whom she mourned as for lost friends.

It speaks well for the race that, within a reasonable area around the village, no traps were set that spring by the hunters, and the following fall the two beaver were located. By common consent, of white hunter and Indian alike, they were spared until a half-breed heard the story. He agreed with the rest not to molest them, but, with the lack of sportsmanship which, unfortunately, characterizes so many of his type, at the first opportunity killed them both.

Up the lake half a mile from my camp there lives a little beaver, the remaining one of a pair one of which died last summer. He spends his nights with me, sharing my bed and board. He seems to miss his small companion that is gone, and has none of the light-hearted devilry of his forerunners. I fixed up an old beaver house, placed a large quantity of feed for him, and turned him loose. But he will not stay loose. Every night until the ice came he was at the camp door at dark.

He is a sad little creature as he sits forlornly on the floor. He has none of the non-subcutaneous beauty that so undermines the talent of certain screen idols, yet who knows but that in the wee old-fashioned brain there is not some dim recollection of happy days of romping and tumbling with just such another clumsy ball of fur in the deep, cool grass on the river bank. And as he regards me gravely, sitting on my feet the while, my heart goes out to the little waif who does not want to be free, and I pick him up and pass my hand over the rich, dark fur, and he sighs contentedly and immediately falls asleep to dream of cool waters, and mud, of poplar leaves and pancakes.

He is small, weighing perhaps ten pounds, but of the two of us he is the better bushman, mainly on account of a few simple things that he can do and I cannot — for instance break ice with my head, cut wood with my teeth, or find my way under half a mile of ice to an unmarked hole in the dark; all very useful accomplishments in this walk of life.

His visits are more irregular now as no doubt it is a ticklish job negotiating that lengthy swim without coming up for air. I was anxious to observe how he was able to do this, so watched him for several hours with a flashlight. His method was to create a considerable disturbance at the water-hole until a bubble of air had formed at its edge under the ice. To this, when large enough, he attached himself, and swam away with it. The bladder of air enveloped his head and most of his back; at intervals he would make holes in the ice, probably to renew the air supply. This occurred three times in the fifteen or so minutes it took him to cover the distance.

When the ice gets thicker this performance will become impossible, and he will pass the winter in the house of McGinnis, who, with McGinty the sly, the capricious, and the inquisitive, has now a lodge of his own designing, on a lake not a mile from this camp. I often wonder if my old-timers remember their trips in a box over many portages, the six-hundred-mile train ride, the journey which they made inside a stove when the canoe swamped and they nearly drowned. Or if they have a passing thought for the torn deerskin rugs, and the cut table legs, and the chewed blankets; the wrestling matches, and the long sleeps on a warm soft bed; or if they will ever know of the big empty space they left when they went away, as they lie in their small mud hut on the little round pond where the Elephant Mountain stands guard.* Today I kill no more beaver, but am bent on repairing in some small measure the damage done in younger and more thoughtless days; replacing at least a part of what I have destroyed,

---

* These beaver are still with the writer, visiting camp regularly several times day and night, and are so domesticated that, even after six months at a time of isolation in their winter lodge, they emerge in spring perfectly tame.

restoring dried-out lakes to their fullness of contented families, bringing life where is nought but desolation. That I may hear in the long evenings, as in the old days, the splash of huge flat tails on the water as the working parties change shift; the queer child-like cries as they wrestle on the leaves beneath the silvery poplars that are their life, the crooning of the mothers within the lodges tending their young. That I may see the dark and gloomy forest shores shining again with Wasacsena,* the brightness of newly peeled sticks, and visit and marvel over the carefully dug canals and the sand pits. And perhaps at times I may glimpse a wise old head, the head of Mishomis, the Old Man, as a pair of bright black eyes, not unfriendly, but always cautious, watch covertly my every move from out the shadows near the shore. And I shall know that I am not, after all, alone in this mighty wilderness, whilst I have for neighbours the happy colonies of Ahmik, The Beaver People.

---

* Indian word for shining appearance of timber, denuded of bark, lying along the shoreline; caused by beaver, ice scraping, or natural driftwood.

X

THE TRAIL
OF TWO SUNSETS

I beheld our nations scattered,
...
Saw the remnants of our people
Sweeping westward wild and woeful,
Like the cloud-rack of a tempest,
Like the withered leaves of Autumn.
— LONGFELLOW

Longfellow sorely grasped the true spirit of the wilderness when he wrote *Hiawatha*, and shows a knowledge of Indian life and customs that is uncommon. So much is this recognized among Indians that, at this late day, and since many years, the poem has been perpetuated by them in the form of a yearly play, held in its natural setting of woods and waters at a place called Desbarato on Lake Huron, where, these people claim, Longfellow spent a long time gathering his material, living amongst them meanwhile. There are some hundred performers, amongst whom no article of white man's clothing, and no word of English is permitted during the week of the celebration. Their rendering of the Indian Songs is worth going far to hear. These are the Garden River Ojibways and Algonquins; I have hunted a good deal with these people in the Mississauga River country, and once on an occasion when I assisted in promoting a tribal celebration at Biscotasing, Ontario, a number of them travelled nearly two hundred miles by canoe to take part in it.

Back in 1876 when the combined forces of the Sioux, the Cheyennes, and the Pawnees defeated General Custer in the ill-advised fiasco which resulted in the demolition of his entire command, the wiser chiefs, having formed by that time a pretty fair idea of the methods of reprisal likely to be handed out, advised the departure from that place of the warriors involved.

Their scheme of holding Custer as a hostage against retaliation by the whites had been thwarted by that General blowing out his brains on the field of battle: a historical fact, long known only to the Indians themselves. And so, like guilty children who have only too successfully opposed the authority of their elders, they fled before the expected retribution, to Canada.

They had learned the bitter lesson that although battle won by the white man's soldiers was considered victory, a combat in which the Indians prevailed was termed a massacre. Their chiefs were hanged for participation in honest battle, whilst atrocities committed by the troops, such as took place at Klamath Lake and Wounded Knee, went unpunished. It speaks well for the policy of the Canadian Government towards Indians that these people saw Canada in the light of a sanctuary. As a result of the just and considerate treatment of the tribes coming under British control the Canadian frontier was, with the exception of the abortive

Rid Rebellion, singularly free from the brutalities, the injustice, the massacres, and the prolonged wars that so characterized the settling of the Western United States. But all that is over now. The Indian is an outcast in his native land, and the Indian population on both sides of the line is at peace for always, if a condition of gradual wasting away and disintegration can be so called.

A moiety have adopted the white man's ways, not always with success, and mostly with attendant degeneracy and lowering of national integrity; although individuals, even so, have risen to remarkable heights.

No longer do they produce great war chiefs, such as Tecumseh, Crowfoot, Dull Knife, and a hundred others, the necessity for them having long passed, but of the large number in the Canadian Expeditionary Force, more than one received a commission, several were NCOs, and as snipers many distinguished themselves, one, to my personal knowledge, winning the VC. Lately in the United States a man of Indian blood, Curtis by name, came close to the Presidential chair, and Pauline Johnstone, or Tekahionwake to give her her tribal name, is Canada's foremost poetess. Dr. Orokonateka became head of the Foresters, next to the Masons the most powerful organized society in Canada; there is an Indian artist of note, and Buffalo-Child Long-Lance is by no means the only Indian author. These are of course outstanding examples and, considering the small number of the race yet remaining, compare well numerically with the white man's achievements; for these people, and some others not mentioned, must be taken seriously, and not at all in the spirit of the old gentleman who once visited a college maintained for the education of Indians. On his tour of inspection he came across a young tribesman who was working away at a carpenter's bench. Astonished at the sight of an Indian engaged in such an occupation, he stared for a time and at length exclaimed:

"This is extraordinary; are you an Indian?"

The young man admitted he was.

"And are you civilized? " continued the old gentleman.

"No," replied the Indian, "are you?"

Another incident of the kind occurred at an exhibition where a Sioux chieftain, attired in the regalia to which his rank entitled him, was displaying some specimens of the handiwork of his tribe. He had much impressed those visitors who had come in contact with him by his quiet and gentlemanly bearing, and one of these, a lady of authentic Puritan ancestry, remarked patronizingly:

"An Indian warrior; how antique."

And the Indian looked at her steadily and replied:

"Yes, madam, 'antique' is correct. As residents of this country our people have at least the merit of antiquity."

Indian Chiefs, however able, have not, and never did have, absolute authority over their bands; they acted in an advisory capacity, and, their ideas being once accepted, the people placed themselves under their direction for that particular battle or journey; but the opinion of a whole tribe might run counter to the chief's policy, in which case the matter was decided by vote. This has given rise to the general impression that Indians are not amenable to discipline, but their record in the late war disproves this, and there is no doubt that had they been able to forget their tribal differences and jealousies and become properly organized, they could have put up a resistance that would have gained them better terms than they received, at the hands of their conquerors.

At the outbreak of war, a number of young men of the band with which I hunted, offered their services. Most of them could speak no English, and few had ever made a journey of any kind, save in a canoe. One patriotic soul, Pot-Mouth by name, offered to provide his own rifle, tent, and blankets. After several weeks in a training camp, where, owing to the retiring disposition of the forest-bred, he fared badly, this doughty warrior showed up one day at the trading post, in full uniform, purchased a quantity of supplies, and hit for his hunting ground. On his return for a second load he found an escort awaiting him and he was brought to trial as a deserter.

Through an interpreter, he stated, in his defence, that the board was poor, and that the officers had too much to say; so, there being as yet no sign of hostilities, he had decided to quit the job until the fighting started. He was leniently dealt with, and served as a sniper until "the job" was finished, having acquired in the meantime a good record, and a flow of profanity that could wither a cactus.

This independence of spirit has prevented the Indians as a race from entering the field of unskilled labour, but the members of some tribes have shown an aptitude for certain occupations requiring skill and activity.

The Iroquois of Caughnawauga are amongst the best bridge-builders in Canada; as canoemen the Crees, Ojibways, and Algonquins can be approached by no white man save, with few exceptions, those they themselves have trained; and although not companionable as guides they command a high wage where serious trips into difficult territories are contemplated.

There exists with a certain type of woodsman, not however in the majority, a distinct hostility towards the Indian, often the result of jealousy of the latter's undoubted superiority in wood-craft. They evince a good-natured contempt for the Indian's abilities in the woods, mainly because, not having travelled with him, they have not the faintest idea of the extent of his powers nor of the deep insight into the ways of the wilderness that he possesses, entailing knowledge of things of which they themselves have never even heard. For the red man does not parade his accumulated knowledge of two thousand years. He is by nature cautious, and an opportunist, seizing on every available means to attain his ends, working unobtrusively by the line of least resistance; and his methods of progress are such that a large band may pass through a whole district without being seen.

He is accused of pusillanimity because he follows the shore line of a lake when beating into a tempest, his purpose being to take advantage of the eddies and back currents of wind which exist there; whilst the tyro plunges boldly and obstinately down the centre of the lake, bucking the full force of the elements, shipping water and wetting his outfit, and often becoming wind-bound, or at least arriving at his destination some hours late.

This people, who knew the fine art of canoeing when in England bold knights fought for the favour of fair ladies, do not need to run rapids to gain experience, and will not do so, thereby risking water-soaked provisions, unless they may gain time by so doing. But, on the necessity arising, they face, without hesitation, white water and storms that their detractors would not for a moment consider. For this is their daily life; the novelty of the game was worn off somewhere around 1066, and they no more pass their time doing unnecessary stunts, than an expert runner would sprint to his daily work in a series of hundred yard dashes.

The genuine woodsman knows these things, and does not disdain to learn from his swarthy brother, attaining often a degree of excellence that causes even his teachers to look to their laurels. The Indian is not to be judged by the standards of civilization, and those who cast aspersion on his skill or manhood, from the fund of their slight experience, know not whereof they speak. In his own line he is supreme, and few know his worth who have not travelled with him. The Indian is rarely seen in lumber camps, for he was never an axeman to compare with the French-Canadian; but in river-driving, the operation of herding a half-million or so of logs down a river swollen with melted snows, and generously strewn with rapids, an occupation requiring a degree of quick-footed daring and swift judgment, he excels.

His knowledge of the idiosyncrasies of swift water is unsurpassed, and although less spectacular than his Gallic contemporary, awakened from his lethargy by the lively competition with his vivacious co-worker, he enters into the spirit of the game with zest. The famous Mohawk drivers are much in demand by companies whose holdings necessitate long drives of timber down rough and dangerous rivers such as the Ottawa, the Gatineau, the Madawaska, and other famous streams.

Civilization has had a certain influence on the more primitive Indians of the north in some districts, but rarely for good, as witness the shiftless, vagabond families living in squalid misery on some of the small reserves, where they are neither flesh, fish, nor fowl, nor yet good red Indian.

The Indian, and I refer now only to him whose life is spent in the Land of Shadows, although a dreamer and a visionary in his idle moments, is a being who lives by constant struggle against the elements, and some very signal virtues are called forth by the demands of his life. As many a business man, on quitting his chosen sphere of activity, becomes more or less atrophied, so the Indian, removed from his familiar occupations, and having no occasion for the exercise of his highly specialized faculties and ideas, loses out entirely.

Those Indians before mentioned who have attained national prominence belong to tribes whose geographical position was in their favour; civilization has made them fairly prosperous, and, excepting Long Lance who is, though educated, a splendid savage, they have two or three generations of civilization already behind them. Some are so fortunately situated as to have oil found on their reserves with the result that they are actually wealthy. But the Indians of the far north live much as their grandfathers did; they are too far behind to catch up in this generation and at the present rate of decrease they will not long outlive the frontier that is so rapidly disappearing.

To effect in a few years an advancement in them that it has taken the white man two thousand years to accomplish would entail their removal; and to wrench them loose from their sur-roundings and suddenly project them into the pitiless, competitive maelstrom of modern life would be equivalent to curing a sick man by hanging him, or loading a sinner into a sixteen-inch gun and shooting him up into heaven. Or, to come back to earth, requesting the Indian to exchange the skilful manipulation of pole, paddle, and snowshoe, in which his soul rejoices, for the drudgery of a shovel on a small backwoods farm, the first step in the reclaiming of which requires him to destroy the forest on which he looks as a home, is to ask an artist to dig graves, for an artist he surely is in his line, and the grave would be his own.

The coming of civilization does not surround the northern tribes with prosperous farmers or the multifarious chances of employment as it did in more favoured districts; it merely destroys their means of livelihood, without offering the compensations of the more productive areas.

Left to his own devices in civilization the Indian is a child let loose in a house of terrors. As a solace he indulges in the doubtful amusements of those only too ready to instruct him, and lacking their judgment, untrained in the technique of vice, he becomes a victim of depravity. Unable to discern the fine line between the evasions and misrepresentations with which civilized man disguises his thoughts, and downright dishonesty, he becomes shiftless and unreliable. The few words of English he learns consist mainly of profanity, so we have the illuminating object-lesson of a race just emerging from a state of savagery turning to the languages of the white man for oaths that their own does not contain. Some few have been brought out to the front and partially educated, but almost invariably they return to the tent or the teepee, and the crackling wood fires, to the land of endless trails, tumbling water, and crimson sunsets.

The Indian readily falls a victim to consumption when he substitutes a poor imitation of the white man's way of living for his own; as he gropes blindly around in the maze of complications that surround him, he selects badly; and undernourished and inadequately clothed, his impoverished system absorbs the first disease that comes along.

Submission to the unalterable facts of a hard life have given the Indian a subdued mien, which his bold and vigorous features belie, quite out of keeping with his fierce and tireless energy when roused. He is the freeman of a vast continent, the First American. Innovation intrudes itself all about him, but he changes not. To those who undertake his regeneration he listens gravely and attentively, whilst retaining his own opinion; inflexible as the changeless courses of Nature which flow around him. If the Indian accepts one or another of the white man's various religions, he does so with reservations. He fails to see what lasting benefit can be derived from a gospel of love and peace, the adherents to the many sects of which are ready to fly at one another's throats over a discussion as to which is the shortest road to hell. An Algonquin once innocently asked me what did I suppose the white man had done in the past that he was unable to approach his God save through an interpreter?

He is Catholic or Protestant with cheerful impartiality, according to whichever minister gets to him first, practising the required rites at intervals, in public, and is easily persuaded to give sums of money for the building of churches. For he is a simple man, he thinks there may be something in this hell business after all, and he, with his bush experience, takes nothing for granted and likes to play safe. Yet he retains his own views, and secretly communes with his omnipresent deity, and propitiates his evil spirit, whilst the white man, too, often works for his own particular devil quite cheerfully, and at times with enthusiasm. I once lived in a small town where the Indians hunting to the north of the railroad track were Protestants and those to the south of it were Catholics; a matter of geography. I remember, too, a Cree Indian, well advanced and able to speak good English, although unable to write, who dictated to me a letter addressed to a Protestant minister in which he reminded the churchman of a promise to help in case of need. The need had now arisen, and the Cree asked for the loan of a hundred dollars, or some such trifling sum, I forget exactly, and to intimidate the good parson into granting his request, he threatened, in the event of a refusal, to turn Catholic.

Under the white man's scheme of existence the Indian is asked to forget his language, his simple conception of the Great Spirit, and his few remaining customs, which if it were demanded of the Hindus, the Boers, the Irish or the French-Canadians, would without doubt cause a rebellion.

And as he sits and glooms beneath the arches of the forest before his little smoky fires, he coughs his hacking cough and stares dumbly out into the dancing shadows, wondering, now that his spirits are forbidden him, why the white man's God that dispossessed them does not fulfill the oft-repeated promise of the missions. Yet their loyalty is such that they recognize no Provincial authority, but look to Ottawa, the seat of Dominion Government, as directly representing the King, who to them is no Royal personage, but Gitche Okima, literally the Great Chief, a father who cannot fail them.

Since the war I have attended councils where no white men were present, the opening ceremony of which was to place on the floor the Union Jack, the assembly seating themselves in a circle around it, and each speaker advanced to the edge of the flag and there had his say.

Very recently I listened to an altercation between a band of Indians and an ecclesiastic who had lowered the dignity of his Church, and entirely lost the confidence of his flock by his extortionate methods of retailing high-priced salvation. During the discussion the "Black Robe" stated that the British Government had nothing to do with the Indians, and that they were directly responsible to the Church for any benefits they had received, including the introduction of moose and beaver into the country. And an old chief arose, and speaking for his assembled people, said with grave emphasis:

"When King George tells us that, we will believe it!"

And no matter how pious, earnest, and sincere a man of God may undertake the task, it will take years of patient labour and devotion to eradicate the effect of this untimely speech on a people to whose minds a statement once made can in no wise be withdrawn.

The Ojibway are probably the most numerous of the tribes that roam the vast Hinterland north of the fifty-first parallel; and regardless of wars, rumours of wars, and the rise and fall of nations, oblivious of the price of eggs, champagne, and razor blades, they wander the length and breadth of the land, which, with the one proviso of game being in plenty, is at once to them a kingdom and a paradise. They overcome with apparent ease the almost insuperable difficulties incidental to a life in this land of violent struggle for existence. By a process of elimination, the result of many generations of experience, they have arrived at a system of economy of effort, a reserving of power for emergencies, and an almost infallible skill in the detection of the weak points in Nature's armour, that makes for the highest degree of efficiency.

Gaunt Crees, in lesser numbers, hollow-cheeked, high-shouldered fellows, skilled in the arts of speed, ranged this region with burning ambition and distance-devouring stride. The light wiry Ojibway, with his crew of good and evil spirits, his omens, and his portents continually dogging his footsteps, packed unbelievable loads over unthinkable trails or no trails at all, and insinuated himself by devious ways into the most inaccessible fastnesses. Then came the white man, cheerful, humorous, undismayed by gods, devils, or distance; working mightily, hacking his way through by main force where the Indian sidled past with scarcely a trace, pushing onward by sheer grit and bulldog courage.

Subdued by no consideration of the passage here before him of the wise and mighty men of former generations, there being in his case none, he forged ahead and lugged the outfit along. And if his lack of skill in the discovery of game left the larder kind of low at times, he starved like the gentleman he was, and dared the wilderness to beat him. And always he left behind permanent works; laboriously hewn trails, log cabins, small clearances, and often large burns, while his russet-skinned, sloe-eyed contemporaries with their easy swing and resilient methods, looked askance at his ruinous progress, and wished him evil. And they retired unobtrusively before him to where as yet, for a little time, the enchanted glades were not disfigured by unsightly stumps, nor the whispering echoes rudely awakened by the crash of falling timber, and other unseemly uproar. The passage of the paleface through his ancestral territories is, to the Indian, in effect, what the arrival of the German Army would have been to a conquered England. To them his progress is marked by a devastation comparable only with that left in the wake of a plague in a crowded metropolis.

His coming changed the short springy carpet of buffalo-grass that covered the prairie into a tangle of coarse wild hay, shoulder high. The groves of the forest became dismal clearances of burnt and blackened skeleton trees, and the jewelled lakes were dammed and transformed into bodies of unclean water, bordered by partly submerged rampikes, and unsightly heaps of dead trees, where, in the event of a sudden storm, landing was dangerous if not impossible. Fish died in the pollution, and game of all kinds migrated to other regions.

For the Indian the woods are peopled with spirits, voices, and mysterious influences. To him the Spirit of the North, a brooding, sullen destroyer who glooms over the land like a shadow of death, is very real. How this destructive demon retains his supremacy over the forces of nature in face of the Indian's ever-present God, to whom he can apply at a moment's notice, is as easily explained as is the uninterrupted prosperity enjoyed by the Satan of the white man. Certain dark ravines are mausoleums in which dwell the shades of savage ancestors. Individual trees and rocks assume a personality, and a quiet glade is the abode of some departed friend, human or animal. The ghostly flickering of the Northern Lights he calls the Dance of the Dead Men, and in the Talking Waters of a rapids he hears the voices of the Old Men of bygone days. The thunder is a bird, and the May-may-gwense, mischievous bush fairies, tangle the traveller's footsteps, spring his traps and put out his fires. Headless skeletons run shouting through the woods at night, and in some dark and swirling eddy dead men swim at the full of the moon. The Windigo, a half-human, flesh-eating creature, scours the lake shores looking for those who sleep carelessly without a fire, and makes sleeping out in some sections a thing of horror.

Thunder Cape rears its thirteen hundred feet of imposing grandeur up out of Lake Superior, fitting bastion to the wall of seismic masonry that swells and plunges its tortuous way across the lone land to add its mass to the Great Divide, which, swinging eastward for a thousand miles and westward for a thousand more, was erected by the Red Gods to be an impregnable rampart to the jealously guarded treasure house of the north. And here beneath this solid mass of the oldest known rock sleeps Hayowentha, or as sometimes called, Hiawatha. He was the great and wise prophet of the Indians, a gentle soul who called the animals Little Brothers, worked for the betterment of mankind, and went around doing good.★

When the first white-winged vessel landed on these shores, he left his people in sorrow at their approaching doom, which they would not take means to avert, with his dogs, his beaver, and his birds, and his canoe, and entered the mighty rock, there to sleep, waking but once a year, until finally he comes forth to effect the emancipation of his people.

Every Fall he releases the Hunting Winds, and opens the Four Way Lodge, coursing for a night through the forest he tried to save, with his furred and feathered familiars, and guarded by a host of wolves. And at such times the Indians can detect in the antiphony of the song of the wolf pack, the deeper baying of Hiawatha's hell-dogs; they can hear the muted swish of wings of ghost-birds, and

★ See note on page 240.

across the hills echoes the clear flute-like call of phantom beaver, from wastes where never beaver was before.

And so we see the Indian cluttered up and retarded by a host of inhibitions, as he was formerly by ceremonial, so that he will put off an important trip on account of a dream, as in former days he delayed a battle to recover a few venerated bones and trinkets, or lost sight of a cause in the fulfillment of some useless vow. The Indian's God does not reside in the inaccessible heights of majestic indifference of most deities. The Indian feels his presence all his waking hours, not precisely as a god, but as an all-powerful, benevolent Spirit, whose outward manifestation is the face of nature. An intimate kind of a Spirit who sends a message in the sighing of the North-West Wind, may plant a hidden motive in the action of a beast for man to profit by, or disturb the course of nature to save a life. They do not fear him, for this God jogs at their elbow, and is a friend, nor do they worship him, save through the sun, a tree, a rock, or a range of hills, which to them are the outward and visible signs of the Power that lives and breathes in all creation.

The Indian believes that his dead are not gone from him, that they live invisible, but ever-present, in selected spots, to which, in trouble, he will repair and spend hours in meditation. The little girl who lost her pet beaver, as related a few pages back, begged the hunter who had killed them to show her where the bodies lay. She preserved the skulls and all the bones, hanging them, in a birch-bark box decorated with porcupine quills, in some secret resort, where she spent hours at a time, and where none were permitted to disturb her.

Great fighting chiefs of former days carried medicine pouches containing a few bits of feathers and small bones, and other apparently useless remnants, as sacred, however, in their eyes, as some religious relics are to a devout congregation.

The band of white thrown across a lake at night by the moonbeams, is, to the red man, the path that little children and small animals take when they die; the Silver Trail to the Land of Spirits. All others take the Sunset Trail.

The conception of the Indian's heaven generally held is erroneous. The Happy Hunting Ground, so called, is not a place of carefree slaughter, but a, let us hope not too mythical, region where hunting is no longer necessary, and where men and the animals live together in amity, as was supposed to be in the beginning. For the Indians were always conservationists, the first there ever were in this country. They are blamed for the existing shortage of wildlife, yet when these people were the most numerous, on the arrival here of the white man, the forests and plains swarmed with game. Few Indians are left today, yet every period of a few years sees some interesting or valuable animal practically wiped off the map.

The Provinces of Canada have at last decided, now that some varieties of animals and timber are on the point of disappearance, to get together and try to evolve some means of preserving Canada's rapidly dwindling natural forest resources. The stable door is about to be closed, the horse having long gone. How slowly we move!

Let us hope that in this judicious and altogether praiseworthy attempt to save something from the wreckage, money will not talk as loud as it generally does when the public welfare and the interests of some branches of big business come into conflict.

There is a kindred feeling between the Indians and the animals which is hard to understand in the face of their former cruel and relentless methods of warfare; but these wars were almost always waged in the defence of those things they held most dear; their freedom, their game, and their sacred spots. Behind a masklike visage the Indian hides a disposition as emotional as that of a Latin. Men who carried dripping scalps at their belts, their bodies streaked with the blood of dead enemies, fought for the preservation of individual trees, and wept at the grave of a friend. When the real bush Indians kill they often address the body before cutting it up, and perform some little service, such as placing the head in a comfortable position or brushing snow from the dead face, whenever they pass that way. They hang up the skull of a bear and place tobacco in it, in propitiation, and if they eat any of the meat they hang the shoulder blades on a tree, first painting two black stripes on them, running parallel to show that their thoughts were not against the bear's, but with them. There is a little bird that stays around campfires, in the trees, hopping from the stem of one leaf to another, as if inspecting them; he is called the Counter of the Leaves, and must on no account be killed. All savagery, no doubt, but not more savage than a civilization that permits the continuance of bull fighting, where worn-out working horses, as a reward for their long service, are, when wounded in the unequal contest, patched up until killed by the bull — blindfolded, that they may not evade the thrust that disembowels them, their vocal chords destroyed so as not to upset by their screaming the delicate nerves of a cowardly and degenerate audience, who, elated by the knowledge that helpless dumb creatures are being tortured for their amusement, shout their brutal satisfaction. And this on the very day they set apart to worship the white man's God of mercy and love! Indians never did these things. Frightful torments they inflicted, or submitted to, according to the luck of war, but to inflict such brutalities on an animal as a pastime seemingly never occurred to them.

Indians are in tune with their surroundings, and that accounts to a large extent for their ability in the old days to detect the foreign element in the atmosphere of the woods and plains. A movement where all should be still; a disturbance of the colour scheme; a disarrangement in the set of the leaves; the frayed edge of a newly broken stick, speak loud to the Indian's eye. They have catalogued and docketed every possible combination of shape, sound, and colour possible in their surroundings, and any deviation from these, however slight, at once strikes a dissonance, as a false note in an orchestra of many instruments is plain to the ear of a musician. An approaching change of weather affects them as it does the animals, and they readily take on the moods of Nature, rain and dull weather seeming to cast a gloom over a whole community. A change of wind they forecast quite accurately and even if sleeping the changed atmospheric conditions brought about by its turning from the South to the North awaken the older people, and they will say, "It is Keewaydin; the North Wind is blowing."

To them the North-West wind is paramount; it is the Wind of Winds; it stands for good trails and clear skies, and puts a bracing quality into the atmosphere that makes any extreme of temperature endurable. They sniff it with distended nostrils as one quaffs a refreshing drink, and inhale deeply of it, as though it were some elixir that cured all bodily ills. From it they seem to gather some sort of inspiration, for it speaks to them of that vast, lone land, down from which it sweeps, which, no matter what advances civilization may make, no one will ever know quite all about.

The red man's whole attitude towards Nature can be summed up in the words of an old man, my companion during many years of travel:

"When the wind speaks to the leaves, the Indian hears — and understands."

The singing of the wolves is not to him the dreadful sound that it is to some. The wolf and his song are as much a part of the great wilderness as the Indian himself, for they are hunters too, and suffer from cold and hunger, and travel long hard trails, as he does.

The wild frenzy of a hurrying rapids, the buffeting, whistling masses of snow whirling across the winter lakes, are to him a spectacle in which he is taking an active part, a rough but friendly contest amid surroundings with which he is familiar, and which he feels will not betray him, does he but obey the rules of the game.

With the heroic atmosphere of war removed and the Cooperesque halo of nobility dissipated by continuous propinquity, the red man loses much of his romantic appeal. But as one gets to know this strange people, with their simplicity, their silence, and their almost Oriental mysticism, other and unsuspected qualities become apparent, which compel the admiration of even those who make much of their faults. Doggedly persevering, of an uncomplaining endurance and an infinite patience, scrupulously honest for the most part, and possessed by a singleness of purpose that permits no deviation from a course of action once decided on, they are as changeless as the face of the wilderness, and as silent almost, and much given to deep thinking, not of the future, but — fatal to the existence of the individual or of a nation — of the past. The future holds nothing for them, and they live in the days gone by. The Indian stands adamant as the very hills, while the tide of progress swells around him, and unable to melt and flow with it, he, like the beaver and the buffalo with whose history his own destiny has been so identified, will be engulfed and swept away. And then all the heart-burnings and endless complaints of the land-hungry over the few acres of soil that are given him in return for the freedom of a continent, will be at an end for all time.

And it almost were better that he so should go, whilst he yet holds his proud position of supremacy in the arts of forest lore, and retains his wild independence and his freedom in the environment for which he is so eminently fitted. It is better that he should follow where the adventurer and the free trapper already point the way, to where the receding, ever shrinking line of the Last Frontier is fading into the dimness of the past. Better thus, than that he should be thrown into the grinding wheels of the mill of modernity, to be spewed out a nondescript, undistinguishable from the mediocrity that surrounds him, a reproach to the memory of a noble race. Better to leave him, for the short time that remains to him, to his recollections, his animals, and his elfin-haunted groves, and when the end comes, his race will meet it as a people, with the same stoic calm with which they met it individually when defeated in war in former times.

The old days are not so far behind. The most stirring period in the history of the old frontier is removed from the present only by a period frequently covered by the span of one human life. I have talked with an old woman who remembered, for she has long joined the great majority, the first matches introduced to her people. They were the kind, still in use in the woods, known as eight-day matches, as on being struck they simmered along for an interminable period before finally bursting into flames. After the interesting entertainment of seeing them lit she retrieved the sticks and took them home to demonstrate the new marvel, but much to her disappointment she could not make them work.

She told me much of the ancient history of the Iroquois and remembered the war parties going out, and as a child, during a battle she hid with the rest of the children and the women in the fields of squashes and corn which the Indians maintained around their villages.

One old man of the Ojibway with the prolonged name of Neejin-nekai-apeechi-geejiguk, or to make a long story short, "Both-ends-of-the-day," witnessed the Iroquois raids of 1835 or thereabouts in the Temagami region. He was a man to whom none could listen without attention, and was a living link with a past of which only too little is known. Although he died in distressing circumstances a good many years ago, I remember him well, as I last saw him; straight as an arrow and active as a young man in spite of his years, he had an unusually developed faculty for seeing in the dark, which accounts for his name, which inferred that day and night were all one to him. I recollect that he carried an alarm clock inside his shirt for a watch, and when once, at a dance, he fell asleep, some mischievous youngster set the alarm, and he created the diversion of the evening when the sudden racket within his shirt woke him up. In reality the first touch of the little urchin had awakened him, but he purposely feigned continued sleep till the alarm should go off, for he had a keen sense of humour, which Indians possess more often than they get credit for. He was also fond of the society of young children, but he once showed me some grisly relics that invested his character with quite a different aspect; and from then on there seemed to lurk behind his cheery smile at times a savage grin.

He would sit for hours outside his camp, tapping a small drum, singing ancient songs in a language no one understood; and sometimes he would lay the drum aside, and to those who had assembled to hear his songs, he would tell of things that students of Canadian history would have given much to hear; of ways and means now long forgotten; tales of the wild Nottaways in bark canoes that held a dozen men; of shaven-headed Iroquois who crept at dawn into a sleeping village and slew all within it before they could awaken. He told of a woman who having crossed a portage some distance from camp, was fishing, and whilst so engaged, saw land at the portage, canoe-load after canoe-load of Mohawk warriors, who secreted their canoes, and effacing the signs of their passage, lay hidden in deadly silence, awaiting the proper hour to strike. That she had been observed she took for granted; but she reasoned, and rightly, that the enemy would not risk killing her, as, if missing, a search for her might reveal the war party. She decided to return to camp by way of the portage, her passport to safety being her pretended ignorance of the presence there of enemies. So this courageous and sagacious woman landed, picked up her canoe, and walked the full length of the trail, knowing that in the dark forest on either hand lay a hundred warriors thirsting for her blood, and that the least faltering or sign of fear would cause her instant death, and precipitate an attack on the village. Her steadiness of mien led the invaders to imagine themselves undiscovered, and she made the trip unmolested. Thus she was able to warn her people who made such good use of the hours of darkness that when at dawn the Iroquois made their attack they found only an empty village.

Judging by some of the old man's narratives, apparently these far-famed warriors were not as uniformly successful as we have been led to believe. It appears that they made a practice of taking along a captive as a guide in his own territory, knocking him on the head when his sphere of usefulness was ended, and taking another in the new district. These conscripted guides sometimes put their knowledge of the country to a good account, as on the occasion when a large canoe, loaded with warriors, arrived near the head of a falls, which was hidden from sight by a curve. The guides, there were two of them in this case, informed their captors that this was a rapids that could be run by those who were acquainted with the channel, and they took the steering positions, formulating, as they did so, a plan, with swift mutterings in their own language, unheard in the roar of the falls. The water ran dark and swift between high rock walls, except at one spot where there was a line of boulders reaching from the shore out into the channel. Increasing the speed of the canoes as much as possible, the Ojibways jumped off the now racing craft as it passed the stepping stones, and the remainder of the crew, struggling desperately to stem the current, were swept over the falls. Those that did not drown were killed with stones by their erstwhile guides, who had raced over the por-tage with that end in view. And great was the glory thereof. The incident obtained for that place the name of Iroquois Falls, which it retains to this day.

During the winter a band of them, arriving back in camp after an arduous and fruitless man-hunt, fatigued by the use of snowshoes unsuited to conditions so far North, asked their guide, a woman, what steps her people took to relieve the cramps that afflicted their legs after such heavy snowshoeing. She informed them that the method generally adopted was to lie with their legs elevated, with the ankles on cross-bars, feet towards the fire. This they did. Exhausted, they fell asleep. The woman wetted and stretched some rawhide thongs, lightly bound their ankles to the bars, and put on a good fire. Soon the thongs dried and shrunk, holding them with a grip like iron, and she killed them all before they could extricate themselves. Taking all the provision she needed, this very able woman proceeded to another war party she knew to be in the vicinity, as vicinities go in that country, a matter of fifty miles or so, and gave herself up as a prisoner. She soon gained the confidence of her captors, and once, coming home tired, they committed the indiscretion of falling asleep in her presence. She thereupon burnt all the snowshoes except one pair, on which she escaped, leaving them as much marooned in six feet of snow as any crew of shipwrecked sailors on a desert island could be, and they were later found and killed by a jubilant band of Algonquins.

The descendants of these same Iroquois today are living near Montreal, and are staging a comeback, reviving their ancient customs, dress, and dances, and this movement is becoming widespread. In the West, blanketted, bonnetted warriors are no longer an uncommon sight, college graduates though some of them may be; and big Indian conventions are being held, to which all the tribes send delegates, where the English language is not permitted, none but tribal dress is worn, and at which the long forbidden Sun Dance is now permitted, minus the self-torturing feature. Always the most interesting thing to me at these revivals is the sight of the old men with their long braided hair, in some cases white with the passage of three-quarters of a century, dressed in the regalia that was at one time the only garb they knew, and wearing war-bonnets that they earned, when each feather represented the accomplishment of some deed of courage, or of skill. They may not be able to compete with the younger men in their supple posturings, but they are living for a while once more the old life that has so long been taken away from them. And I often wonder what stirring memories, and perchance what melancholy recollections of the past, are awakened behind those inscrutable old eyes and wrinkled faces, as they raise their quavering voices in the "Buffalo Song" in a land of cattle, or tread, in mimic war-dance, measures to which they stepped in deadly earnest half a century ago.

Many years ago I cast in my lot with that nation known under the various appellations of Chippeways, Algonquins, Londucks, and Ojibways. A blood-brother proved and sworn, by moose-head feast, wordless chant, and ancient ritual was I named before a gaily decorated and attentive concourse, when Ne-ganik-abo, "Man-that-stands-ahead," whom none living remember as a young man, danced the conjurors' dance beneath the spruce trees, before an open fire; danced the ancient steps to the throb of drums, the wailing of reed pipes, and the rhythmical skirring of turtle shell rattles; danced alone before a sacred bear-skull set beneath a painted rawhide shield, whose bizarre device might have graced the tomb of some long-dead Pharaoh. And as the chanting rose and fell in endless reiteration, the flitting shadows of his weird contortions danced a witches' dance between the serried tree trunks. The smoke hung in a white pall short of the spreading limbs of the towering trees, and with a hundred pairs of beady eyes upon me, I stepped out beneath it when called on. And not one feral visage relaxed in recognition, as, absorbed in the mystery of their ritual they intoned the almost forgotten cadences.

"Hi-Heeh, Hi-Heh, Ho! Hi-Heh, Hi-Heh, Ha! Hi-Hey, Hi-Hey, Ho! Hi-Ho, Hi-Ho, Ha!" and on and on in endless repetition, until the monotony of the sounds had the same effect on the mind that the unvarying and measured markings of a snake have on the eye. The sensation of stepping into the motionless ring was that of suddenly entering a temple, devoted to the worship of some pagan deity, where the walls were lined with images cast in bronze; and there I proudly received the name they had devised, which the old man now bestowed upon me.

At that the drums changed their rhythm and the whole assemblage, hitherto so still, commenced to move with a concerted swaying, rocking motion, in time to the thunder of the drums, and the circle commenced to revolve about me. The chant broke into a series of rapidly ascending minor notes, which dropped from the climax to the hollow, prolonged hoot of the owl whose name I now bore.

"Hoh-hoh, hoh-hoooooo! Hoh-hoh, hoh-hoooooo!" The weird cries trailed off into the empty halls of the forest, while faster and faster grew the dance before the bear skull; and the drummers, and those who played the rattles, and the circle round about, moved in unison to the constantly accelerating tempo that the old man gave them, till the swift thudding of many feet made a thunder of its own, and the glade became a whirling mass of colour; and ever the chant grew louder, until with a long-drawn out quavering yell, "Ahi, yah-ah-ah-ah-ah," all movement ceased, and like the dropping of a curtain, silence fell.

This band is sadly reduced. The lonely graves beneath the giant red pines are more numerous today; they are a fading people. Not long from now will come one sunset, their last; far from the graves of their fathers they are awaiting with stolid calm what, to them, is the inevitable. To leave them, to stand from under, to desert the sinking ship, were a craven act, unthinkable. All of whatsoever I may know of the way of the wild they have taught me.

Neganikabo, my mentor, my kindly instructor, my companion in untold hardship and nameless tribulation, has pulled back little by little, the magic invisible veil of mystery from across the face of the forest, that I might learn its uttermost secrets, and has laid open before me the book of Nature for me to read; and in my bungling way I have profited by his lessons, but the half is not yet done.

I have followed him when snowshoes sank into the soft snow halfway to the knee, mile after weary mile, to sleep at night behind a square of canvas; this for five days and nights, it snowing steadily most of the time, and with nothing to eat but strips of dried moose-meat, and teas made from boiled leaves of the Labrador sage. I have negotiated dangerous rapids under his tuition, when at each run, after the irrevocable step of entering, I doubted much that I would make the foot alive. He has led me many hours of travel with birch bark flares at night, and more than once entire nights in an unknown country without them. Once, soon after the freeze-up, and with the ice in bad condition, we returned late in the evening to our sahaagan,* to be greeted by a heap of charred fragments, and bare poles on which small portions of canvas were still smouldering.

Our fire, which we supposed we had extinguished, had worked under the peaty forest soil, and sprung up in the centre of the camp, destroying every last ounce of provisions, the blankets, and the shelter itself. Greatest of our losses was that of several mink and a red fox, the latter not entirely destroyed, but now scorched black; my first black fox, and, I might add, my last. As a storm threatened the old man started on the day and a half's journey to the village in the darkness, over ice that few would have attempted by daylight, judging it by the sound only, singing in bad spots in an undertone, a song suitable to the conditions; such as "I see the trail like a thread, I see it, I see it," or "I feel water close, I feel water." Meanwhile all I could see was the surrounding blackness, and the only thing I felt was a sinking sensation in the pit of my stomach when the tap of his pole indicated bad ice.

I have seen him, in the spring of the year, when all ice is treacherous, after half a day of juggling between canoe, sleigh,

* Semi-circular canvas shelter.

and snowshoes, walk out on to the next lake, that by all the law should have been as bad as the last one, and glancing casually across it say:

"This ice is good."

His faculties of observation, as with most Indians, were very keen; nothing seemed to escape him. He could detect game invisible to me, yet his gaze was not piercing, rather it was comprehensive, all-embracing, effortless, as is the eye of a camera, registering every detail in a moment of time. He often made fire with bow and spindle, habitually carried flint and steel, and seemed to have knowledge of the speech of some animals, calling them almost at will in the right season. He carried a beaded pouch which contained, among other trinkets, some small beaver bones. In spite of the unprecedented advances in latter years of the price of beaver skins, on account of some belief he held he would not kill these animals, even when in want; and he would stand at times outside their lodges, seeming to converse with them. Not a good shot with firearms, yet he would get so close to his quarry without their knowledge, that an old muzzle-loading beaver-gun (so called from the method of purchase) fulfilled all his requirements for game of all sizes, partridges included. For your Indian, in common with the white hunter, shoots his birds sitting; but he uses a bullet, and the mark is its head, a sporting enough proposition for a man with an empty belly. He showed me, in the course of years, did I but have the head to hold it all, what a man may learn in a long life of observation and applied experience.

He had his humorous occasions, too. With a party of moose-hunters we were standing on the abrupt edge of a hill, the face of which had fallen away and lay in a mass of broken fragments at the foot, crowned with a few small jackpines, shoulder high. Across the valley was a ridge crested with a row of immense white pines, seedlings, perhaps, in the days when the Plymouth Brethren dodged flights of arrows on their way to church. One of the tourists had shown great curiosity with regard to the venerable guide, and had pestered me with endless questions regarding him. The old man knew no English, but I think he got the gist of the conversation, for at last, on being asked his age, he pointed across to the big pines.

"Tell that man," he said, "that when I was a boy those trees were so small that I could reach out and shake them — so!" and grasping one of the jackpine saplings he shook it violently back and forth.

He who lands his canoe at a semi-permanent Indian village at any hour after daylight will find few, if any, of the men at home. At the first sign of dawn the hunters are away, for more game may be taken in the two hours after the break of day than in all the rest of the twenty-four together.

Returning at noon the visitor is very apt to find the inhabitants all sleeping, and the camp basking silently in the sunlight without a sign of life; save perhaps some old woman who sits smoking and dreaming by the slowly smouldering fire; and he will hear no sound save the drowsy hum of insects and the metallic shrilling of the cicadas★ in the treetops. For this is the hour of rest. Quite often these people have done half a day's work when the rest of the world was in bed, and when an Indian is not actually engaged in some branch of his strenuous occupation, he relaxes utterly and completely. The women do all the camp work, and this is what no doubt gives rise to the legend of Indian laziness. Did a man lay his hand to the maintenance of camp, once it is erected, he would be laughed out of countenance by his womenfolk and sent about his business.

These villages are all movable, for this is a nomadic people. Rarely do they build cabins save in the vicinity of a trading post.

★ This insect resembles an enormous house-fly about two inches long, with the wings obliquely down the body. It sucks the sap of trees.

Tents, wind-breaks, and birch-bark shelters are scattered amongst the growth of umbrella-topped jack-pines, on a low point midway of a lake set deep into an amphitheatre of emerald hills. Here and there a tall teepee, its upper half dyed a deep umber by the smoke of years, looms above its lesser brethren. On the foreshore a variety of canoes are drawn up, the canvas-covered type predominating, but some of them are of birch-bark, dyed red with alder sap, with black strips of gum at the seams. And in the background is the inevitable dark, towering wall of evergreen forest.

Hudson Bay blankets, half an inch thick, and green, blue, black, red, or white, according to the owner's taste, hanging out on poles to air before each lodge, give a brilliant note of colour. Women in voluminous plaid dresses and multicoloured head shawls, move from tent to tent, sewing, baking endless bannocks, or working everlastingly at half-tanned hides. In an open space near the centre of the village is standing a rack of poles, ten feet long and six high, festooned with numerous strips of moose-meat, and on it, split open from the back, hangs a giant sturgeon the length of a man. Beneath this rack a long slow fire is burning, the cool smoke hovering in amongst the meat and fish, adding to it a savour and a zest that no bottled condiment can impart. Men, some with clipped heads, others bobbed, older men with long black braids, gather around this central place, whittling out muskrat stretchers★ with crooked-knives, mending nets, sitting around and smoking, or just sitting around. Half-naked children play in the dust with half-tame huskies; a crow, tied by the leg with a length of thong to a cross pole, squawking discordantly at intervals.

Two tumbling bear cubs run loose; one, his face covered with flour, chased by an enraged woman with a cudgel; a month-old wolf, his nature already asserting itself, creeps up on a cat, twice his size, which lies sleeping, its head in the shade of a small square

★ Frames for stretching hides.

of birch-bark it has found; for so do even domestic animals adapt themselves to this manner of life and turn opportunist; next winter some of the dogs will feign a limp, or unaccountably fall sick, on being hitched up for the first trip.

As the sun climbs down towards the rim of hills the men bestir themselves, and at intervals, in parties of two, or singly, take their guns and light axes, slip down on noiseless moccasined feet to the shore, and paddle silently away. Some will be back at dark, others at midnight; a few have taken small neat packs and will be gone several days. No goodbyes have been said, no stir has taken place; they just steal away as the spirit moves them; when one turns to speak they are not there; that is all.

As the day falls, smudges are lit to the windward, a protection from the swarms of mosquitoes that now descend on the camp, and volumes of smoke envelope the point, through which the tents are dimly visible. Tiny beavers are brought down to the lake for their daily swim, whilst young boys stand guard with clubs to keep the dogs away, or take canoes and herd the stragglers in, for there are voracious pike of immense size in these waters that would make short work of a month-old kit. Nets are set, everything eatable, and many things not considered to be so, are hung up out of reach of the dogs, and the business of the day is ended. Little, twinkling fires spring to life and the pale illumination of tallow dips within the lodges gives the village from the distance the appearance of a gathering of fireflies. And on the canvas wall the shadows of those within depict their every movement, and through them every sound escapes, so that one's neighbour's doings are so obvious, and his conversation so audible, as to be no longer intriguing. The same principle that is the doom of prudery and prohibition, in this case ensures a privacy that four stone walls do not always give.

Then some morning at daybreak the whole village is in motion. Blankets are folded and teepees pulled down, fires are extinguished with countless pails of water. Children, now fully dressed, commence carrying down the smaller bundles to the canoes. The tenting place has become monotonous; the fish have moved to deeper water, also a woman heard a squirrel chittering during the night; a bad omen. So the camp is to be moved.

The dogs, viewing the preparations with disfavour, howl dolorously, for to them this means a long and arduous journey around the edge of the lake to the next stop, whilst their masters sit at ease in the smooth-running canoes. For Indians, unless on a flying trip, travel within easy reach of the shore line, as offering better observation of the movements of game; and this is a country of sudden and violent tempests, a consideration of some account, with women and children aboard. Should the shore deviate too far from the line of travel, room will be made, temporarily, for the dogs.

There is no unseemly haste in this breaking of camp. Every individual has his or her allotted task; not a move is wasted. Quietly, smoothly, without bustle or confusion, the canoes are loaded, and in little more than an hour from the time of rising nothing remains of a village of perhaps ten or fifteen families, save the damp steam rising from deluged fires and the racks of bare poles, piled clear of the ground for future use.

The scene at a portage is a lively one. Colourful as a band of gypsies, men, women, and children are strung out over the trail, decked with inordinate loads of every imaginable description. Men with a hundred pounds of flour and a tin stove take a canoe for a binder; others take from two hundred pounds up, of solid weight. Women carry tents and huge rolls of blankets with apparent ease, their hands filled with light but irksome utensils. The squaws take their share of the labour as a matter of course, and to suggest to them that packing is no job for a woman would be to meet with instant ridicule.

Children carry their own packs with miniature tump lines, taking their work as seriously as do their elders.

Some women carry infants on their backs, laced on to flat padded boards fitted with an outrig in such a manner that the child is protected in case of a fall, from which dangles a wooden homemade doll or other simple toy. These mothers carry no other load, but to them, having their hands free, is delegated the difficult and diplomatic task of herding, leading, and hazing along the trail those of the multifarious pets that cannot be carried in bags or boxes, assisted by the children. I have seen cats perched contentedly on top of a roll of bedding, stealing a ride, crows carried on poles like banners, full grown beaver led on a chain, tiny bears running loose, not daring to leave the outfit, and once a young girl with an owl laced tightly into a baby's cradle, the poor creature being supposedly highly honoured.

The younger men vie with one another in tests of speed and endurance, while the seasoned veterans move along with measured step and a smooth effortless progression that never falters or changes. These people are considered to be half-savage, which probably they are, yet contrast their expenditure of effort on behalf of the young of wild animals that fall into their hands, with the behaviour of a family of civilized Indians, who bought a bear cub from some of their more primitive brethren, expecting to sell it at a high figure to tourists. Failing in this, they had no more use for it, and unwilling to let it go, as it had cost them money, they neglected the poor little creature, and it died of thirst chained to a tree within a few feet of the lake shore.

A large percentage of the Indians of mixed blood who live near the railroad (this does not include those bush Indians who of necessity trade at railroad posts) are rascals; their native cunning in the chase is diverted into improper channels, and they become merely sly and lazy. They lack the dignity, the honesty, and the mental stability of the genuine forest dwellers, whose reputation as a race has suffered much at the hands of this type.

Indian winter camps in the Keewaydin district differ little from their summer villages. They erect their habitations in more sheltered places, but tents and wigwams are the only shelters, the former warmed by small tin stoves that give a surprising heat, and the latter by an open fire inside, with sometimes the stove as well. The lodges are banked high with snow and are a good deal warmer than would be supposed. But once the stove dies it is only a matter of a few minutes till the cold swoops down like a descending scimitar of chilled steel, down through the flimsy canvas, on into the ground beneath the sleepers, freezing it solid as a rock, searching out every nook and cranny in the weak defences, petrifying everything. And over the camp hangs a mist of hoar frost, whilst the wolves beyond the ridges bay the moon, and the trees crack with reports like gunshots in the iron grip of ninety degrees of frost. Although permanent for the period of deep snow, the entire camp may be loaded on toboggans and moved at an hour's notice. Stretched out in file across the surface of frozen lakes, half hidden by drifting snow, these winter caravans travel sometimes hundreds of miles. They literally march, these people, and almost always in step, each stepping between the tracks of his predecessor, an action which in time becomes second nature, so that the trail, by the packing of many snowshoes, becomes a solid springy road, on which the dogs are able to put forth their best efforts. And in the van, leading a procession perhaps a quarter of a mile in length, are the trail breakers, often young girls and boys of from twelve years of age up. This seems like cruelty, but it is no colder at the head of the caravan than at the rear, and these children pass lightly over the snow without hardship to themselves, packing the trail; and the entire outfit travels easily behind them, where otherwise men would have to take turns to break a trail a foot in depth, at the rate of a mile an hour. These youngsters take a pride in their work and contest hotly for the leadership, a coveted honour.

Every night camp must be made in any weather. A heavy carpet of spruce or balsam boughs supports the tents and provides a floor on the surface of several feet of snow; stoves are quickly put up, wood cut, and the cooking done, and the dogs, once fed, dig themselves in for the night. The various tasks are all performed with the speed and efficiency of long practice; and in a remarkably short space of time the camp assumes an appearance of permanence and comfort; only, in the morning, to be taken down and loaded up for the next leg of a journey that is never quite completed, summer or winter.

To follow these restless people in their ceaseless wanderings, is to spend long weeks of terrific labour, alternating with lazy days of basking in the sun, and games, and dancing. Periods of want are offset by days and nights of feasting. I have seen times when small birds and squirrels were snared for their meat, dogs were eaten as they died of hunger, and wailing children cried for the food their starving mothers could not give. And on a day a lucky hunter found a herd of moose, and pinched faces became broad with smiles, and people ate, and ate, till they could eat no more, and a herd of brown youngsters with laughing shoe-button eyes, sat around a fire of their own, each with his broiled moose-rib, hands and faces well smeared with grease. Juicy steaks were impaled on sticks planted at an angle before the fires, and when they had sizzled awhile, one ate the meat with his fingers, and wiped his hands on the stick.

Generally the more primitive Indian camps are well regulated and the housekeeping, although often untidy, is clean, but in cases of this kind, aboriginal standards are the only ones followed for the time being, and everybody is happy — until the next time. In these communities, provision, on becoming short, becomes common property, as meat is at any time. No one claims a kill as his own exclusively, each family sending a representative to collect their share and those unable to leave have it brought to them. Each also takes his turn to supply, and on this account, another young fellow and myself, our turn arriving, undertook to do our bit.

It was the time of first ice, and the travelling was of the best, with less than six inches of snow. We took two days' provisions, intending to return by a shortcut the third day. And here is where the mice and men, so often mentioned, sustained their well-known reputation. We were poor prophets. The second night it turned soft, and there was an unprecedented snowfall of at least two feet. The lakes slushed up and the bush was clogged with wet snow. We had brought no snowshoes, we had not killed a moose, we had nothing to eat save the remains of our last meal, and were at least twenty miles from the village; an interesting problem any way you look at it. It took us four days and a half to get back, during which time we ate one partridge and two squirrels. These last we ate raw in order to get all there was in them. Once we found a thin strip of dried moose-meat hanging on a rack at an old campground; it was no bigger than your thumb, and must have been old enough to vote, being much like a stick of wood.

We commenced to become weak, taking long rests which ate into our time, and when it was necessary to cross over a log larger than common, we sat on it and looked at one another for long periods. I thought frequently of the squirrel skins which we had thrown away; apart from the hair there had been nothing wrong with them. We were much tempted to commit the indiscretion of eating snow, and sometimes chewed the scrapings off the inside bark of yellow birch. This, however, induced thirst, and drinking ice water under these conditions is sometimes fatal. In the course of our wanderings we arrived at a spot where a moose had been killed that Fall, and we dug the bones out of the snow, scorched them for a while on a fire, broke them open, and devoured the rotten marrow with relish.

These exercises occupied four days. At noon on the next day we met a rescue party supplied with snowshoes, but we were unable to use them, as we were now deathly sick from our last meal, and had to ride the dog teams. But for an old woman who understood the use of herbal medicines we should probably have died. I can never be caught in precisely the same predicament again, as since that experience I keep my snowshoes within reach whilst there is ice on the lake.

But the pitfalls are many and various. Violent and unseasonable changes of weather may catch unprepared those who live precariously on the edge of things, and inflict severe hardship; and even Indians, who have made the weather a separate study, are not altogether immune.

Five canoes of us, all heavily laden, were caught on a river that was rapidly freezing up, and thinking to beat out the ice, we made no camp, but continued on our journey in the darkness, until, unable to break ice any further we were actually frozen in near the shore. We had to chop the canoes out by firelight, make a cache, and wait for daylight. This was only the middle of October, and one of the party froze the ends of all the fingers of one hand.

The next day, taking what we could carry, we started overland on a twenty-five mile journey to our destination, where we had camps already built, walking on good ice all of the last day. On our arrival we commenced setting traps, intending to return with toboggans, at the first snow, for our goods. We had worked only a couple of days, when the unnatural conditions changed, the ice went out with heavy rain, and we were well marooned on a large island, on which the camps were situated, with but little food and no canoes.

We stayed here for three weeks living mostly on fish, until the second and permanent freeze-up released us, when we drew in our huge loads by relays, losing the early Fall hunt in the process.

As is common with all savage peoples, and some not so savage, there was prevalent amongst the Indians, not so long ago, the practice of the arts of the medicine man, or conjuror, and even today every Indian community has at least one exponent of the black arts. Undoubtedly most of these wizards are nothing more than quacks and charlatans who, working on the credulity of their less well-informed tribesmen, have indulged a taste for the occult with attendant increase in prestige. This exploitation of the ignorant is common enough in the administration of most of the many religions with which man has seen fit to cloud his clear perception of things infinite; but in the case of the Indian these practices have no bearing on religion, and the medicine-man is simply a magician. In most cases he is merely tolerated on the off-chance that there may be something in it, since nobody wants to be caught with his boots off, yet amongst the Indian mystics are men who sincerely believe in their own powers; and powers some of them have without a doubt, over and above those of common men.

I have seen some startling performances, but believe that they all come under the heading of either sleight-of-hand, or hypnotism, or perhaps in some instances, telepathy. In the first place the Indian is by the nature of his environment psychic and imaginative to the last degree. The ceaseless and monotonous beating of a drum for hours, which precedes nearly all these seances, exercises an influence on him which leaves him in a very receptive condition for the hypnotic influence. I was present at a gathering where an old medicine man caused a handkerchief to be hidden, by a stranger, at a distance but in his presence. Taking from the crowd a youth of his own race, he placed both hands on the lad's shoulders and gazed steadily into his eyes perhaps for a minute. At this point the beating of a drum, which had continued without a break for at least an hour, ceased. On being released the young Indian walked out of sight as though dazed, but without hesitation, soon returning with the handkerchief. This was repeated with several different articles in various hiding places, with only one failure.

Collusion between the conjuror and the stranger was impos-sible, as the former could speak no English, and the latter was a tourist passing by on a trip. No word passed the old man's lips, but the boy seemed to fall very easily under his influence, and was no doubt a familiar subject.

On another occasion, before a small but skeptical assemblage, a noted conjuror sat facing a disc of stretched rawhide, distant from him about ten paces. I assisted in hanging immediately in front of the disc, about a foot apart, three tanned moose hides, which suspended loosely from a beam, formed a target that was almost bulletproof. Yet before the eyes of all, this man took a shaftless bone arrowhead, and with a quick flirt of his hand drove it apparently through the hides. On pulling them aside the arrowhead was seen to be imbedded in the disc, and no hole or other mark could be discerned on the skins. None present were able to detect the trick, and it was suggested that the performance had been an example of group hypnotism, of which, in that case, I was one of the victims together with several highly mystified tourists.

There have been cases where a conjuror has put a curse on one who has offended him, such as bad luck in hunting, accidental maiming with an axe or knife, sickness, or even death. Fear of the supposed power, causing a lack of confidence in his ability to break the spell cast on him, has caused many a victim unconsciously to bring about his own undoing, and so fulfill the curse. The hypnotic power of a drum at a certain pitch of sound, beaten regularly and without intermission, is not generally known. Some of these magicians claim the uncanny ability of calling to them by this means those who are far out of earshot of the sound. It is not beyond the realms of possibility, perhaps, that reduction to a clairvoyant or psychic condition — if such a condition exists — by voluntary starvation, the monotonous beat of the drum, and continuous mental concentration on the one idea over a period of thirty hours or more, may enable a strong-willed man to project his thoughts through space, forcing his ego in waves across the ether, willing himself to be felt hour after hour, until the object of these intense mental efforts to be heard feels an influence, he knows not what, that inevitably draws him to a certain spot.

An experience, yet very fresh in my mind, befell me not long since, and, although not offered as a proof of these things, yet could be of interest to those who make a study of telepathy or thought transference, and might give food for thought to others. My opinion in the matter is of no value, and the occurrence could easily be accounted a coincidence, or the result of a reaction to nostalgia. It was in autumn, a season when everyone is more of less tempted to indulge in reflection and recollection, and I was taking a few days of relaxation between the finish of a strenuous summer's exploration in search of a hunting ground, and the commencement of the Fall trip in with my supplies. I passed the peaceful lazy days of Indian Summer gathering up energy for the trials to come, mostly sitting before my tent, smoking and thinking, as our custom is when idle. Meanwhile I found my mind constantly dwelling on the scenes of my younger days, and particularly on a certain lake, now widely known for the picturesque beauty of its shores. More and more frequently my thoughts reverted to the well-remembered scene, until I thought of little else in my waking hours, and sleeping, dreamed of it. Recollections crowded down upon me, and there rose vividly and persistently before my mind the image of my wise and ancient companion of former days, whom I should never see again. It was on those waters that I had embarked on the restless wandering life of a trapper, and a feeling akin to homesickness, which I found myself unable to conquer, at last decided me to visit that place once more, although I knew the inhabitants had long ago departed. Little more than a day's travel by canoe brought me to the last portage, which comes out on to the lake I sought at the deserted camping ground.

As I neared the end of the carry I became conscious of some peculiar quality in the silence, which I felt but could not define. Coming out onto the open lake shore and my hearing no longer impeded by the canoe, I knew this for the measured, persistent throbbing of an Indian drum, which, whilst distant, seemed to come from no particular direction. The sound brought back a flood of reminiscences of long-departed days amongst the simple, kindly people of my adoption, of whom no recent sign remained, though the graveyard showed a pitiful increase.

Here, under these very trees I had feasted, and gamed, and danced with those of whom many now rested in that silent grove, with its miniature birch-bark huts which had contained food, and its remnants of personal belongings, laid in bark receptacles by trusting friends, for use on the journey to the Other Side.

Only the teepee and tent poles, rotten and fallen long since, and the shallow moss-grown depressions left by the fires of many years, marked the site of what had once been a populous village of human souls. And as I gazed on the familiar scene, my feelings reflected the mood of the place, which seemed immersed in a brooding melancholy.

The leasing of the surrounding waters to a fishing concern, resulting in a shortage of the food supply of the Indian, and the proximity of a new railroad with its attendant horde of amateur trappers, leaving in their wake a ravished area of poison and broken beaver-dams, had driven the occupants of the glade from their ancestral home forever. I thought of my old associate, and what his feelings would be were he alive to see the ruin and decay that had encompassed his little band; he whose rigid adherence to the customs of his race had long kept his people from that contamination of the wilderness and its dwellers, which seems to be, only too often, inherent in the advance of civilization in its earlier stages. A feeling of sadness pervaded me, and I began to wish I had not come.

I had felt influenced in some unaccountable way to make this pilgrimage, and, now, having arrived, I decided to make the best of it, and proceeded to make fire and prepare my shelter for the night. And as I worked the monotonous beat of the drum, at first merging itself into the scheme of things, as does the ticking of a clock in a silent room, so as to be at times unnoticed, became insistent, obtruding itself on my senses, weaving a spell about me, until I found myself moving about my various tasks in time to it. During the still night the sound, now fainter, now louder, never ceasing with its changeless rhythm, dominated my consciousness, sleeping and waking, and the figments of my half-formed dreams danced in the darkness to its tune.

Unable to rest I went down and sat by the water's edge. The ceaseless hypnotic throbbing permeated the air with its magic of a bygone day, and in the amphitheatre of the dusky hills that rimmed the lake, seemed to sound a chord to which the tympans of Nature vibrated, to strike a master note which, if prolonged enough, could rock the fabric of the wilderness to its foundations. I felt as one must who is becoming hypnotized. Education and the influences of civilization slipped from me like a discarded garment, as the atavistic syncopated pulsing thrilled me, arousing half-forgotten instincts, and stirring my blood with impulses long supposed to be dead. Back down the years the memories trooped upon me, effacing the veneer of semi-culture I had acquired; memories of barbarous nights when the lines of half-naked dancers postured and side-stepped through the figures of the Wabeno, between the long fires; bowed, and writhed, and stamped as they chanted a chorus that was old before the white man came, to the thudding of one-sided drums, the thin wailing of reed whistles, the piping of hollow wing-bones of eagles, and the clinking rattle of dried deer-hoofs. High-pitched yells and ululations rang sharply against the roof of the forest, and long quavering whoops trailed off into the recesses of the mountains, echoing back and forth across the empty hills in fading repetitions; dying away at times to the whisper of wind through the dry grasses of the fenlands, swelling again to a rhythmic uproar; continuing without intermission, until after two nights and a day the drums were stilled; and then the feasts of moose-meat —

Late the next day the sound abruptly ceased, and towards evening a bark canoe drifted gently ashore at the landing-place, and with a guttural exclamation of greeting there rose before me my friend of many days — Ne-ganik-abo, Stands First.

My emotions were not a little mixed, as I had thought of him as long ago gathered to his fathers. Many years had passed since we first had bent to the paddle and slept beneath the stars together. An aged man from my earliest recollection of him, he now seemed of another day and age, which indeed he was, and changed beyond belief. Dressed in old and faded overalls and shirt, he retained only the footwear of his people, a pair of beautifully beaded moccasins, and a medicine pouch decorated with porcupine quills. His hair, now white, framed a face the colour of old mahogany, patrician in cast, and almost fleshless; the eyes alone lent life to the mask-like visage, which was seamed with a thousand wrinkles. He sat at the fire and smoked awhile, seeming to rest, for he was very feeble.

He refused my offers of food, and, it not being customary for younger men to open a conversation, I waited until he first should speak; which, his smoke finished, he did, standing, and emphasizing his remarks with the restrained but expressive gestures of an Indian.

"Washaquonasin, Grey Owl, I see you do not forget. I called, and, of them all, you came."

Up to this moment I had thought of no such thing, but there now flashed through my mind the tales I had heard. Was this the explanation of my unaccountable urge to visit the lake? I remembered that this place had been accessible to me any day for years, yet I had chosen this particular time to come. Coincidence? I became conscious of a slight feeling of uneasiness. He continued:

"Three days have I called and none came; this is the last day, the day of Two Sunsets; tonight I go away from here; tomorrow you would not have found me. My son, I have seen many snows come and go; to me you are a young man, and most of what I say will pass by your ears like the piping of frogs, or the tapping of a woodpecker on a hollow tree; yet of all my people, you are the only one who remembers the way of our race. I was a warrior once, and fought the blue-coated soldiers on a day when a river ran red with blood, and none escaped. This is many years past.

Three of us returned here; we formed ourselves into a blood-brotherhood, that of the Beaver, called after our bravest warrior, killed in the battle. Of them, I alone remain. When you were named, I made you a blood-brother of the clan; remember that."

He looked searchingly at me for a moment. This, then, was the reason for his attitude towards these animals, and I knew that I might never set another beaver trap, did I choose to remain true to the creed of this society of the Dead. For the old man's weakness was such that it was evident that soon, not he, but I, would be the last of the clan of the Beaver.

He said a few words in a language unintelligible to me and resumed:

"Since then I have seen many changes; I have seen the skin teepees replaced by houses; the snowshoe trail by the railroad; and now the winged canoe of the white man flies with the wild geese amongst the clouds. I am now very old. Old age is a time of rest and meditation, yet I find myself surrounded by changes that keep me moving; at no place can I rest, and ponder peacefully on the past. Long ago my people left this lake where I was born. I played as a child on this very beach, and in these forests I learned the wisdom of the Old Men. Here I will leave my bones that the Medicine Spirits may see that there is one that has not forgotten that he is an Indian."

He paused and seemed to listen.

Came a sound, a murmuring from the distance, a wind that stirred the treetops overhead; the sleeping forest half-awakened, sighed, and as the sound passed onward, slept again. And all around the golden and red leaves of the birch and maples, the spots of sunlight on the forest floor; and the thin blue wisp of smoke trailing up and up from the dying fire, up through the leaves and on beyond them. And far overhead the Unseen Musician improvised a low rambling melody in the many-stringed lyre of the pine-tops, and its soft humming, and the quiet lap, lap of the wavelets on the sandy shore, mingled with the old man's voice as he intoned in soft gutturals, with all the imagery to which his language lends itself.

"I hear a sound: the wind speaks to the leaves. No! It is the spirit of an Indian, looking for a place to rest, and there is none! The sky is red at night with the fire of burning forests. The beaver are gone, and there are no more singing birds; they cannot sing in the dry limbs of dead trees, and the Indian cannot live in a land of rotting stumps. The setting sun throws a red path across the water; there lies the trail to the Land of Spirits; along it I soon must follow my people. When the deep snows come I will dance the Dance of the Dead Men in the northern sky."

The latter part of his speech seemed only indirectly intended for me; rather he thought aloud. He spoke of his past life, his old-time friends, and of days beyond the memory of living man. He dwelt on the time when his band could count half a hundred lodges, and told of his struggles to keep his people steadfast; and he seemed to wander a little, till I got the purport of his words: he was painting the picture of a vanishing race. He seemed no longer aware of his surroundings, and somehow gave the impression of talking to an invisible audience, of which I was not one. And his voice gathered some arresting quality from his theme, so that even the motionless trees about him seemed to stand and listen. And my previous intimacy faded into the background; and he seemed no longer a man, but a prophet, the patriarchal ruler of a vanished people, a reincarnation of the fabled Hiawatha.

And from his words there seemed to spring a pageant in the air behind him, of days gone by; of mighty men, long dead, whose deeds now lived again; of lines of naked braves filing by in the crouching hop and shuffle of the war-dance; of clouds of mounted warriors with waving ghostly bonnets, passing in review to strains of wild unearthly music. Of a buckskin-coated figure, with long yellow hair, surrounded by the bodies of dead men dressed in blue, standing alone in an inferno of screaming, racing savages, painted ponies, and whirling dust-clouds; in his ears the terrible shuddering chorus of the death-hulloo;* a pistol raised to his head for the last act.

His voice lost its martial note, and the fire died from the old eyes, momentarily aflame with the memory of the historic combat. And then the scene changed. Endless forests marching, marching, tops swaying to the tune of the Hunting Winds; brigades of yellow bark canoes loaded high with skins, floating down swift rivers walled with granite; four-footed creatures, now rare, trooping by in all their rich variety; the quiet lodges of a peaceful people, lodges before whose doors stood racks of sturgeon, moose, and deer-meat. Then — the coming of the railroad; unnumbered leagues of noble forest falling before a sea of flames; scattered bands of a broken, bewildered people driven like leaves before the wind and then — today! And as he ceased the scenes faded, and the figures were gone; and he stood again alone; a forlorn, lonely old man.

I fumbled in my mind for words to express my thoughts, when turning, he walked the few steps beyond the edge of the forest to the sandy lake shore, and stood facing the glimmering ribbon of red cast on the still water by the now rapidly setting sun. In the crimson glow, the broken, patched canoe became a thing of beauty, and the withered, time-worn figure in its tattered clothing, silhouetted against the brilliance, seemed to take on again something of the wild freedom of his youth in its posture. With the simple dignity of a savage chieftain he raised his right hand, palm out, and bowed his head, as though in benediction of the scene before him, saluting the western sky with that greeting with which the Indian met the first white man, the ancient and almost forgotten Peace Sign. And as he so stood, embracing into his audience with a single gesture, the peaceful sleeping lake, the dark legions of the forest, and the brooding hills, he cried in a loud, clear voice, as to a vast and unseen assemblage:

---

* So called by the whites. A rhythmic yelling, almost a chant, used by Indians to signalize victory and the taking of scalps.

"I stand on the Trail of Two Sunsets. Tonight the sun sets for the White Man for a day. Soon another sun will set for the Indian; and it will be forever. There is a cloud across the face of the sky, and it shadows our trail to the end."

He dropped his head, and sitting down beside his canoe, seemed lost in reverie. And the rim of the burning sun sank behind the distant hilltops, and the last vestige of the red beam disappeared from the surface of the water.

I waited respectfully till the aged chieftain should see fit to address me again, when another thought struck me, and with a chill not altogether accounted for by the cool of evening, I walked quickly over and laid my hand on his shoulder.

His arm slipped gently down from the gunwale to his side. He was dead.

I buried him the next day in his old canoe, with his muzzle-loading gun, his old-fashioned axe, and his beaded pouch of relics by his side, in the smooth ground beneath the birches near the lake-shore, where he may hear the singing birds trill in rippling melody their evensong, in the sad days of the Fall of the Leaf, and the North-West wind may bring a message from the Great Lone Land beyond.

And there he will always be, facing towards the West, so that the rays of the setting sun to which he turned so wistfully in his last moments, may, at the close of every summer day, bathe his resting place, in the Glory of his Sunset Trail.

EPILOGUE

At the brow of a high eminence stood two men, their figures etched sharply against the sky of a day now near its close. Beside them lay two bundles, rolled as though in readiness for a long and immediate journey.

To the south lay spread out a smiling valley of farmlands, dotted thickly with the habitations of man; and at the foot of the declivity far below, were half-cleared fields, in which lay piles of burning roots and prostrate tree trunks. And there came up faintly to the ears of the men the ring of axes and the crash of falling timber, as an antlike swarm hewed at the face of the forest, eating into it, as a rising flood eats into a wall of sand.

Beyond the valley, in the distance, stood a mighty city, its tall buildings rising in huge piles of masonry heaped up against the skyline, whilst from its bowels rose the dull roar and whirr of massed machinery, and a confused hum as of a myriad bees within a gigantic hive. Towering smokestacks belched forth heavy clouds of rolling black smoke, which hung over the city like a dark canopy, and spreading out over the farm lands, shadowed them.

On the other side the mountain descended in a gradual slope to the level of the dark waves of an endless forest, the tree-covered hills rolling into the north, row on row, rank on rank, sweeping on in ever-lessening undulation until they merged into the dimness of the horizon. The ocean of evergreens opened out as it neared the foot of the descent, to flank a long open meadow of beaver hay, down the full length of which there wound a long ribbon of a trail, winding and twisting its way amongst the yellow grasses towards the north, until, visible only as a thread where it entered the woods, the trees crowded down upon it, engulfed it, and swallowed it up, so that it could be no more seen.

The man nearest the edge of the cliff stood leaning on his rifle, gazing out over the tilled fields, towards the city beyond. His grey eyes were narrow, and stamped at the corners with crow's feet, hallmark of one who has peered into the glare of a thousand suns, and faced the blizzards of many winters. His face, tanned to the colour of leather, was hollow-cheeked, ascetic almost. Once his glance strayed involuntarily to the panorama of forest that lay spread out behind him, but his eyes again sought the distant city, as though drawn by some powerful attraction.

The other, a tall spare man, his long black hair confined at the temples by a buckskin band, and with the vigorous features and calm bearing of an Indian, regarded not the city, but stood motionless, his gaze roaming over the sweep and swell of the wilderness; and at his feet were the charred sticks of a fire, now extinguished. He had the air of one who waits.

Presently he turned and touched the white man on the shoulder, and pointing to the west, spoke in his native language.

"The sun is setting, my ears are filled with the sound of falling trees; it is enough. See! The shadows lengthen; let us go."

And as the slow wind of evening passed over the land, there seemed to come an answering murmur from the hosts of the forest, saying, "Let us go: let us go."

And the concerted waving movement of the myriad treetops in the breeze likened them to an immense and restless concourse, gathered together for some great migration, awaiting but the signal for departure.

For a moment longer the frontiersman stood irresolute, and then with a gesture of finality, his face set in the stern lines of one who has made a sweeping and unalterable decision, he assumed his pack, and turning his back forever on the haunts of man, followed the Indian, now already on his way.

And their moccasined feet left no track as they followed the winding trail, and as they marched steadily away, their figures grew smaller and smaller, diminished, dwindled, dwindled, until at last, no longer distinguishable in the gathering dusk, they vanished into the shadows amongst the trees.

And there nothing remained of their passing, save the empty trail, and the ashes of their long-dead fire.

In the darkness from over all the length and breadth of the wild lands there came a murmur, and the air was filled with the sound of a mighty rustling and a crepitation, as of an innumerable multitude in motion. And the dark masses of the forest seemed to roll up behind those who had already gone before, to recede like the outgoing waves of an ebbing tide, as though, defeated at last, they retired before the Juggernaut that was now upon them, fleeing in the face of the doom that had threatened them for now three hundred years.

And with them went all of the wild that had life, following the last fading line of the Vanishing Frontier, Northward, Northward, ever Northward, back into the days that are long forgotten, slipping away over the hills into the purple distance, beyond the Land of Shadows, into the sunset.